Joseph Powell

Two Years in the Pontifical Zouaves

A Narrative of Travel, Residence, and Experience in the Roman States

Joseph Powell

Two Years in the Pontifical Zouaves

A Narrative of Travel, Residence, and Experience in the Roman States

ISBN/EAN: 9783337006792

Printed in Europe, USA, Canada, Australia, Japan

Cover: Foto ©Andreas Hilbeck / pixelio.de

More available books at **www.hansebooks.com**

Two Years in the Pontifical Zouaves.

ROCKY CHASM NEAR ACQUAPENDENTE. *Front.*

TWO YEARS

IN THE

PONTIFICAL ZOUAVES,

A NARRATIVE OF

TRAVEL, RESIDENCE, AND EXPERIENCE

IN THE

ROMAN STATES.

BY

JOSEPH POWELL, Z.P.

Anima mia, anima mia,
Ama Dio e tira via.
Motto of Julian Watts-Russell.

LONDON:
R. WASHBOURNE, 18A, PATERNOSTER ROW.
1871.

[*The Copyright is Reserved.*]

TO THE
HON. AND VERY REV. MONSIGNOR STONOR,
THE ENERGETIC, DEVOTED
CHIEF CHAPLAIN OF THE ENGLISH-SPEAKING ZOUAVES,
This Work is Respectfully Dedicated,
AS A PROOF OF
THE SINCERITY OF THE WRITER'S ATTACHMENT
TO THE GRAND CAUSE OF
OUR HOLY FATHER, PIUS IX.,
TO THE ETERNAL CITY,
AND TO THE PONTIFICAL ZOUAVES.

SONG OF THE ENGLISH ZOUAVES.

" Anima mia, anima mia,
Ama Dio e tira via."

Saint George and old England for ever !
Once more her sons arm for the fight,
With the cross on their breasts, to do battle
For God, Holy Church, and the right.
Twine your swords with the palm branch, brave comrades,
For as Pilgrims we march forth to-day ;—
Love God, O my soul, love Him only,
And then with light heart go thy way.

We come from the blue shores of England,
From the mountains of Scotia we come,
From the green, faithful island of Erin,—
Far, far, from our wild northern home.
Place Saint Andrew's red cross in your bonnets,
Saint Patrick's green shamrock display ;—
Love God, O my soul, love Him only,
And then with light heart go thy way.

Dishonour our swords shall not tarnish,
We draw them for Rome and the Pope ;
Victors still, whether living or dying,
For the Martyr's bright crown is our hope ;
If 'tis sweet for our country to perish,
Sweeter far for the cause of to-day ;—
Love God, O my soul, love Him only,
And then with light heart go thy way.

Though the odds be against us, what matter ?
While God and Our Lady look down,
And the Saints of our country are near us,
And Angels are holding the crown.
March, march to the combat and fear not,
A light round our weapons will play ;—
Love God, O my soul, love Him only,
And then with light heart go thy way.

PREFACE.

THESE pages are principally the 'work of an old Zouave, and are founded on letters and notes written in Rome and the Pontifical States. These suggested to me the idea which has resulted in the present book; at the same time I am greatly indebted to W. C. Robinson, Esq., Z.P., both for the stimulus he has given me to carry out my idea, and for the valuable and interesting matter he has generously sent me, and which I have used in these pages, on "Life in Detachment at Bolsena," "Visit to Subiaco," "Siege of Rome," and the following chapter. I am also much indebted to Captain De la Hoyde, for his kindness in furnishing me with notes on the early history of the Corps, and the later events in connection with it. Next, I must acknowledge my obligations to the '*Tablet*' for much valuable information on the events and victories of 1867, related in the first four chapters. Again, "Rome, its Churches," by Rev. W. H. Neligan, M.A., has been largely quoted in reference to the churches and monuments mentioned.

Some other works made use of will be mentioned in notes. I am indebted to "Personal Recollections of Rome," by W. J. Jacob, Esq., Z.P., for a description of the opening of the Vatican Council, and to some other kind friends for assistance.

The title has been chosen as the most appropriate to the idea which originated the work, and because I belonged for *two years* to the Corps; but the period of the principal events related extends over upwards of three years.

Although the principal part of the book will be found to refer to the Zouaves, yet many subjects incidental to this Corps, and to a residence in Rome and the Roman States, have been introduced. As the work may be considered one of travel and experience related in letters and notes, it is necessarily somewhat fragmentary in its character; but this feature will, I hope, meet with indulgence at the hands of its readers, who may be asked to pardon the faults of a novice, now appearing in print for the first time.

Much care has been taken to compare dates, narratives, and statements of fact, and I trust that those given will be found generally correct. The miles spoken of are Roman—a Roman mile consists of 1000 paces, or 1611 English yards—thus twelve Roman miles are nearly equal to eleven English.

To the Corps to which I had the honour to belong, I beg to submit this work, hoping that it will meet with approval at the hands of my comrades in arms, and that the recital of some of the heroic deeds which have so much adorned the history of the Zouaves, may not be unacceptable to the general body, and particularly to its English and Irish members.

The many friends and well-wishers of the Corps will, I hope, feel an interest in the details here submitted to them.

To the general public I hope that the work may prove to be interesting, first, because the subject of the Pontifical Zouaves lays claim to a general interest on account of the courage and heroism they have displayed, not only in the Roman States, but also during the late disastrous war in France, where they have singularly proved their real discipline and organisation. Secondly, because the variety of subjects introduced may have an interest for many classes of readers.

CONTENTS.

CHAPTER	PAGE
I. ORIGIN AND EARLY ACHIEVEMENTS OF THE CORPS—VICTORIES OF 1867	1
II. SECRET SOCIETIES OF THE CONTINENT—CRITICAL STATE OF ROME—COURAGE OF AN IRISHMAN—CAPTAIN DE LA HOYDE ON MENTANA	15
III. GENERAL KANZLER'S REPORT OF THE BATTLE OF MENTANA ADDRESSED TO THE POPE	25
IV. FRENCH OFFICIAL REPORT OF THE BATTLE—MGR. DUPANLOUP ON THE VICTORIES—DE QUELEN AND DUFOURNEL—EVIDENCE OF THE DISPOSITIONS OF THE ROMANS—CARDINAL DONNET ON THE POPE—HEROISM OF A LADY	35
V. JOURNEY TO ROME—ENGAGEMENT IN THE ZOUAVES—LIFE IN THE DEPOT—EASTER IN ROME—DISCIPLINE OF THE CORPS	45
VI. FEAST OF CORPUS CHRISTI—AT MONTE ROTONDO—PROMENADE TO MONTE LIBRETTI—LIFE IN THE COMPANY AT CECCANO—PIPERNO	57
VII. MARCH TO THE CAMP OF ANNIBAL—ROCCA DI PAPA—LIFE IN CAMP—LAKE NEMI	64
VIII. RETURN TO ROME—LIFE AT THE SORA—MONTI AND TOGNETTI	72
IX. IN HOSPITAL—LIFE IN ROME AT THE CASERMA DEL GESU—THE VATICAN—ST. PETER'S	81
X. SANTA SABINA—FEAST OF ST. JOSEPH—JUBILEE OF THE HOLY FATHER—ST. GEORGE	91

CHAPTER	PAGE
XI. MARCH TO MONTEFIASCONE—LAGO DI VICO—BEAUTIFUL SCENERY—FEAST OF SS. PETER AND PAUL IN ROME—LIFE AT MONTEFIASCONE	99
XII. THEORY—BOLSENA AND THE MIRACLE OF THE MOST HOLY SACRAMENT—ACQUAPENDENTE—FEAST OF SANTA CHRISTINA—LIFE IN DETACHMENT AT BOLSENA	108
XIII. FEAST OF ST. ROSE AT VITERBO—BOATING EXCURSION ON LAKE BOLSENA—EXCURSION TO ORTE, CIVITA CASTELLANA, SORIANO	119
XIV. RETURN TO ROME—AT SAN MICHELE—TARGET FIRING	125
XV. THE OPENING OF THE COUNCIL OF THE VATICAN	132
XVI. CHRISTMAS — PASTORAL MUSIC — A FEW WORDS ABOUT LEAVING THE CORPS—SANT' ANDREA DELLA VALLE—CONFESSION IN ST. PETER'S	141
XVI*. THE "WEEK" IN THE ZOUAVES—PARADE—CORPORAL OF THE WEEK—THE EXHIBITION OF CHRISTIAN ART—SANT' ONOFRIO—SANTA PUDENTIANA AND SANTA PRASSEDE—PRÆTORIAN CAMP	146
XVII. LIFE AT SANTA GALLA AS CORPORAL—CHURCH OF SAN MARTINO AI MONTI—OF SANT' AGNESE—"VERSEMENT"	156
XVIII. DIARY DURING HOLY WEEK—BASILICA OF ST. JOHN LATERAN—EASTER FESTIVITIES	161
XIX. THE VIA APPIA, COLUMBARIA, AND CATACOMBS	170
XX. VISIT TO TIVOLI	181
XXI. DIARY CONTINUED—BATHS OF DIOCLETIAN—SANTA CROCE—CONGE	190
XXII. THE COLISEUM—CHURCHES ON THE CŒLIAN, ETC.—THE CAPITOL—ARA CŒLI—ROMAN FORUM—ARCH OF TITUS—ST. SEBASTIAN	194
XXIII. THE PANTHEON—COLUMNS—OBELISKS—AQUEDUCTS	208
XXIV. THE KIRCHERIAN MUSEUM—CHURCHES OF S. MARIA IN TRASTEVERE, SAN PIETRO IN MONTORIO, AND THE GESU—CAMPO SANTO AND TOMB OF JULIAN WATTS-RUSSELL	215

Contents.

CHAPTER		PAGE
XXV.	REMARKS ON THE ANCIENT HISTORY OF PLACES VISITED NEAR ROME	222
XXVI.	RETURN TO ENGLAND—VOYAGE—MARSEILLES—PARIS—BOULOGNE—LONDON, ETC. . .	232
XXVII.	THE ZOUAVES AT MONTEFIASCONE—THE MASTERLY RETREAT OF LIEUT.-COLONEL DE CHARETTE .	243
XXVIII.	EVENTS OF SEPTEMBER, 1870—DIARY OF A ZOUAVE OFFICER DURING THE SIEGE OF ROME—COMBAT OF SERGEANT SHEE WITH ITALIAN LANCERS—THE CAPITULATION—A LADY UNDER FIRE—ASSASSINATION OF A ZOUAVE OFFICER—BRAVE CONDUCT OF GENTLEMEN RETURNING TO THE CORPS	254
XXIX.	THE SIEGE FROM ANOTHER POINT OF VIEW—FAREWELL OF THE ZOUAVES TO THE HOLY FATHER—THEIR RETURN HOME—ITALIAN SOLDIERS AND IRRELIGION IN THE ITALIAN ARMY . .	270
XXX.	VISITORS TO ROME—A SAD INCIDENT—ORGANISATION AND DISCIPLINE	283
XXXI.	THE USURPATION—THE POPE A PRISONER—FRANCE—LIBERTY, EQUALITY, FRATERNITY, CONSOLATION, HEROISM—CONCLUSION . .	293

ERRATA.

Page 72, chapter line, *for* "Toqnetti" *read* "Tognetti."
,, 110, line 32, *for* "in charming country" *read* "in a charming country."
,, 132, line 26, *for* "2000 bishops" *read* "upwards of 800 bishops."
,, 200, ,, 12, *for* "Cominius" *read* "Cominus."
,, 201, ,, 28, *for* "Sybil" *read* "Sibyl."

LIST OF ILLUSTRATIONS.

ROCKY CHASM NEAR ACQUAPENDENTE . *Frontispiece*
BAGNOREA . . . . page 110
LAKE OF BOLSENA . . . . . . „ 120
TIVOLI—LE CASCATELLE . . . . . „ 184

The Author has received for his work the warmest encouragement and best wishes of the Hon. and Very Rev. MGR. STONOR, of the Earl of DENBIGH, and of Major W. F. GORDON. He also begs to acknowledge, with thanks, the support of the distinguished names which follow :—

Most Rev. the Lord ARCHBISHOP OF WESTMINSTER.
Most Rev. the Lord ARCHBISHOP OF CASHEL.
Hon. and Right Rev. the Lord BISHOP OF CLIFTON.
Right Rev. the Lord BISHOP OF BRISBANE.
Right Rev. the Lord BISHOP OF NORTHAMPTON.
Right Rev. the Lord BISHOP OF SOUTHWARK.
Right Rev. the Lord BISHOP OF ROSS.
Right Hon. the Lord HERRIES.
Right Hon. the Lady CAMOYS.
Right Hon. the Lord PETRE.
Very Rev. Dr. NORTHCOTE.
Very Rev. Dr. WILLIAMS, Prior Park.
Very Rev. Dr. KIRNER.
Very Rev. Father E. I. PURBRICK, Stonyhurst College.
Very Rev. F. CRANE, Provincial O.S.A., Dublin.
Very Rev. RECTOR, Clongowes Wood College, Kildare.
Very Rev. RECTOR, S. Stanislaus' College, Tullamore.
Very Rev. RECTOR, Carlow College, Ireland.
Very Rev. PRESIDENT, S. Vincent's College, Castleknock, Dublin.
Very Rev. Canon MOORE, Sedgley Park.
Very Rev. Father PRIOR, Woodchester, Stroud.
Very Rev. F. PETER MACKEY, Woodchester.
Very Rev. F. GREGORY KELLY, O.P.
Rev. Father J. HENRY BARTLETT, O.P.
Rev. MOTHER, S. Benedict's Convent, Colwich.
Rev. MOTHER, Convent of Mercy, Handsworth.
Rev. MOTHER, Convent of Mercy, Swinford, Co. Galway.
Rev. MOTHER, Convent of Mercy, Ballinrobe, Mayo.
Rev. MOTHER, S. Augustine's Priory, Newton Abbot.

Rev. E. R. Martin.
Rev. J. Canty.
Rev. A. B. Gurdon.
Rev. S. W. Allen.
Rev. C. Robinson, O.S.C.
Rev. J. P. Brady.
Rev. C. Bowen.
Rev. C. Macauley, Maynooth College.
Rev. Dean Hughes, Maynooth College.
Rev. T. Seddon.
Rev. F. Loughnan, Clifton.
Rev. F. Stanfield, Hertford.
Rev. G. Akers.
Rev. Father W. Lockhart.
Very Rev. Canon Neve, Taunton.
Rev. Father Faure, Leicester Square.
Rev. Father J. E. Bowden, Cong. Orat.

Rev. C. Collingridge.
Rev. P. Doyle, Dublin.
Rev. W. B. Scruton.
Rev. Father W. Waterworth, S.J.
Rev Father M. Watts-Russell.
Rev. F. Daniel, Dublin.
Rev. F. Byrne.
Rev. C. J. Moncrieff Smith.
Rev. J. Flanagan, Dublin.
Rev. J. M. Donnell.
Rev. A. Russell.
Rev. M. Coxon.
Rev. A. Peter.
Rev. Father Coffey, Dublin.
Sir G. Bowyer, Bart.
Sir C. Clifford, Bart.
Lady Pollen.
Captain D'Arcy.
Captain De la Hoyde.

Mrs. Leigh, Woodchester Park.
Mrs. Plummer, Woodchester.
Keyes O'Clery, Esq.
John G. Kenyon, Esq.
Joseph S. Hansom, Esq.
J. R. W. Lloyd, Esq., K.S.G.
C. C. Woodward, Esq.
Arthur Coombs, Esq.
Alfred F. Blount, Esq.
Fauconberg De Selby, Esq.
Alexander Fletcher, Esq.
A. R. Saraiva, Esq.
Thomas Fowler, Esq., Waterford.
J. F. Maguire, Esq., M.P.
J. T. Power, Esq., M.P.
F. J. Morgan, Esq.
Mrs. Robinson.
W. C. Robinson, Esq., Z.P.
R. Greenhalgh, Esq.
A. C. Scoles, Esq.
W. J. Jacob, Esq., Z.P.
G. Collingridge, Esq., Z.P.
J. Connolly, Esq.
D. Shee, Esq., Z.P.
P. Vassar Esq., Z.P.
W. T. Raymond, Esq.
E. V. Thornton, Esq., Z.P.
Mr. D. Ricks, Z.P.
Mr. H. B. Vrain, Z.P.
Mr. B. Holtham, Z.P.
Mr. H. Weetman, Z.P.
Mrs. Elder.
Mr. C. Atkins, Z.P.
The Lady Manager, S. James' Registry, Manchester Square.
R. C. Hanrott, Esq.
Miss Greame.
Donat Sampson, Esq.
Mrs. James.
Mrs. Newsham, Darlington.
Mrs. Coulston.
Mr. G. G. Bartlett.
Mr. T. Flannery.
John Hanly, Esq., Churchtown.
Alexander Drake, Esq., J.P., Rathvale.
Miss Annie White.

Miss Monks.
Mrs. Atkins, Atherstone.
Miss Astley.
Mr. M. Beakey.
W. E. J. Vavasour, Esq.
James Knill, Esq., M.D.
Mr. J. Macken, Dublin.
Mr. C. Parker.
Miss Bayliss.
Mrs. Allen.
J. Lennox Power, Esq., 84th Regiment.
F. M. Spaight, Esq.
Mr. J. Arkell.
Miss Arkell.
Mrs. Arkell, Whelford.
Mrs. T. Arkell, Whelford.
Mrs. Arkell, Loughborough.
Mr. W. Arkell.
Mr. R. A. Iles.
Mrs. W. Arkell, Frogmore Farm.
Mrs. Wakefield.
Mrs. Dancey.
Mrs. Gibbs.
Mr. Whitty.
Mrs. Townley.
Mrs. Alcock.
Mr. S. Hughes, Liverpool.
The Misses Iles, Fairford.
Mrs. Councer, Cheltenham.
Mrs. Sargent.
P. Burchett, Esq.
G. Keogh, Esq.
M. Brophy, Esq.
F. Bowler, Esq.
John Kidd, Esq.
Mr. Hooker.
Mrs. Smith.
Mrs. Chard.
Mrs. Moore.
Mr. J. Bratt.
Mrs. W. Boardman.
Mr. Beeck.
Mr. H. Phipp.
Mr. M'Carthy.
And other kind friends, whose names are withheld at their desire.

TWO YEARS IN THE PONTIFICAL ZOUAVES.

CHAPTER I.

ORIGIN AND EARLY ACHIEVEMENTS OF THE CORPS—
VICTORIES OF 1867.

As this is not intended to be a history of the corps but the relation only of my own experience in connection with it, a lengthened description of its origin and early achievements is unnecessary, nor will any elaborate eulogium of many great names connected with it be attempted. I will content myself at present by saying that I esteem it a great honour to have belonged to a corps which has acted with so much real *heroism* in rallying round the throne of the great Pontiff, Pius IX., in defence of the rights of the oldest sovereignty in Europe, which was formed under that great general De Lamoricière, and contains in its annals the names of such men as Guérin, Guillemin, De Quelen, the Dufournels, De Vaux, Julian Watts-Russell, and Collingridge.

I presume that a few introductory chapters descriptive of the victories and events which have shed so much lustre and renown on the annals of the corps, will not be deemed out of place before I commence my own narrative.

The Pontifical Zouaves were originated by the heroic De Lamoricière in 1860, and were known at first as "Tirailleurs Franco-Belges," the corps being composed principally of French and Flemish gentlemen of good family and others, who, following the noble example of their general, ranged themselves on the side of religion and right, to do battle against injustice, represented by the invading forces of Victor Emmanuel—who had already taken forcible possession of a portion of the States of the Church. Count Major de Becdelièvre, an old African and Crimean veteran, was appointed to command the Franco-Belges, and under him the little battalion, about two hundred and fifty strong, was organised at the Camp of Terni, and took part in the battle of Castel Fidardo on September 18, 1860.

General De Lamoricière was there betrayed by false promises, and although the Franco-Belges fought desperately and carried at the point of the bayonet the farm-house of Le Crocette and the hill beyond it, they were overwhelmed by numbers, and had the mortification of seeing themselves treacherously fired upon by some of the Italians on their own side. Almost every third man, it is said, was struck. De Charette received two wounds, Captain Guelton was killed, Lieut. Moncuit lost his left arm, the celebrated Guérin was mortally wounded, and Corporal Arthur Guillemin received a bayonet thrust. The result of the unequal contest is well known; but it is said the victor, General Cialdini, declared that, had all the Pontifical troops fought as well as the Franco-Belges, the fortune of the day would have been reversed, and this notwithstanding that his own forces outnumbered the Pontifical army in the proportion of nearly ten to one.

On the 1st January, 1861, the corps was reorganised by Count de Becdelièvre, and it received, through his exertions, the picturesque uniform of grey with red facings and cincture, and the name of the "Zouaves Pontificaux."

A "smart and successful service" was effected by Colonel de Becdelièvre during the same month; he surprised and took prisoners the Italian force which had posted itself at Correse, in the Comarca and Patrimony of St. Peter. Correse is an important point at the junction of the two roads of Terni and Rieti, and the only passage from the Comarca into Sabinum. "The Pontifical Zouaves, favoured by the night, attacked the Sardinian volunteers at Correse. Two

Sardinians were killed and six wounded, fifty were made prisoners, and were conveyed to-day to Rome."*

Colonel de Becdelièvre resigned the command of the corps about Easter, 1866, and Lieut.-Col. Allet, an old Swiss officer, was appointed its chief, De Charette being major.

In 1862 Lieut. Mousty, commanding an advanced post of sixteen Zouaves, drove back an Italian company, which attempted to violate the frontier on the Neapolitan side. In December, 1865, two new companies and a company of depôt were added to the little regiment. Brigandage became rife in the provinces of Frosinone, and particularly in the Volscian hills, and Sezze, Piperno, and Prossedi, and other towns were occupied by detachments, and part of the regiment was employed during the spring and summer of 1866 in constant hunting after the brigands. The most remarkable combat took place on November 22nd on Monte Lupino, one of the Volscians. Several bands, amounting altogether to sixty brigands, had beaten three detachments of Swiss Carbineers, when finally a detachment of twenty-seven Zouaves under Captain Adeodatus Dufournel and Lieut. De Coüessin, fought them for four hours, and put them to flight.

On the 1st January, 1867, the Zouaves were constituted a regiment of two battalions, of six companies each; Colonel Allet commanded, the Baron de Charette being Lieut.-Colonel, Vicomte de Lambilly and Baron de Troussures, Chefs de Bataillon. During the summer of this year several Englishmen joined the corps, which now included in its rolls two Irish officers, and men of good position and rank from many different countries.

In the month of August the cholera broke out in the Eternal City. Albano had always as yet been free from this epidemic, and certain strong-minded individuals there mocked at the affliction of Rome, naming dishes of fruit of the three colours, red, white, and green, combined, *piatto di colera*, &c., and tried to excite the people against the coming of a proposed detachment of Zouaves, saying that they would bring the infection. The detachment was delayed,

* *Tablet*, January, 1861.

as part of the company had to be sent to Velletri, where some disturbances had arisen. When the other part of this company were on the march to Albano they met crowds of fugitives; the cholera had broken out the night before. The visitation was sudden and awful, and about eighty persons are said to have died the first night; the authorities fled, the natives in crowds took to the woods. The neighbouring town of L'Ariccia formed a cordon of its inhabitants on the approaches, threatening to shoot any fugitives who attempted to enter it. Lieut. de Resimond made an appeal to the good will of his Zouaves, and every one of the forty responded to it: he himself was the first to carry off a dead body. The *Zouaves* were for two days the only *nurses, doctors,* or *gravediggers* of the town; they organised the burial service as best they could. Three men were victims of their charity.

Cardinal Altieri, the Bishop, came out at once with a staff of doctors, Sisters of Charity, and infirmarians; he also died a victim to his zeal. The royal family of Naples were there in *villegiatura;* the Queen Dowager and Don Gennaro, her youngest son, died of the epidemic; their funeral was attended by Zouaves, and their remains carried to the tomb by officers, sergeants, and others. Lieut.-Colonel de Charette came out several times to encourage his men. In Rome the cholera made itself severely felt amongst the troops; every Sunday the officers, headed by the colonel, visited the hospital, and this had a good effect on the *morale* of the sick. Albano suffered fearfully for about three weeks, after which the mortality decreased; the inhabitants, numbering about nine or ten thousand souls, were decimated, a number estimated from six hundred to eight hundred having died. Lieut. de Resimond was decorated with the Cross of Pius IX., and that of Francis I. of the first class, by the King of Naples. Several others were also decorated by the Holy Father and the King, both of whom thus recognised the heroic conduct of the Zouaves at this trying emergency, the privates receiving gold medals of *bene merenti*.

In the end of September, and commencement of October 1867, began the Garibaldian invasion of the Pontifical States, which was connived at, more or less openly, by the Italian Government, as it is certain that the latter permitted many of its regular soldiers to enter the Garibaldian army.

The Garibaldians entered the States at four points, viz., Grotta San Stefano, on September 29th; Acquapendente, Canino, and Valentano on September 30th. The sixteen Pontifical gendarmes, who occupied Acquapendente, retired before the superior force of the enemy, towards Montefiascone, and the Garibaldians advanced, and took possession of the town of Bagnorea, which is a strong position, on a rocky height surrounded by deep defiles. I copy the following authentic account of the action of recovering Bagnorea, from the *Tablet* of October 26th, 1867.

" Here they—the Garibaldians—were attacked on October 3rd, by a detachment of the Papal forces, who were repulsed, being unable with their numerical inferiority to make head against the enemy. But General de Courten arrived from Rome with two pieces of artillery and twenty horses, and setting out from Montefiascone at seven a.m., on October 5th, with 170 Zouaves and 150 Romans of the line, attacked Bagnorea at eleven a.m."

A letter from a Pontifical Zouave to his sister, dated Bagnorea, October 6th, says :—" On receiving the order to attack, we advanced at the *pas gymnastique*. The enemy occupied the heights round the town, but retired before our skirmishers and abandoned the position. We had scarcely gained the heights when a shower of balls rained upon us. The Garibaldians were under shelter in the vineyards, and we were exposed; so, crying 'Vive Pie IX.! En avant les Zouaves ! A la Baionette !' we charged and dislodged them, and got among the vineyards under the ramparts. The Garibaldians took refuge in a convent, and kept up a sharp fire on us from the windows and from the clock tower. We attacked the gate with the butt-ends of our muskets, our lieutenant, though wounded in the arm, dealing formidable one-handed blows with an axe. As soon as the gate was forced we rushed in with levelled bayonets. The Garibaldians threw down their arms and surrendered. We took fifty-six of them, and several officers in the convent. As they still held the town, our commander had the cannon pointed at the gate. We got in. The enemy fled. The inhabitants cried, ' Viva Pio Nono !' ' Evvivano i Zuavi !' White handkerchiefs waved from the windows, and the doors were all thrown open. They clasped us in their arms and called us their liberators. The women wept for joy and gave thanks to the Madonna. The action had lasted four hours, and they had not ceased praying for our victory. The Garibaldians had thirty killed and fifty wounded. We made 130 prisoners, They were 708 strong; we were only 340. If you knew the sacrileges they had committed in the Benedictine convent! They smashed the altars, flung down the sacred relics, and stabbed at the sacred images with their bayonets. They stole two ciboriums, sacked the seminary, and burned the town registers and the Papal arms. Pray for me. If the powers do not intervene, some of us will be in heaven before the year is out. We shall be glad to give our blood for the Holy Father and the Church."

On October 11th a detachment left Subiaco to explore the neighbourhood of Cervara and Camerata. A strong band of Garibaldians, profiting by their absence, came down from the mountains and occupied the town. The few gendarmes left there were obliged to fly. Lieutenant-Colonel de Charette, on being informed of what had passed, diverged from his march on Nerola and moved upon Subiaco; but before his arrival, the detachment, which had left in the morning, had returned, and an obstinate engagement ensued in the town.

The Garibaldians were completely beaten, fifteen prisoners were taken, several were wounded, and three were killed, among them one Emilio Bressio, of Milan, their commander.

A correspondent of *L'Univers*, gives the following account of the action at Monte Libretti, on the 13th of October :—

" Monte Libretti is a fortified village with gates.—(Its natural position flanked on either side by ravines is a strong one.) Some two hundred yards from the gate is a wide and deep ditch, crossed by a stone bridge. It was guarded, and the ninety Zouaves commanded by Lieutenants Guillemin and de Quelen received the enemy's fire at this point and carried the bridge in an instant. They took here ten prisoners, and rapidly ascending the slope towards the gate received the fire of three hundred Garibaldians concealed amongst the vines to the right and left of the road. Charging them with the bayonet, the Zouaves dislodged them and entered the village, but the fire in the streets from the windows was too hot, and they had to retreat to the gate, where an obstinate fight took place. The Garibaldian Major Fascri and his aide-de-camp animated their men, who vastly outnumbered the Pontificals; both of them were wounded and dismounted.

"The brave Zouave, Lieutenant Arthur Guillemin, was one of the first killed at the gate of Monte Libretti. Sergeant de la Bergassiere received a bullet in his arm, another bullet carried off his *kepi*, which he replaced by the red and green *kepi* of the fallen Garibaldian Major. A Zouave from Marseilles had a wound in the head, a bullet in each arm, and lost two fingers of the right hand. He had slain several of the enemy before he retired from the front. In the hospital he said next day, 'I don't understand these Garibaldians. At the first ball they drop. I have had four, and here I am.' An English corporal named Collingridge performed prodigies of valour. He was killed after being seen with his back to the wall defending himself desperately against six Garibaldians. His brother joined the Zouaves the week before. A Belgian corporal (Mercier, from Namur) is named as having distinguished himself extraordinarily. He is among the wounded. A Roman bugler, called Mimi by his comrades, had one hand shattered by a ball; he continued throughout to sound the charge, holding his bugle in the other hand. Sergeant-Major Bach, a German Swiss, was particularly conspicuous. He was bathed in blood, but it was the blood of the enemy. He himself did not receive a scratch.

"The Dutchman De Yonghe, a gigantic Hercules, was slain after killing fourteen Garibaldians. Bareheaded, and with his uniform torn to ribbons, he was seen dealing fearful blows with the butt-end of his musket, until, breathless with fatigue, though unwounded, he fell upon his knees and was pierced by a dozen bayonets. Two other Dutch Zouaves, brothers, were also slain. The Sous-Lieutenant de Quelen fought till the last, in worthy emulation of his friend and brother officer Guillemin. He was killed at the end of the action. The fight began at half-past five p.m., and at eight p.m. the Zouaves still held their ground in front of the gate. The night was beautifully calm, and a full moon lit the scene of so much valour.

" At eight p.m., the Garibaldians inside the village closed the gate, leaving a number of their comrades outside who were slain by the Zouaves under command of Sergeant-Major Bach, who kept his ground until four a.m. next day, when, just as he was about to retreat upon Monte Maggiore with his prisoners and wounded, the inhabitants opened the gate, announcing that the Garibaldians had retreated through the opposite gate making for Nerola."

The accounts of the number of the opposing forces in the engagement of Monte Libretti, do not all agree in every particular, but all concur in stating that the Garibaldians were in immensely superior strength to the Zouaves; the numbers I have seen stated in two different quarters, represent the Garibaldians to have had 1200 men, while the Zouaves had only ninety men, or one small company.

It will have been noticed from the foregoing narration, that although the ninety Zouaves did not succeed at once in dislodging twelve hundred Garibaldians from a strong position, yet it was certainly a *victory gained by the Zouaves*, as, the Garibaldians having stolen off under cover of the night, the field of battle and the position both remained in the possession of the Pontifical troops. This engagement and victory, having thus been won against such fearful odds as *thirteen* to *one*, is worthy of being ranked by the side of the most glorious achievements recorded in history, for although the engagement may not have been so very important in its immediate results,—on account of the small number of men engaged on both sides,—yet it is not always on account of its *results* that an achievement is immortalised—witness the devotion to death of Leonidas, and three hundred Spartans, at the pass of Thermopylæ—but it is heroism and valour which cause a brilliant action to shine with lustre, and to adorn, in vivid colouring, the page of history.

On reading the authentic accounts given above, who will be found to deny that the Zouaves displayed the greatest *heroism,*—both their commanding officers, one after the other, falling at the head of their company, others, like De Yonghe and Collingridge, fighting like lions, till they fell literally exhausted with fatigue?

The Pontifical gendarmes also did their duty, and showed their fidelity to their Sovereign, as may be seen from the following report of the fighting at Vallecorsa, copied from the Roman correspondent of the *Tablet*:—" Vallecorsa was attacked on Tuesday by a band of Garibaldians, but the gendarmes behaved nobly and drove them back, taking sixty-six prisoners, among whom were their commanding officer and four subalterns. Ten were killed, while two gendarmes fell mortally wounded."

Here follow a few other interesting particulars:—" The bands—of Garibaldians—are entirely composed of Milanese, Florentines, Romagnoli, Marchezziani, and a very few Roman emigrants. Not a single inhabitant of the country has joined, and although no excesses of the kind that took place at Bagnorea—these have been before related—have occurred at Nerola or Monte Libretti, the people do not disguise their dislike of the invaders, nor do the chiefs of the bands pretend that they have any support from the country itself."

The assertions just made by the correspondent, of the dispositions of the Holy Father's subjects, are fully borne out by authentic accounts from every quarter, of which sufficient proof will be here given, in General Kanzler's official report of the entry into Monte Rotondo after the battle of Mentana, by letters from different persons quoted, and also by the *remarkable fact*, that the Garibaldian and Mazzinian revolutionists—notwithstanding their putting in motion all the machinery of the secret societies—signally failed in their efforts to excite a rising within the walls of Rome during the crisis of the Garibaldian raids.

We gather the following details of the engagement at Nerola from the same source as the last—the correspondent being an eye-witness of the victory:—

"The column of Colonel de Charette was already in movement from Monte Rotondo on the Garibaldian post, when about eleven o'clock we observed an unusual excitement among the Garibaldians. Their out-sentries were withdrawn, and their forces concentrated in the fortress. The bugles sounded to arm a few moments later, and through the yellowing woods to the left of the position we distinguished clearly the flash of the Zouave bayonets, the gay uniform of the Antibes Legion, and the oxen dragging the battery of artillery under M. de Quatrebarbes, which was to help the assault . . . . . From the look-out we could easily distinguish the advance. Colonel de Charette and Major de Troussures, his second in command, led the van on horseback, and the 1st, 2nd, and 5th companies of Zouaves followed and halted on the eminences. The place having been summoned and replying by a rifle shot and a shout of 'Viva l'Italia!' the Antibes Legion advanced to the front, and took up a skirmishing position close to the ambulance in which we were placed. The first volley from the Garibaldians was a spirited one, and three of the Legionaries fell desperately wounded. We threw open the door of the ambulance, and three or four young soldiers immediately offered themselves to carry the wounded, draw water, and prepare beds, and a moment or two after the chaplain of the Legion, Mgr. Bastide, the Père Wylde, S. J., the Dutch and Belgian confessor, and the Pères Legier, O. P. and Daniel came up, and taking their places at the beds of the wounded, commenced their pious mission. Mgr. Stonor had been there from an early hour in the morning, devoting himself to the care of the wounded of the previous encounters. The Zouave companies soon came up the steep ascent, and then the action became general. I had the great pleasure of seeing several of our English Zouaves rivalling their French and Belgian comrades in courage and *elan*. Among them were the two brothers Watts-Russell, and the brother of Mr. Collingridge, who has just joined Mr. Cary; and having seen them under a severe fire, I am most happy to be able, as an eye-witness, to testify to their gallantry. The company of Captain Toudien scaled the heights from the further side, and kept up a tremendous fire 'en tirailleur' on the fort. MM. de Lusignan, de Montbel, de Gatebois, all distinguished themselves in the attack. The 'Batterie Quartrebarbes' came up at last, and then a tremendous fire opened on the 'Place,' which was returned fiercely by the Garibaldian rifles.

"A terrible cry of rage broke from the Zouave ranks as a ball struck M. de Charette's horse, and the Colonel fell to the ground. He was, however, up again in a moment, unhurt, and waving his sword to M. de Quatrebarbes, whose next shot from the battery brought down the tri-coloured flag from the castle, and amid a burst of cheering, the Zouaves charged up the hill crying "Vive Pio IX.!" their officers leading them on several paces in front of the column, which was formed en tirailleur. Suddenly a white flag was displayed on the ramparts of the fortress, and we knew that the battle was ours. The Compagnie Tourmelin, with its gallant Belgian sergeant-major, M. Caullier, was the first to arrive, and the terms having been refused, the garrison laid down their arms and surrendered at discretion.

"The wounded of the Garibaldian party were immediately cared for, and it was most touching to see the repentance and piety with which several of them received the last sacraments at the hands of Monsignore Bastide, and Monsignore Stonor. The medical staff behaved admirably on both sides, and were impartial in their care of the wounded of either party, and the Zouave officers ordered that every kindness should be shown to those who had 'cared for our men when in their hands.'"

The correspondent is here referring to the consideration

shown to the wounded Zouave prisoners carried off from Monte Libretti to Nerola, by the orders of the brothers Garibaldi.

"Dr. O'Flynn, of the Zouaves, was left in charge of the Zouave ambulance in conjunction with a Garibaldian surgeon. The Antibes Legion alone suffered on this occasion. A young officer, M. Eschmann, was dangerously wounded with three of his men, and one killed. A Pontifical gendarme officer and one of his soldiers were severely wounded. None of the Zouaves received a wound."

One hundred and thirty-four Garibaldians were taken prisoners, and amongst them was the Garibaldian commanding officer. Thus far the Garibaldian raid has been a complete failure, and the chief organiser, Garibaldi himself, has been deceived in his thinking to drive the Pontifical soldiers before him with the "*butt-ends of their muskets;*" and now his volunteers have completely disappeared for the present from the Pontifical States.

The victory of Nerola was gained on Oct. 18th, after which the revolutionary bands retreated to the Italian States.

The correspondent before quoted, writes as follows from Rome, Oct. 27th:

". . . . The march—from Nerola to Monte Rotondo—had been a fearful one across the mountains, and it was only possible to bring back part of the wounded, as the carriage-road, by which alone they could be transported, runs through Corrèse on the Italian territory, and this circumstance necessitated my return the next day with the ambulance to Nerola, no military, not even the surgeons of the corps, being allowed to go in search of our unfortunate soldiers. On reaching Nerola next day, I found that Mr. Collingridge had died the night following the engagement of Nerola, surrounded by his companions-in-arms, and receiving the last consolations of religion at the hands of Father Wylde, with the most heroic sentiments of piety and resignation. He lived a hero and died a martyr to the good cause, and his blood, the first shed for it by an English Catholic, will be the seed of a race of manlier and braver defenders of the Church than our Catholic youth has yet afforded to Rome. His obsequies, which I had the honour of assisting at, were performed in the little church of Saint Antonio the next morning, with those of an Antibes soldier who died the same night.

"The surgeon of Montorio Romano, who assisted in the removal of our few remaining wounded, assured me that on the first fire of the Papal cannon, five hundred of Menotti's band, who witnessed the combat from an adjoining height, threw down their arms and deserted. Menotti, who had ordered Mattia Valentini to hold out two hours at Nerola, then abandoned all idea of relieving the place, and left the garrison to its fate. Such cowardice, with 2,500 men, is utterly inconceivable, especially as he held a flank position, most perilous for our column.

"At Correse, we were, in consequence of this inhuman order (of the Italian lieutenant not to allow the ambulance to enter an Italian 'Osteria'), obliged to go on to a miserable cottage on the Pontifical side, to get ready, under great difficulties, what was necessary."

The Garibaldians had acted with humanity to our wounded, in comparison with what they met with from the Italian regular troops, and it speaks little for the military spirit of the army of Victor Emmanuel. Amid the revolting sacrileges and impieties practised by the Garibaldians,—as for instance at Bagnorea already related,—it is a pleasing relief to hear of their care and humanity for their wounded opponents, displayed particularly at Nerola, where their forces were commanded by Menotti and Ricciotti Garibaldi, sons of the old revolutionary general. Another relieving feature of the otherwise dark aspect of the picture is the repentance exhibited by many of these misguided youths—entrapped into the meshes of the secret societies, and into the revolutionary army—when they are wounded and have to face eternity; the piety which many of them exhibited on receiving the last sacraments and consolations of the Catholic religion on their deathbeds, has been beautifully described by the correspondent before quoted, in the last letter but one.

The following interesting paragraphs relate to a critical period:

"On reaching Rome we found the city preparing for its defence *à l'outrance*. Barricades were raised at all the gates, cannon placed at every embrasure of the earthworks, and a movement was known to be organised for the evening of Wednesday. . . . At the Campidoglio all had been prepared by the conspirators to proclaim the republic, and there, too, the guard was attacked. The troops fired and killed ten Garibaldians. Later in the evening the caserne of Serristori, near St. Peter's, exploded with a fearful report. It had been mined, and one whole side was blown into the air, burying thirty men under the ruins. The dead are eighteen, and the wounded twelve or fourteen, but they are still disinterring bodies."

This explosion took place on the 22nd of October. It was planned and directed by the secret societies to assist the Garibaldian invasion, and the other Zouave barracks being also mined, it was a cowardly conspiracy to destroy in cold blood those whom the revolutionary bands were unable to conquer on the field of battle. Such dastardly outrages as these are surely worthy of the execration of Christendom, and of every civilised nation.

CHAPTER II.

SECRET SOCIETIES OF THE CONTINENT—CRITICAL STATE OF
ROME—COURAGE OF AN IRISHMAN—CAPTAIN DE LA
HOYDE ON MENTANA.

THE secret societies spread through Italy and France, with connections in other countries of the continent, are known by different names, such as the *Carbonari, Francmaçons,* &c., but the objects of the chiefs, and of those admitted to the higher grades of each of these secret organisations, are all more or less the same, and they are, first, the destruction of the order which the Providence of God has established in the world; next, the destruction of religion, of Christianity, and even of the belief in a Supreme Being. The doctrines of these pretended regenerators of the human race, being equality, *i.e.*, possession of everything in common, and implying no superiority of anyone in dignity or authority —a principle subversive of all government; liberty and license; fraternity; atheism; and a belief and worship of the goddess, Nature.

Although I should be sorry to accuse even the majority of the members of these secret sects of holding all these frightful doctrines, yet I am fully convinced that they are held more or less by the chiefs, and that the objects named above are those for which the societies exist, and particularly the *Carbonari*. Two works published by Father Bresciani—"The Jew of Verona," and "Lionella," a sequel to the former—let great light into the fearful machinery by which the latter sect is worked, and especially with regard to its operations in the Roman Revolution of 1848-9.

As a proof of the truth of what I have brought forward,

I beg to refer the reader to a French work, "Les Francmaçons," by Mgr. Segur, Paris. If the reader is not able to refer to this work, I can sincerely assure him that the French prelate cites facts and authorities of indisputable weight in support of the statements I have given of the objects and doctrines of the secret sects. It may be asked —how comes it that many professed Catholics join these societies, if the objects are those I have given? The reason is, that they are entrapped into the meshes of the sects by the specious cries of *liberty, equality, fraternity,* without knowing the real objects of the organisation they have been drawn into; then afterwards, when once initiated, it appears too late to retrace a false step, especially as, if they retreat, they must be prepared to face the dagger— which is the punishment awarded by the sect to all whom it fears to trust longer with its secrets.

On the 23rd of October the citizens of the Eternal City were kept in a constant state of alarm by the efforts of the secret sects to provoke a revolution; their efforts to destroy the Zouaves in their barracks on the previous day have been already mentioned, and in the same letter from Rome which I last quoted we read: "Bombs were thrown in every direction, at the Zouave Club, the gendarmerie barracks, and the quarters of the Antibes Legion, and the alarm at length became so general, that the provisional measures preparatory to a state of siege were published. Cordons of military were drawn across the Corso and principal streets, patrols traversed the city in every direction, and the citizens were warned to retire to their houses. Still, throughout the next day our outposts were attacked. At Papa Giulio there was a very severe encounter, in which the Legion d'Antibes and Swiss killed ten, and took fifteen prisoners, all leading men of the party of action, among whom are Cairoli, Colloredo, and several young men of education."

The following interesting account of the taking of the revolutionary depôt of arms in the Trastevere has been furnished by an eye-witness, who was one of the attacking party: "On the 23rd of October, 1867, at two, p.m., a piquet was formed of twenty-one Zouaves and twenty-one gendarmes, with the intention of seizing a house supposed to be one of the revolutionary depôts of arms. The piquet dividing into seven patrols of three gendarmes and three Zouaves each, left the barracks of San Calisto in the Trastevere. Each patrol took a different street to avoid observation, and if possible, to surround the house without the knowledge of the inmates. However, this was not to be, for scarcely had the patrol to which I belonged got in sight of the house, when a shot was fired by a man (a *supposed sentinel*) which struck the head of one of the gendarmes. This was the signal for the conflict. The revolutionists—fifty-six in number—immediately flew to the windows and commenced a very heavy fire on the different patrols, which had now united. Not content with that, the enemy got on the top of the house, on which there was a spacious terrace, and from there threw *bombs*, slates, melted lead, &c., on our heads. Our position being much to our disadvantage, and our forces inferior in number, we were obliged to send for a reinforcement, which speedily arrived. The fire was kept up on both sides with great animation. About half-past four, p.m., the commander, seeing that our remaining outside was of no avail, gave the necessary order for an assault. The order was received with a cheer, and the Zouaves, like the true heroes they have always proved themselves, rushed forward without hesitation through the fire of the enemy, and were soon engaged in overthrowing and breaking through the barricades thrown up. Very little resistance was made on the stairs. On arriving at the apartment occupied by the revolutionists, the panels of the door were immediately broken through with the butt ends of our muskets. A stoppage now ensued. The captain asked: 'Who will go in first?' The answer was not long forthcoming. An Irishman, the only one of his countrymen engaged in this affair, immediately answered: 'I will.' He entered, and was soon followed by his comrades, who, furious at the prolonged resistance of the enemy, now commenced the fight in earnest. Random shots were fired, but without much effect to either party, but frightful havoc was performed with the bayonet, with which our fellows rushed on the revolutionists, and made awful but short work of their business: seventeen of the enemy were killed, and the rest taken prisoners.

"The Zouaves, although excited and furious almost to madness at seeing their comrades shot down beside them, yet when those very men who had done this, throw themselves on their knees and beg for their lives in the name of the Madonna, listen to the cry for mercy, and their enemies are spared, and made prisoners. In the house were found immense quantities of ammunition, thirty or forty breechloaders, several cases of bombs and stilettoes, with several hundred pikes, torches, and everything necessary to help a republican demonstration. The salvation of Rome in 1867, partly dates from the glorious success of the 23rd of October; in fact, it may be said that that day the grave of the revolution was dug, to be finally filled up after the glorious victory of Mentana."

This narrative shows in glorious colours both the courage and the gentleness of the victors. The Irishman here mentioned behaved so admirably, that he received a gold medal and the rank of sergeant for his bravery. They fought as long as any resistance was offered, and then, like true soldiers, they showed mercy to those who craved it.

It appears from another account that all the revolutionists were natives of the North of Italy, and not *Romans*.

On or about this day a Zouave of the depôt who was carrying the soup to his comrades on guard, was fired on and killed in cold blood by a revolutionary hand.

All the outrages and conspiracies mentioned in this and the preceding chapter, were conceived and carried out by the agency of the secret societies, with a view to frighten the peaceably inclined Romans and their defenders the Pontifical soldiers, and to stir up a rising in Rome, and to proclaim there the red republic, while in the meantime the Garibaldians did their share of the work by entering again the Pontifical States, in order, as they thought, to crush all opposition in the field, and to march on the Eternal City, in order to proclaim the republic from the top of the capitol.*

How the whole design was frustrated will be shown by the sequel.

I have been, through the kindness of a Zouave friend, furnished with the following very interesting paragraph, letter, and official reports, of the defence of Monte Rotondo and battle of Mentana, which were published in the *Freeman's Journal* of November 18th and November 22nd, 1867:—

"One of the first to volunteer from this country in defence of the glorious and holy cause of Pius the Ninth, was Lieutenant Albert Delahoyd, second son of our estimable fellow-citizen Mr. Robert Delahoyd. Even before the formation of an Irish Brigade was spoken of, he was in communication with friends in Rome, with a view of entering the Pontifical army.

"However, as the great sympathy meeting of 1860 gave practical effect to its resolutions in sending out the Battalion of St. Patrick, he obtained a sub-lieutenant's commission in that corps, and as staff officer to General De Lamoriciere, in Ancona, shared the perils of the siege. That brief and unequal campaign being ended in the manner we are all acquainted with, instead of returning home he retraced his steps from Marseilles to Rome, and, content to enter the remnant of the brave Franco-Belgian legion as a private soldier, remained in Rome ever since, and worked his way through the several military grades until he reached his present proud position of a first lieutenant in the immortal Zouaves, a position which he has now filled for nearly two years, and is soon likely to exchange for a captaincy. The subjoined letter from him, written after the battle of Mentana, in which he took a part, and giving details of that glorious day, will, we are sure, be perused with interest:—

" ' Rome, 8th November, 1867.

" ' In my last letter I gave you a hurried sketch of our

* Speech of Garibaldi.

expedition to Nerola. On the following Wednesday three companies of Zouaves, with cavalry and two guns, made a reconnaisance outside the walls, beginning at Ponte Molle, near which, at Monte Parioli, the site of the celebrated Acqua Acetosa, there had been a skirmish the evening before, between a small detachment of Swiss and a band which had dropped down the Tiber at night in small boats. This band contained many young men of good family, chiefly Lombards and Venetians, who were to have entered Rome in small groups and raise the row. They were well armed, but quickly dispersed. The Swiss had three wounded, and we found in a house several dead and wounded, and made some prisoners; we destroyed about fifty stand of arms, and captured thirty-five revolvers. These gentlemen had been pitching into a fine dinner when attacked, and we found a quantity of choice wines, &c. We scoured the vineyards, tore up the rails of the iron bridge, and mined the Ponte Salara and Nomentana. My feet blistered after the forced march from Nerola, got cut again, and lamed me for two days. Friday, Garibaldi, with four thousand men, attacked Monte Rotondo, defended by two companies of the Antibes Legion, one company Swiss, two guns, and about thirty dragoons and gendarmes. This little garrison repulsed four assaults, and only surrendered for want of ammunition, after twenty-seven hours. The Garibaldians had about three hundred *hors de combat;* we had an artillery sergeant killed. Lieutenant de Quatrebarbes, nephew of Count de Quatrebarbes, Governor of Ancona in 1860, got a ball in the left elbow, and lost a joint of the second finger of the right hand; seven Swiss were wounded, of whom one has since died. Dr. O'Flynn was unhurt, but made prisoner. Saturday our colonel (Allet) started with nine hundred men and two guns, but arrived too late. The Garibaldians say that but for the old fellow himself they would never have persevered, and had the garrison held out another hour (they had no more ammunition), or Allet's column been some hours earlier, they would have been obliged to retreat. Saturday I slept at home, having a slight feverishness from fatigue.

Sunday, 27th, I was on piquet at Piazza Colonna, and at night was sent to reinforce the advanced post of Porta Salara (forty Zouaves). I passed the night on a chair, against the wall of the little police station, in the rain. Towards morning we finished the mine, blew up the bridge, tore up the railway bridge, and retired. Monday night, 28th, I slept with my company under the colonnade of St. Peter's, and on Tuesday was off to Ponte Molle for three days, during which (as nearly always since the 16th of October), I never took off my boots nor washed my face. Sunday morning we started to beat up Garibaldi at Monte Rotondo. Our force consisted of the regiment of Zouaves (fourteen companies), the Swiss (eight companies), six guns, and one and a half squadron of dragoons. In reserve three French battalions (one Chasseurs and two of the line, which latter had the chassepots), and two guns. We crossed Ponte Nomentana at half-past six, a.m. Five or six hundred men were detached under Major De Troussures, of the Zouaves to act on Garibaldi's rear. Our march was necessarily slow, being about to throw out scouts. At ten we halted to take coffee and repose. We expected to find five hundred men at Mentana, whom we should drive in, and have a severe fight at Monte Rotondo, but the bands having devoured all that was in the town, had set out that morning for Tivoli. About three miles before the village the road winds up and down four hills, pretty steep, and covered with oak woods and brush. Here, at half-past twelve o'clock, the first shot was fired; we halted, threw out the four companies, first battalion, as skirmishers, second battalion remaining in column. At one the firing got smart. I made a final act of contrition, and we dashed on in support.

"The ravines and underwood rendered a charge in line impossible, so we went on where we could, with fixed bayonets and firing constantly. In less than an hour we had driven them from three strong positions. A certain number retired into two houses, firing from the windows. One of these was taken '*a la baionette;*' twenty were bayoneted and at least as many taken, the others fled from the house on the left of the road, leaving a number dead, wounded and prisoners. A moment before Captain De Veaux fell, shot through the heart. One of my sub-lieutenants Dujardin (promoted three days before) got a shot in the hand, but we had few struck. The Colonel ordered halt, to let the artillery come up, for the village is so placed that one can only enter by the narrow street. Garibaldi himself arrived just then, but seeing the 'run,' returned to the village (two o'clock p. m.) and directed the defence till four p. m., when he '*evaporated.*' The artillery plied the village with shell and grape, every window was occupied by Red Shirts. The Swiss, and some stragglers of ours, and the Legion extended behind a rising ground on the right; a crowd of fellows fleeing fell in the trap; the artillery sent them a shot of grape, and the Swiss finished driving them into the town. The French began about half-past three p.m. driving them from an olive wood. A French battalion of the line tried to enter the town, but from the nature of the ground, was obliged to content itself with plying them with the chassepot. Meantime De Troussure's column came on their rear; as the enemy was nine or ten thousand the havoc was awful. Night came on and put an end to the affair.

"We expected to continue the next day, but they evacuated on the right, carrying off upwards of 500 wounded.

"At six a. m. on Monday some skirmishing took place, and the rest soon surrendered. They lost at least 300 killed (it has since been ascertained the loss in killed amounted to 600): we took 1,500 prisoners, of whom about 150 wounded, and a quantity of arms. About nine o'clock, General De Polhès arrived with his brigade, and we marched on Monte Rotondo, which had been evacuated in the night. There we found our wounded prisoners, captured a number of Red Shirts, and at least 8,000 muskets. The Zouaves lost twenty-three killed and two officers, and about sixty men wounded, mostly without danger. We bore the brunt. The Legion had eight wounded, the Swiss and French lost but few. Our total loss in dead does not exceed forty, and in wounded about seventy. On Wednesday we returned to Rome, and there were still dead lying about. Many wretches, doubtless, fleeing wounded, have died miserably in the woods.

"On our arrival at Rome, we were received by a crowd of all classes, and got an enthusiastic cheering. Don Alfonso, Count of Caserta, brother of Francis the Second, with two other Neapolitan colonels of artillery, were on General Kanzler's staff, and directed several of the guns. Monte Rotondo was devastated. When we arrived we could get neither meat, bread, nor cigars. The commissariat got something prepared and distributed. I passed Sunday with a cup of soldiers' coffee, some biscuit, and a little water, which latter was exceedingly difficult to get, as there was but one well. At night I lay on the ground in my mantle, sleeping perfectly from eight till two, when I awoke unable to walk from cold. I then slept about an hour and a half before a camp fire. On coming to Monte Rotondo, I went to a family where I had lodged before, got from them some smoked ham, wine and bread; got to bed at eight and slept till six. On Tuesday, with a young Calabrian friend, a sergeant, we ferreted out some cheese and macaroni, and in the evening we had cheese and salad. It was droll to see the officers, as well as the soldiers, trotting about with bundles of salad, radishes, &c., under their arms.

"The churches were devastated, chalices, &c., stolen. We found a broken chalice on one wretch, the ostensorium, with particles of the Host on another; everything plundered; the altar, furniture, crucifixes, &c., smashed and burned, a scene which brought tears to all our eyes, and then the poor people of the town looking horror-struck at the wreck, 'twas horrible.

"There are but few stragglers now on the territory, and they are busy plundering as they go off.

"We are likely to have peace till the spring, when we may hope for a general war, when Italy will certainly break up, if, indeed, the Red party do not upset everything before them. In all we have lost two captains, one lieutenant, (my poor friend Guillemin) and two sub-lieutenants (Emanuel Dufournel and Urban De Quelen.) The captains killed were De Veaux and Adeodatus Dufournel, brother of the sub-lieutenant. Two new companies have been formed, and two more soon will be; so I think I shall have another stripe ere Christmas.

"By the blowing up of the corner of the Serristori barracks, we lost sixteen men, and at Monte Libretti ten; our total loss is fifty dead, but the Garibaldians have got a lesson, of which I do not think they will risk another. Two Englishmen have fallen, Corporal Collingridge, wounded at Monte Libretti, died at Nerola; and young Watts Russell killed at Mentana; a Westmeath man, Curran, was slightly wounded in the arm. .... I put all in order (this is in allusion to his preparation for the next world) to have as short a quarantine as possible, 'in case'—and got my passport viséd every eight days, so my only preoccupation was on your account."

CHAPTER III.

GENERAL KANZLER'S REPORT OF THE BATTLE OF MENTANA
ADDRESSED TO THE POPE.

" MOST HOLY FATHER—Whilst hoping at some future day to lay at your Holiness's feet a more circumstantial report of the several engagements victoriously sustained by the Pontifical troops against the sacrilegious invaders of the States of your Holiness, I hasten to present this report on the combat at Mentana, in which the French allied troops valorously co-operated, to the end that the truth about this decisive engagement, so much disfigured by the revolutionary press, may be declared as speedily as possible.

" The threat of an invasion by the regular army, concerning which a rumour was circulated of the confines having been actually passed on the Monte Rotondo side, and the continual increase in the provinces of the Garibaldian hordes, which, on several points had begun to be massed in formidable corps, induced me to propose to your Holiness on the 27th of October last, the extreme measures of abandoning the provinces and concentrating all the troops in Rome, and not expose them to the danger of being attacked in isolated positions and overwhelmed by such an invasion. No sooner were the provinces abandoned than they were immediately occupied by the bands of Garibaldi, which, meeting with no opposition, became every day more numerous and more oppressive.

" On the 26th ult., the little garrison of Monte Rotondo was assailed by forces ten times more numerous. It surrendered after a most heroic resistance, and these bands, emboldened by success, pushed their outposts up to the very walls of Rome, disturbing the city and suburbs, and threatening to give a helping hand to the many hired assassins who had been secretly introduced into this capital, the better to insure that it also should become a victim to their sacrilegious desires. It therefore became a matter of urgent necessity to strike some decisive blow to repress their audacity, and put an end to their bandit enterprise. I determined, in consequence, to put myself at the head of a column of troops, not too inferior in numbers to the Garibaldians, and give them battle at that very spot whence they boasted they would march to the conquest of Rome. Having communicated this project to the Commander-in-Chief of the French troops, Count de Failly, he manifested a desire to support us with a column of French troops to secure us against a surprise from other bands, which mustered in considerable numbers around Tivoli, and which, if informed in time, might have attacked us in flank whilst we were operating on Monte Rotondo.

"The Pontifical column placed under the command of General Count de Courten was composed of the following troops, viz.:—

Two battalions of Zouaves, commanded by Colonel Allet	1,500 men
One battalion of Carabineers (Swiss) under the orders of Lieutenant-Colonel Jeannerot	520 „
One battalion of Antibes Legion, commanded by Colonel Count d'Argy	540 „
One battery, six pieces of artillery, commanded by Captain Polani	117 „
One squadron of four platoons of dragoons, under the orders of Captain Cremona	106 „
One company of sappers	80 „
Gendarmes	50 „
Total	2,913 „

"The French column which followed as a reserve,

commanded by Brigadier-General Baron de Polhès consisted of :—

Second battalion of foot chasseurs
First battalion of the 1st regiment of the line,
  under the orders of Colonel Fremont
First battalion of the 20th of the line, commanded by Colonel Saussier
Second battalion of the 59th of the line, under
  the command of Colonel Berger
A platoon of the 7th mounted chasseurs, commanded by Commandant Wederspach-Tor
A platoon of Papal dragoons commanded by
  Sub-Lieutenant Belli
Half a battery of artillery
  Forming a total of .   .   .   .   2,000 men

Thus the two columns numbered very near 5,000 men.

"We started at four in the morning from Porta Pia, and, crossing the Ponte Nomentana, marched along the road that leads to Mentana. Having crossed the bridge, I ordered Major de Troussures of the Zouaves to go with three companies of his regiment along the Anio to the Via Salara, and advancing cautiously by that road, to create a diversion for the enemy, whilst I would make the attack from the opposite side. The advanced guard of the principal column, preceded by a platoon of dragoons under Lieutenant de la Rochette, was made up of three companies of Zouaves, under the command of Major de Lambilly, and a section of artillery directed by Lieutenant Cheynet. The enemy we went to encounter was militarily encamped, expecting an attack, and, so far from giving any indications of retreat, was disposing his principal corps in the direction of Tivoli. Warned by his outposts of the movements of our columns, he prepared to meet us. The barricades which were afterwards discovered, as well at Montana as at Monte Rotondo and his advanced posts, evidently proved that he had well entrenched himself in a strongly fortified position to await us. At about three quarters past twelve o'clock, and at a distance of four kilometres from Mentana the advanced guard came upon the first Garibaldian posts, situated in most favourable positions upon hills commanding the road along which we marched.

"Our Zouaves, without a moment's hesitation, threw themselves upon this first line of the enemy, with which little by little the entire regiment of Zouaves became seriously engaged. In this first encounter very few shots were fired, because the enemy, so quickly surrounded by bayonets, was driven from the heights to others not far distant. In this first attack Captain De Veaux fell a glorious victim, struck by a ball which passed right through his heart whilst heading his company. This more than impetuous onslaught was supported by the Swiss Carabineers, one company of which took the left of the road, whilst the others were thrown out along the right. At the same moment two companies of the Legion by a well-directed fire drove the Garibaldians from a neighbouring wood, from which they annoyed the left wing of our column by a continuous fusillade. The enemy being routed in disorder from his first positions, endeavoured to reform under cover and in strong masses behind the walled enclosure of the Santucci vineyard, but there, too, the [Zouaves with irresistible *élan* attacked the vineyard and farmhouse, and were soon masters of both. Lieutenant Colonel de Charette was on this occasion at the head of the Zouaves in the attack and his horse received three balls, whilst Colonel Allet throughout the whole action was endeavouring to maintain the compactness of his too ardent soldiers.

"From the beginning the combat was seconded by discharges from one piece of artillery which, placed on a hill at the left of the road, was pointed at the masses of the enemy that endeavoured to reform in the Santucci vineyard and was only silent when the rapid advance of our infantry rendered a continuance of fire dangerous. When the entire column had reached the summit of the Santucci vineyard, a howitzer was placed on a hill at the left of the road, about

800 metres from Mentana, and was speedily joined by two pieces of French rifled artillery escorted by two companies of foot chasseurs; this artillery whilst firing on the Castle of Mentana disabled the guns of the enemy. Almost at the same moment another piece of Pontifical artillery was placed on the road at a distance of 500 metres from Mentana, and judging also that the Santucci vineyard was favourable ground for establishing a section, I ordered the third section of the Polani battery to post itself there, which united its fire with capital success, to that of the pieces posted at a short distance on the hill to the left. Meanwhile, our brave infantry, with ever increasing ardour, advanced towards Mentana, seeking to gain ground as well on the left as on the right of this most solid and almost unassailable village. The enemy, perceiving this move, deployed two strong columns to attack us on both flanks, and partially succeeded, especially on the right wing, so that the battalion of Swiss Carabineers which had pushed on through an olive grove to within a very short distance of the village, suddenly found itself between two fires, but it did not on this account, although suffering heavy loss yield one inch of ground that it had gained. It was then about half-past three in the afternoon, and not having any more of my own column in reserve, since Colonel D'Argy of the Antibes Legion who had all the responsibility of watching our centre, was left with a very small force, I invited General de Polhès to support both our wings.

"The French, who were up to that moment but spectators of our progress, and very impatient ones, in an instant, with their habitual bravery, threw themselves upon the enemy's columns which were threatening to surround us. Colonel Fremont of the 1st of the line, in fact, and aided by three companies of the Chasseurs-à-pied not only arrested the enemy's column, but having arrived at the extreme left of the Garibaldians opened such a deadly fire on them that they were compelled to beat a hasty retreat. This Colonel moreover had the daring to push on at the rear of Mentana itself, to within a very short distance of Monte Rotondo, which doubtless he would have entered with his column before the Garibaldians, but that he feared he should be isolated from the rest of our forces. Lieutenant-colonel Saussier of the 29th of the line, accomplished a similar movement on our left wing. Having encountered an enemy's column, which with the force of about 1,500 men, crowned the heights of Monte Rotondo, notwithstanding the inferiority of his strength, he took up an advantageous position to keep them at bay and repulse them. Most opportunely at this moment the detachment of Major De Troussures arrived on the field, by the road running along the Tiber, and by the dexterous movements executed by only three companies of Zouaves, contributed in a great measure to intimidate the Garibaldians, and paralyze their attacking movements on our right wing. Moreover, Major De Troussures got upon the road leading from Monte Rotondo to Mentana, and penetrating to the rear of this last named village, made some prisoners. Meeting however a stout resistance, and knowing that Monte Rotondo was also occupied by bands, with great daring and equal success, he traversed the entire enemy's line till he got upon our extreme right, close beside the French battalion of the first of the line, and there bivouacked for the night. Meanwhile a section of artillery, commanded by Captain Daudier, pushed on within three hundred metres right under the walls of the Castle of Mentana, against which it opened a steady fire; but these pieces being too much exposed to the enemy's musketry, ran great risk of being overpowered. Bravely seconded, however, by a company of Zouaves, they maintained their position for some time, not without heavy loss, having had Marshal Count Bernadini killed, and two *guides* and several horses wounded. Nevertheless this section was safely removed and placed in a more advantageous position. The infantry who, through several hours, with unequalled bravery, had sustained and repulsed every attack, by degrees was closing round Mentana, which was now enclosed as it were within a circle of steel, despite the active, uninterrupted fire of its defenders lying behind its walls. I considered therefore that the moment had arrived, for attempting a decisive assault, and so terminating the action before night set in. I gave the necessary orders, and informed General de Polhès, who, with Colonel Berger moved on valorously at the head of the 59th, and second battalion of Chasseurs-à-pied, and advancing by a sheltered road on the right of the high road to within a very short distance of the walls of Mentana, succeeded in driving the enemy from the surrounding vineyards, but despite the most heroic endeavours he could not penetrate into the village, fortified as it was with barricades, and flanked by isolated houses, all strongly occupied by the enemy.

"Having observed that the principal scope of that day's battle was attained, because the enemy, driven from all his positions and after suffering immense loss, had retired into Mentana and there remained demoralized and frightened; I concluded (as night was just setting in) to postpone a renewal of the attack till the following morning; especially as there was no free exit from Mentana, and it was evident the enemy would ask to surrender without waiting for another assault, which would have infinitely increased its loss. Our troops therefore, scattered about on the several conquered positions, and mixed up with the French, were called together, and the necessary precautions being taken, we bivouacked for the night on the very ground which the enemy had occupied at first, guarding by strong advanced posts all round Mentana against any sortie.

"The night passed without any incident occurring, and the facts of the following day proved exactly the correctness of my calculations, for at an early hour ·on the morning of the 4th, a "parliamentaire" was conducted to head quarters to propose the surrender of Mentana, on condition that the enemy might be permitted to retire with arms and baggage, a condition which I naturally declined to agree to. Major Fauchon, of the 59th of the line, had in the meantime made a number of prisoners in the houses surrounding Mentana; and as this multitude of Garibaldians, along with so many others captured in preceding engagements, created an embarrassment, I considered it less inconvenient to allow the remaining defenders of the Castle of Mentana to retire without arms beyond the frontier. It was ascertained also that Monte Rotondo had been evacuated during the night, and Colonel Fremont, with a battalion of the 1st of the line, followed by the 2nd Chasseurs-à-pied, entered Monte Rotondo at an early hour, without having to strike a blow, and was welcomed with the most enthusiastic "Evvivas" for the Holy Father and the Emperor of the French.

"The spectacle which the city of Monte Rotondo presented to the eyes of our troops was sad in the extreme—churches devastated, profaned, the citizens terrified with the extortions and cruelties they were subjected to. The allied troops were hailed by them as the deliverers. Garibaldi, who, with his sons, was present at the battle of Mentana, was never seen in the first line, and when he beheld his followers yielding, driven in at all points by our brave troops, we have been told that he fled in all haste for safety to Monte Rotondo, and thence in the course of the evening passed the frontier, thus exchanging his impious cry of '*Rome or death*' for '*Sauve qui peut.*'

"On the other hand it must be acknowledged, that the movements of the enemy were well directed, and that confiding in their numerical superiority, and their favourable position, they defended themselves bravely at several points, especially from behind the walls and barricades.

Our losses were as follows:—

	KILLED.	WOUNDED.
De Courten column—Regiment of Zouaves, (including Captain De Vaux, killed, second Lieutenant Jacquemont and Sub-lieutenant Dujardin wounded),	24	57
The Roman (Antibes) Legion, privates	—	6
Battalion of Swiss Carabineers, (including Major Castella and Sub-lieutenant Dewerscheen, wounded)	5	37
Artillery	1	2
Dragoons	—	1
Total	30	103

	KILLED.	WOUNDED.
The De Polhès column—2nd battalion Chasseurs-à-pieds	—	6
1st Regiment of the line	—	2
25th Regiment of the line	—	5
59th Regiment of the line (including Captain Marambat and Lieutenant Blanc, both wounded) one missing	2	22
Regiment of Chasseurs mounted	—	1
Total, 1 missing	2	36

"According to the information gleaned from the inhabitants of Mentana and the prisoners, and arguing from the quantity of arms found, both in Mentana and Monte Rotondo, the Garibaldians numbered about 9,000, of which number more than 1,000 were put 'hors de combat,' and 1,398 were made prisoners. Several hundreds were escorted to the frontiers, the rest fled, breaking and throwing away their arms, and leaving one cannon behind. The result of the victory was therefore the most complete that could be hoped for. The humanity of the allied troops was equal to their valour. Soldiers of every arm, though worn out by the fatigues of the march, and the ensuing battle of four hours, set to work that very evening to search for the wounded, and resumed the following morning, bringing in, in the most careful manner, the Garibaldian wounded, as well as their own companions, to the ambulance, where all were equally cared for, not only by the military and sanitary officials, and the infirmarians belonging to the ambulance, but also by the heroic and charitable Mrs. Catharine Stone, by three Sisters of Charity, by the Messieurs Dr. Ozanam, Vicomte de St. Priest, Vrignault, Benoit D'Azy, and De Luppé, who came out expressly for this pious purpose. In gratitude I feel bound to signalize the cordial concurrence, valour and ability of General de Polhès, and I may be permitted to add also the name of Colonel Fremont, who distinguished himself for daring and military skill. I must also mention Colonel Berger, of the 59th of the line, and Lieutenant-Colonel Saussier of the 29th, who took a share, the first in the attack on the right, the second in that on the left. Amongst our troops, General de Courten with his aides-de-camp, Captain Eugene de Maistre, Captain Pietramellara, and Sub-Lieutenant de Terves, the heads of corps, officers and soldiers, all did their duty gloriously, and it would be too long a report if I were to note down every individual act of heroism.

"I cannot, however, pass over in silence the names of those, who, animated with the noble desire of combating for the sacred cause of your Holiness, voluntarily united themselves to the corps of operation. In the first place I must mention his Royal Highness the Count of Caserta, who, from the very beginning of this iniquitous invasion, placed himself at my disposal, beseeching me to employ him wherever danger should be greatest. His Royal Highness in the action at Mentana was admired by our troops for his courage, and gave unmistakable proof of military discernment and skill. Colonels Afan de Riviera and Ussani were worthy to follow their Prince. Colonel Sonnenburgh, commanding the Swiss Guard of your Holiness, was on the staff and rendered great services as staff-officer. Finally I must specially mention the courage, zeal, and services rendered by the officers of my staff, Major Ungarelli, aide-de-camp; Captain Francis de Maistre, Captain Bourbon de Chalus, and Captain Maumigny, as also the indefatigable activity of the Sub-Intendant Monari, who by his judicious foresight, provided the column with valuable resources. I am very happy to be able to conclude this my report, with the assurance that the Pontifical troops, as they have shown themselves throughout this campaign, worthy of the noble mission entrusted to them, so they will be glad to seize their arms with equal ardour every time the enemies of the Holy See may challenge them to new combats.

"In fine, I implore for the little army of your Holiness, for the allied troops and for myself your apostolic benediction.

"Of your Holiness the most humble, devoted, and obedient servant and subject,

"HERMAN KANZLER,
"*General, Pro-minister of Arms.*"

CHAPTER IV.

FRENCH OFFICIAL REPORT OF THE BATTLE—MGR. DUPANLOUP ON THE VICTORIES—DE QUELEN AND DUFOURNEL—EVIDENCE OF THE DISPOSITIONS OF THE ROMANS—CARDINAL DONNET ON THE POPE—HEROISM OF A LADY.

THE other official report which is signed by the Commander-in-chief of the French forces, General de Failly, corroborates that of General Kanzler in all important particulars. On taking the two reports and looking through them, we may make the following summary:—

The battle of Mentana was a glorious victory for the allied forces engaged; it was a complete and decisive victory, for in consequence the Garibaldians all quickly retired from the Pontifical States; the forces engaged numbered 2913 Pontifical, and 2000 French soldiers, against about 9000 revolutionary troops; the Garibaldians had the advantage of strong positions, from which to defend themselves, both, on the heights commanding the Via Nomentana, and in the fortified villages of Mentana and Monte Rotondo; all the troops, both Pontifical and French, fought bravely—and *particularly the Zouaves*. The *Pontificals* undertook the *chief attack*, and suffered more considerably than the French in consequence; the French troops acted as the reserve, and were only brought into action three hours after the commencement of the battle.

Thus the statement that the victory was *entirely* owing to the presence of the French troops, is not borne out by the facts. I do not deny to these brave men their due meed of praise, and General Kanzler has rendered testimony to their good services in the report given in the last chapter; all that

I contend for is, the right of the Pontificals to claim the honour of having made the attack, and driven the enemy from very commanding positions at the point of the bayonet, in fact of having sustained the *brunt of the battle.*

In proof of this, I subjoin the following extracts from General de Failly's report:—" These troops—the Pontificals —under the orders of General Kanzler, solicited the honour of marching first to the attack . . . . The Garibaldians' advanced posts, who occupied the thicket which fringes the road, opened fire on the advanced guard of the Pontificals. The thicket was stormed and carried in a brilliant manner by the Zouaves, who succeeded in establishing themselves on the heights which command Mentana . . . . . . Our loss in this brilliant affair was two officers wounded, two soldiers killed, thirty-six wounded, and one missing. The Pontifical army, which undertook the chief attack, suffered much more considerably. As regards the losses of the Garibaldians they are enormous, compared with those of the allied troops. The number of dead taken from the field of battle exceeded 600; that of the wounded is in proportion, and that of the prisoners amounted to 1,600 . . . . . I cannot conclude this report better, Monsieur le Maréchal, than by pointing out to your Excellency the daring and bravery of the Pontifical troops. It is a homage which the French army is happy to render them. DE FAILLY, *General-in-chief.*"

I make the following extracts from the Pastoral Letter of Monseigneur Dupanloup, Bishop of Orleans; they relate to the victories of the Pontifical army:—

" It has been needful, alas! that their blood should flow; but across the billows of that blood spilled, God has conducted them to glory . . . Victors in twenty battles, even when they are one against ten, they earned the triumph they have obtained. Soldiers of the right and of honour, they have made justice triumphant, and have torn the spoils from the wicked . . . . What voice issues from their triumph? They proclaim, with resistless eloquence, these champions of the most beautiful of causes, that there are still noble hearts capable of devoting themselves for the weak and justice, and that this sacred cause of the Pontiff thrills in the Catholic world, the most profound and delicate fibres of men's souls. They have conquered not only armed violence, but calumny and lying; they have crushed the sophisms of the revolution; they have shown by the side of a faithful people, a devoted army, a sovereign that is venerated and defended; and it needs must be that in the councils of Europe their voice shall be heard."

In the *Tablet* of November 9th, 1867, we find the following particulars relating to MM. de Quelen and Dufournel, two sous-lieutenants of the Pontifical Zouaves, who died gloriously in defence of the Holy See;—

"It is a sacred duty to assist in spreading the praises and holding up the examples of these heroes of the Church, of these brave martyrs of the Christian cause. Urbain de Quelen, was the son of M. Prosper de Quelen of Kerhoan, near Le Faou, in Brittany. Having enlisted in the Pontifical Zouaves, he obtained his promotion as sous-lieutenant last summer in reward for his bravery in succouring a gendarme attacked by two brigands. M. de Quelen killed one and wounded the other, but received a severe wound himself. He had not recovered from it, when he was attacked by cholera and compelled to send in his resignation."

It appears that at the time of the Garibaldian invasion he had obtained his congé, and was still suffering from his wound and from the cholera, when he rejoined the service to share the dangers of his comrades and to offer up his life in defence of the Holy See. "He was mortally wounded at Monte Libretti, and died next day a death worthy of a descendant of the Crusaders."

The *Impartial* says:—"In 1249 a Quelen was killed by the side of a brother of St. Louis, at the battle of Massoura. In 1270 another Quelen perished before Tunis with St. Louis himself. In 1867 another Quelen lays down his life for the rights of the Holy See, and the liberty of the Church. Honour to the family! It justifies its proud Breton motto, *En pel amzer* Quelen. 'There are always Quelens.' Yes, there are Quelens to defend religion and right. Honour to them, and honour to all who follow their example."

The *Union* of Franche Comté says:—"The death is announced of M. Emmanuel Dufournel, wounded in the affair of October 20th, near Farnese, and who died next day . . . . . This young and brilliant officer had been on sick leave, when the news of the dangers of the Holy See called upon his faith and honour to rejoin his flag . . . . . He had been in the service of the Sovereign Pontiff for five years, and had won every step by his valour and good conduct."

Another account says:—"Lieutenant Dufournel was at Velletri on October 18th, with a detachment of the Zouaves, where he and his men confessed and communicated. On the 19th, he was sent with forty of his men under the command of a Captain of Carabineers, to occupy the little village of Farnese, near Valentano. A band of Garibaldians were there, and M. Dufournel was ordered to take a large house at the entrance of the village. This order was executed, but being soon attacked by a superior force the Pontificals barricaded themselves. To avoid having to surrender, M. Dufournel resolved to sally forth, and cut his way through the enemy. He severed with his sword the rope which kept the boards of the barricade in their place, but they fell so as to leave room for one man only at a time to pass] from the house. The Garibaldians were drawn up in front, and death was certain, but Emmanuel Dufournel rushed upon their bayonets, and fell pierced by twenty wounds. His immediate follower fell also, but the rest of the Zouaves got out, formed, and charged the Garibaldians, who fled. One of M. Dufournel's many wounds had pierced the lungs, and he died next day after receiving all the rites of the Church."

A letter in the *Univers* says:—"I have just seen at the hospital the Rev. Father Gerlache, who attended Lieutenant Dufournel. He died like a Christian hero, happy to see his blood flow from his fifteen wounds for the glory of the Church. 'We are living,' said Father Gerlache, 'in an atmosphere all redolent of Christian glory and martyrdom.'"

The *Times* Florence Correspondent makes the following unexpected admissions regarding Mentana and the other events of this period:—"If there had not been a French Brigade in support, there would have been one of Pontifical troops, and it is impossible to believe that the result of the conflict would have been different. Rejecting the exaggerations rife on both sides as to the number of the Pope's men and of the Garibaldians during the late warfare in the Roman States, and taking into account the superiority of the former in armament, drill, artillery, and organisation, one fact seems established by the events of the last few weeks, and it is that the Pope's army suffices (which has often been doubted) not only to maintain his authority amongst his own subjects, but to repel any attack that could be made upon him from the side of Italy, without the cognizance or manifest connivance of the Italian government. This belief is linked with another fact, clearly resulting from recent occurrences, and which is, that the Pope's own subjects are not disposed to risk their lives for their liberties, or to strike the blow which the 'hereditary bondsman' is warned by the poet must be the condition of his freedom. There is no denying that the *Romans*, whether of town or country, *lent no aid worth mentioning* to the Italian invaders. Viterbo, a large town slenderly garrisoned, was attacked by the Garibaldians, but they found no support from a population we have always heard spoken of as the most malcontent and resolute in the Pope's dominions." Thus far the *Times* correspondent; we find the opinion here expressed as to the disposition of the inhabitants of the Roman States corroborated by the following extracts:—" On the 5th instant, at 5·30, a.m., the Piedmontese troops evacuated Frosinone. All the houses were decorated, and in the principal streets an immense crowd assisted with enthusiastic exclamations at the re-installation of the Pontifical escutcheon. In the afternoon the Pontifical troops entered amid demonstrations of joy by the inhabitants, who, headed by the magistrates, went out *en masse* to meet them with white and yellow banners. In the evening there were brilliant illuminations."*

" Palestrina was evacuated by the Garibaldians on the 6th.

* Giornale di Roma.

The population were so hostile to them, that, except by force, they were unable to make the peasants help them to throw up their fortifications at Tivoli. The Garibaldians, under the command of Piancini, retired precipitately on the approach of the Pontificals, after setting up their colours in the square, with threats of vengeance against any one who should touch it. These threats, however, did not prevent the inhabitants from tearing down the Piedmontese flag and hoisting the Pontifical colours. The French were welcomed with cheers."*

The Roman correspondent of the *Standard*, writing from Rome on the 6th November, says of the magnificent demonstration in favour of the Pontifical troops which took place on their return to Rome after the victory of Mentana:— "Half-past two had been fixed for their reception at the Piazza del Termini, and before that hour the whole road from the Quirinal to the Porta Pia was blocked up by carriages filled with the families of the Roman aristocracy, and every window was crowded, every balcony draped with the gay hangings usual on solemn occasions in Rome. About half-past two General Kanzler appeared, and mounting his charger, rode out to the Porta Pia, accompanied by the General de Failly. Very soon they returned at the head of the victorious column, and General Kanzler was the object of a most enthusiastic ovation as he took his place in the square and waited the defile of the troops. The Zouave companies formed the *avant-garde*. Dusty and war-worn, as troops returning from active service ever are, their gay and proud bearing was the theme of universal admiration, and the whole crowd broke into enthusiastic cheers as M. de Charette and the Commandants de Troussures and Lambilly appeared at the head of the regiment, their gallantry at Mentana having become a household word in Rome. It was a beautiful sight to watch company after company of noble volunteers, many of them mere children in years, but with the chivalrous resolution of veteran soldiers in their

* Tablet.

gait and countenance as they passed before General Kanzler; and even the French general was so evidently moved at the sight, that we observed him repeatedly turn to General Kanzler and wring his hand, as our neighbours say, 'avec effusion,' as 'les enfants de la vieille France' passed. Madame Kanzler's carriage driving up at the moment, her excellency was received with a burst of cheering; and her name, dear to the Romans as one of themselves, since it has been associated with the courage and self-devotion of her gallant husband, whom she has so nobly seconded in the moment of supreme difficulty.

"The Legion of Antibes were admirably received, as were also the Swiss Carabineers, the artillery, and the gendarmerie, and dragoons. Flowers were scattered on the troops as they passed, handkerchiefs waved, and the enthusiasm of the citizens is the best answer to those who state that the army is unpopular in Rome. Of the army, foreign and native, it may be fairly said—

" ' The city cast its people out upon it,'

for such a crowd has scarcely ever been seen in Rome as assembled to greet its triumphal entry yesterday. . . . The Italian troops have, I believe, evacuated Viterbo during the night, Villetri and Frosinone have also called in the Papal troops, and quiet is everywhere restored."

Thus from every quarter we have the most *conclusive* evidence that the inhabitants of the Roman States were perfectly contented to remain subjects of the Pope, that they looked with gratitude on the *foreign* soldiers, *i.e.* the Zouaves, the French Legion, the Swiss, who had defended their city and country from the Garibaldian bands, and thus prevented a repetition of the crimes and tyranny of 1849 ; and further, that they have no wish to be united to the rest of Italy under the sway of King Victor Emmanuel.

From the *Monde* we learn as follows as to the object of Garibaldi's march on Tivoli which brought about the battle of Mentana:—" In a council of war held at Monte Rotondo, it was resolved to march to the Abruzzi and raise the standard of revolt against Victor Emmanuel. An insurrection was to have broken out at Milan, and Pavia, and at Florence. The Pontifical army, therefore, rendered a great service to Victor Emmanuel by annihilating Garibaldi's corps at Mentana. Garibaldi's intention in ordering his troops to march on Tivoli was evidently not to attack Rome, which he knew to be beyond his reach, nor to dissolve his army. "It results, from all the documents which we have had before us (and the *Nazione* itself of November 6th discloses it) that the chief of the Red Shirts was endeavouring to gain the Apennines, with the intention of flinging himself into the Southern provinces, where the fire of insurrection against the existing order of things still smoulders under the ashes."*

The following extracts are taken from the Pastoral of H. E. Cardinal Donnet, Archbishop of Bordeaux, and from the *Gazette du Midi*:—

"Energy, dear brethren, energy carried up to heroism, is the necessity of our day. The Sovereign Pontiff, against whom the shafts of hell are directed, because the whole church is summed up in him, is a magnificent example of it. How noble his attitude in the midst of his trials! How his constancy attests his divine mission! How his magnanimity honours humanity! The Castle of St. Angelo, in which were confined the daggermen of the invasion, who had been taken prisoners, witnessed the other day a sight to move earth and heaven. The Garibaldian prisoners, to the number of more than two hundred, were in the basement story of the castle, when the door opened suddenly and they saw appear one clothed in white. It was the Pope. He entered alone, and calm and radiant with holiness and majesty. He stood in the midst of them and said, 'Here I am, my friends; you see before you the *vampire* of Italy, of whom your general speaks. What! you all took up arms to attack me, and you find only a poor old man.'

* Tablet.

"Not a word was spoken; all the volunteers of Garibaldi had instinctively knelt down. Pius IX., deeply affected and glowing with benevolence, stood amidst the poor creatures all kneeling round him, and affording a striking picture of Italy repentant, of Italy of the future.

"He accosted several and said, 'My son, you want clothes; you, shoes; you, linen. Well, the Pope whom you marched to attack will see about clothing you, and sending you back to your families, to which you shall take his blessing.' The Pope blessed them.

"What a picture, my brethren! But at Rome the sublime invokes the sublime. Pius IX., surrounded by his little army, displaying his mildness and resignation amid the warlike enthusiasm of his defenders, who were asking his blessing before going to die for his flag, was not that a magnificent spectacle? O soldiers of Pius IX., you teach us what to care for life when the defence of eternal truth is in question. O martyrs of the holiest of causes, every Christian heart repays you with gratitude and love. When you fight and die for our Father, you are fighting and dying for us. All our soul is with you. We bleed from your wounds —we rejoice in your triumphs. Heroes of Viterbo, of Monte Libretti, of Bagnorea, if further conflicts are before you, your courage will rise equal to every danger, and if you fall the Church will build for you in her heart a shrine of immortality."*

These words of thrilling eloquence will find an echo in the hearts of all those who were thoroughly acquainted with the intentions and motives of the Pontifical Zouaves of this time.

The *Univers* publishes a letter dated Rome, November 4th. M. de Veaux was killed near the Villa Santucci. This young officer, one of the most amiable and accomplished in the corps of Zouaves, was shot dead by a ball through the heart. He lay near a little chapel where the first ambulance had been established. Not a drop of blood had

---

* Pastoral of H. E. Cardinal Donnet.

stained his uniform. The hole made by the bullet was the only evidence of the wound. His lips still smiled. The gracious, cordial expression was unchanged. By his side was the corpse of a red-bearded Garibaldian, bathed in blood. . . . . Many Garibaldian officers wounded, taken, or killed, are dressed with great foppishness. Among the dead was a very handsome young man. His pocket-book contained his cards—' *Giuseppe—commis-voyageur en cotonnerie, mercerie, et passementerie.*' The pocket-book of this poor haberdasher's clerk contained the following letter: ' Oh, pardon me, my mother, the crime I have committed, and the pain I have caused you. I am not here of my own accord. I am forced to choose between dying in battle or dying by the dagger.'

" One cannot read without emotion, one cannot but commiserate these unhappy youths, whom the Italian sects entangle in their dark conspiracies, and devote to the alternative left to Giuseppe Gabrielli."*

The Baron de Becquilley writes to the *Univers*—

" Madame Stone was at Mentana with the most advanced ambulances, preserving, amid shells bursting, and bullets whistling, the impassibility of a true Briton. She behaved splendidly under fire, and was wholly devoted to her wounded."

The heroism and charity of this lady has been already mentioned in General Kanzler's report; from other sources we gather that she was also particularly attentive to the wounded of Monte Libretti and Nerola, undertaking the organization of the ambulance. I can testify myself to her great kindness to the inmates of the hospital of Santo Spirito, in Rome; in fact, she has long proved herself a faithful imitator of those heroic daughters of St. Vincent of Paul—the Sisters of Charity.

* Tablet.

CHAPTER V.

JOURNEY TO ROME — ENGAGEMENT IN THE ZOUAVES — LIFE IN THE DEPOT — EASTER IN ROME — DISCIPLINE OF THE CORPS.

> O ROME! thy very name awakes
> Within my soul a thousand thrills;
> Upon the slumb'ring mem'ry break
> Thine echoes sweet of classic hills.
>
> Thou once wert mistress of the world,
> As nations far and near proclaimed;
> Thy banners Cæsars oft unfurl'd,
> And conquer'd all, and made thee fam'd.
>
> Again, how changed is all the scene!
> The mighty Pagan Rome is gone;
> Triumphant everywhere has been
> Christ's victory for ever won.
>
> The Cross aloft! behold it stands
> O'er grandest monuments of skill;
> The Holy One by peaceful hands,
> The people taught, and teaches still.

1868.—I LEFT home Sunday, March 8th, and saw Captain Mullings on arriving in London. The next day he kindly gave me letters of introduction to parties in Rome. Monday evening I left London for Newhaven, went on board the steamboat the same night, and arrived at Dieppe the following morning.

Paris, March 11th.—The voyage was splendid, there was a pleasant swell on the sea, and I had no sea sickness; I had the pleasure of meeting a very kind young Frenchman at Victoria Station, we travelled to Paris together, and he has been of great assistance to me. I get on pretty well with the language and can generally make myself understood, though I cannot yet understand much French spoken by natives. I obtained my passport yesterday, and have passed a doctor's examination satisfactorily. On my way from Dieppe I had two hours' delay at Rouen, and spent them very pleasantly in visiting the mediæval remains and Cathedral, a splendid old Gothic pile. In Paris I have visited Nôtre Dame des Victoires, La Trinité, La Madeleine, and St. Sulpice.

Rome, March 18th.—I avail myself of my first leisure moments to tell you of my safe arrival here, and of the great success—with the blessing of God—of my efforts to enter the Pontifical army. I started from Paris on Thursday afternoon in the company of five Frenchmen—recruits—and a sergeant who was returning to Rome. We left at three p.m., and travelled all the following night and next day without intermission, except for refreshment.

A few words on the fine city we left will doubtless be interesting. Paris is indeed a beautiful city, far before London in point of beauty; the houses generally grand, the churches fine, the city interspersed with beautiful gardens, trees, and promenades; the Palace of the Tuilleries, the Palais Royal, the Place de la Concorde, and the Cathedral of Nôtre Dame are especially fine; the river Seine and its bridges are also very beautiful, especially by gaslight. On my way to the Lyons Railway I passed the Jardin des Plantes, part of which is a promenade, the other being a Zoological Garden; very near to it are vineyards and wine stores.

In the church of St. Sulpice there is a very beautiful and famous statue of Our Lady of the Immaculate Conception which I much admired; the exterior of Nôtre Dame de Paris is most beautifully carved with statues of saints and kings, it is all in the Gothic style. I had not time to see the Lady Chapel, but the prettiest gem of Gothic I saw in Paris was La Sainte Chapelle, which I believe was built by Saint Louis.

Beyond the fine rivers and vineyards there was nothing particular to remark on the journey through France until nearing Lyons, where the views became grand; what with majestic mountains, pleasant valleys, dotted here and there with cottages; near Chateauneuf we saw several picturesque ruins of old castles on nearly perpendicular rocks, then here and there a peach tree in blossom on the lower slopes of the mountains; as we neared Avignon vegetation was very much advanced, peaches, apricots, nectarines in blossom, and unfolding their leaves, at least a month earlier than in England; as we began to approach Marseilles, we saw the olives, which are the principal fruit trees cultivated on the rocky mountains near the railway.

About six p.m., Friday, we had the first glimpse of the beautiful Mediterranean, and about seven we reached Marseilles. I was rather tired after this first long journey by train, for I had felt the cold the previous night, having lent my rug to one of the recruits with whom I was already friendly.

At Marseilles I began to experience some of the difficulties of being entirely amongst foreigners, and being able to speak but little (that little, however, very useful) of their language, and to understand none except spoken slowly and in distinct sentences; I also found the accent of Marseilles more difficult than that of Paris. While there I saw the grand Rue Canebière and much admired the fine buildings and port, also the renowned sanctuary of Nôtre Dame de la Garde. The present church is in process of building, the situation is magnificent, and Nôtre Dame overlooks the city and harbour like a guardian angel. We heard Mass, had our breakfast, then started on board a steamer for Civita Vecchia. I enjoyed the voyage very much on the whole, the accommodation for the night was very rough—a good breaking in for my future life—that was all; we were nearly two days at sea, arriving at Civita Vecchia yesterday morning at nine o'clock, and here at seven in the evening. At the station we were met by a sergeant, who conducted us to the barracks, where I was warmly received by the English and Irish recruits. I think that I shall choose to enlist in the Zouaves, as the dragoons are mostly Italians.

I do not anticipate any difficulty in getting in. The Zouaves whom I have met are on the whole a noble body of men; the grey dress I like very much; they are for the most part young, some of them under twenty; the average height is above my own. I must further describe the life when I know more; it is not so hard as it has been represented, from what I have seen and heard as yet.

March 28th.—I must only write a few lines this time, as I am in the guard-room, waiting my turn to go on guard for the first time. It is not at all hard work; here, for instance, take the sentry work, it will come to my turn once in about eight days; nine of us take twenty-four hours, three being on guard as sentinels for two hours, then we rest, but must be within call; then, after four hours' rest, we take turn again.

The introduction I received from the Hon. and Right Rev. Dr. Clifford greatly facilitated my admission to the Zouave Corps. I like the life very much, and think it will suit me. As to the food, it is much as you have heard it described, except that we get a tin of coffee the first thing in the morning. The dress is grey cloth, trimmed with red cord; it looks very well. March weather here in Rome is far preferable to March weather in England. I am well, save a slight cold.

April 13th.—I have delayed writing a letter in order to tell you something about Holy Week in Rome. Since my last letter we have removed from the barracks of St. Callisto, which was situated at the foot of the hill on which St. Peter was crucified—on the spot is a small church dedicated under his invocation. The Basilica or Cathedral of St. Peter is built over the tombs of the Holy Apostles, not on the spot where they died.

We are now at the Torlonia barracks, only six minutes' walk from St. Peter's, which is an advantage. I have had a little to do in the sewing line lately, stitching on buttons, &c., and I take my turn at other kinds of work; as, for instance, to-day I am *garde de chambre*, my duty is to be on the watch for thieves and to serve out the coffee at five a.m., and sweep the rooms. At four p.m., I shall be at liberty to go out and see the fireworks. In the meantime I am employing my time in writing this to you on my trunk, the latter on my bed.

We are rather crowded in this barracks just now, forty-seven in one large room, but we expect to remove shortly, and the weather is not very hot yet.

Now for a few words about Holy Week. I had no military duty on Palm Sunday, so was able to hear two Masses and to be present at St. Peter's to see the Pope, the procession, and to hear the singing of the Papal Choir. I could not for the great crowd get very near to see the ceremonies performed. The procession was very fine, the singing very fine also, the visitors very numerous, and amongst them a great proportion of the higher classes. I generally go to the English College for vespers and benediction, which are there sung as in England. I was able to hear six Masses in St. Peter's last week, also to be present for the ceremonies of Good Friday and Holy Thursday, and at St. John Lateran for the Tenebræ, and to mount on my knees the *Scala Sancta* (or Holy Stairs) down which Our Lord descended to death from Pilate's house; to be present at the Coliseum for the Stations of the Cross, as well as to visit other churches for the Exposition of the Holy Sacrament, and the Holy Sepulchre. But the great feast of Easter was the day of days in Rome beyond everywhere else, and I had the great pleasure of being placed on picket in St. Peter's for the function of the day, viz., the Celebration of Mass by the Pope. Was not that a great honour for me so soon after my arrival?

I will now tell you all about yesterday. After going out to early Mass and Holy Communion, and then getting breakfast we assembled for the *appel* and inspection by the officer who commands the depôt; the officer after the *appel* passes down the ranks and looks to see that all the men are clean in body and dress, also to see if their arms are bright and in good condition. We arrived at St. Peter's at nine. After entering the Basilica we formed into line on either side of the nave (or rather in two lines down the middle of it); we were about six hundred in number (Zouaves); above us, near the Confession, stood the Palatine Guard, composed entirely of civilians in a pretty uniform, viz., blue coats, red trousers, gold scarves and epaulets; we were all armed, and our duty was to keep a passage clear for the procession.

After some few preparations, the procession came in from the Vatican. A more magnificent one can hardly be imagined; first came the senators and suite, most brilliantly attired, then the servants bearing the hats of the Cardinals, the different Religious Orders, and the secular Clergy, including the Canons of St. Peter's, next the Bishops, the Cardinals attended by their gentlemen, and then the Holy Father borne aloft on the *Sedia Gestatoria*, attended on either side by the Noble Guard in their full dress uniform; as he passed between our lines the commands of "*Portez armes*," "*Presentez armes*," "*Genou à terre*" were given, and we presented arms, knelt on one knee, and saluted him with our right hands, and received his blessing. I saw him perfectly, the sight was a striking one, the face most benignant and yet so noble; I think it would be difficult to imagine how a *man* could be a better representative of our Lord; none of his portraits that I have seen do him justice. On his way to the High Altar the Pope passes the Altar of the Blessed Sacrament, on arriving before it he alights and goes on foot to adore Our Lord. However high a man may be raised, he must acknowledge his nothingness before God, and no other teaches us this truth so well as the Catholic Church.

The crowd of persons who were in and about St. Peter's yesterday was very great. At the Elevation was heard the exquisite sound of the silver trumpets, and we presented arms, knelt and saluted Our Lord in the Sacred Host. Soon after twelve o'clock the procession re-formed and the Pope ascended the Balcony of the east front, facing the Piazza of St. Peter's, for the Benediction and Plenary Indulgence "Urbi et Orbi," that is, "On the city and the world;" we could not get out far enough to see the Holy Father, but received his benediction kneeling under the balcony. The

Piazza of St. Peter together with the Piazza Rusticucci—which opens out beyond it—stands on about seven acres (I should judge); they were nearly filled with soldiers, carriages, and people. Last evening the façade and dome of the Basilica were illuminated, many persons declared it to be the best they had ever seen.

The so-called *silver trumpets* played in the balcony over the vestibule of St. Peter's on the entrance of the Pope, and again during the Elevation, are not really of silver, but have obtained the name from some cause, probably from the beautifully mellow and silvery tone, descending from the dome and spreading over the whole building, which is produced from the position in which they are played.

In the procession on Easter Sunday the Pope is always accompanied by some of the Noble Guard, who walk on each side of him, and there is also an assistant prince, besides which, there are other princes, ambassadors, the generals of the army, as well as officers of all the different corps, who take part in the procession. Other officers, either pontifical or foreign, who choose to go in uniform are always admitted inside the cordon of soldiers, there are usually a great number, including several English; and there are always reserved seats in a good position for the ladies, but it is necessary to be veiled and dressed in black to gain admittance.

The difficulties of the climate here in summer will be compensated by the absence of hard work, and by being out in the country, where we are expecting to be sent in a few days. As regards hard work I have done none since my arrival, at the same time you must not imagine that the greater part of our time is at our own disposal for studying languages, visiting interesting places, &c. In the depôts our time is divided between drill, duty, such as picket, guard, keeping our clothes in order, cleaning our arms, belts, &c., making up our knapsacks, with our overcoats, tent, rug rolled round; then we march out with all our kit for inspection by the lieutenant, who remarks if even a buckle is out of place. This morning our lieutenant and sub-lieutenant inspected all our effects in the barrack room; we had to brush up and arrange everything on our tent beds. On passing the inspection we were each asked if we wanted anything, if so, our names were entered and we were supplied with all necessaries; so you will see that between all these several duties I find very little time for studying. As for French, I learn it from conversation, but my progress is slow, I find the pronunciation difficult, but I can catch enough of the commands given to learn my drill nearly as quickly as the Frenchmen who perfectly understand the language. Several of the Englishmen who received me so kindly at first are gone into companies in the country. At first the recruits form a depôt, to be drilled, and to learn the details of a soldier's life; as they advance they are drafted off into companies. Of course I am still in depôt, and expect to be until I know my drill perfectly, when I can choose my own company. Our barracks are called *Caserma Torlonia*. Although we have some inconveniences, we are not now so crowded as we were, and we are very near to St. Peter's, where I can go every Sunday. Some of those who are gone into the country are nice fellows, and I miss them now they are gone; they came to Rome for a flying visit on Friday last, they spoke of the life and food in the company as a great improvement on those of the depôt.

I was able to visit the Catacombs in Easter week, at least that of S. Calisto, part of which was never entirely lost sight of; it is entered from the Church of St. Sebastian. I much enjoyed my visit there—but more another time on the subject. The other day I descended to the tomb of the Apostles in St. Peter's, and heard mass over it. I much enjoyed the Feast of St. Joseph here; also the fireworks and illuminations in honour of the Pope in Easter week.

May 13th.—I expect to leave the depôt very soon for the 2nd company, 1st battalion; I have asked the Colonel to pass me into that company and such requests are usually granted. For the regular company arrangements are all better than in the depôt, where men are continually coming and going.

Four of my friends have been passed into the 2nd of the 1st, at Ceccano. At their invitation, I took the opportunity of the absence of most of our men (who were on picket for the fête at Velletri) to go down and visit them, having previously obtained forty-eight hours' permission. I arrived there at 6.30 p.m. on Monday week; Mitchell met me at the station; all appeared pleased to see me, and we enjoyed ourselves together very much, especially as we were amongst such magnificent scenery. I made up my mind, after visiting them and a little reflection, to ask to be passed into their company.

Ceccano is situated about sixty-three miles south-east of Rome, on the railway to Naples, in an immense valley between two chains of high mountains, some of them on the north-east even now snow capped; the valley is by no means flat, but is diversified with hill and dale, prettily varied by vineyards, gardens, and fields; the towns help also to complete the beauty of the view, being built on the tops and sides of steep hills, the houses appear to rise perpendicularly one above the other; the whole completed by a pretty brook washing the foot of the hill, the top of which is crowned by Ceccano.

Amongst the most remarkable objects one sees from this town are Monte Cacume (a cone-topped mountain), Monte Lupino, the towns of Frosinone, Padrico, and Polfi; the high mountains in the north-east forming the boundary between the Pontifical States and the Piedmontese. The manners of the people here are simple and industrious; the women appear to be courteous and modest in their deportment. Good crops of maize are grown here, and the fields seem to be well cultivated.

It should have been mentioned before that the strength of our regiment was raised to three battalions on Nov. 15, 1867, Captain D'Albiousse being appointed commandant of the third battalion.

So great was the enthusiasm aroused among the Catholics of France, Holland, and Belgium by the achievements of the Pontifical army during the autumn of 1867, that no less than fifteen hundred recruits for the Zouaves arrived in Rome during little more than a fortnight. One account says that on the day above-named there were eleven hundred men in the depôt, and among them were the Baron de Farelle, the Comte de Montmorin, Mr. Vavasour, Mr. Hansom, M. Henri de Riancey, and a number of young men belonging to the first French and Belgian families.

About this time (May, 1868), a fourth depôt was formed in order to prepare the way to raising the strength of the regiment to four battalions—the latter was accomplished during the course of the summer.

In our army every one enters the ranks, no matter what his station [in life may be, so that we number a prince and men of noble blood amongst the privates, as well as a good many of high family, and a great admixture of the middle classes. The Englishmen here are generally intelligent and well educated; every one takes his chance of promotion, those who understand the French language and know their drill, and are the best educated stand the best chance of promotion for the lower grades, but no one is excluded from further advancement who has the requisite ability. Amongst the officers are two Irishmen (Captains D'Arcy and De la Hoyde); then there are Dutch, Belgians, Italians, Germans, Spaniards (Prince Alphonse de Bourbon belonged to the corps in 1869-70), not to mention the French, who are in great force—most of them are of well-known Breton and Vendean families. The commander-in-chief, General Kanzler, is a Bavarian, and the Colonel (M. Allet) of our regiment is a Swiss.

I am still in the first depôt; the third depôt includes all the Canadians who came out in the first detachment, the Captain insists on their being thoroughly drilled, and they promise to turn out good soldiers.

The drill was somewhat interrupted by the ceremonies of Holy Week and festivities of Easter, but we get it regularly again now once a day, and sometimes twice, the morning drill lasting from 6 till 9 a.m.; some remain in the depôt as long as six months. It has sometimes been said a man is no soldier until he has been in the "*Salle de police*," viz., a mild kind of prison for slight breaches of discipline; whatever truth there may be in this, I have been *inside* already, and the reason was this—The barracks are generally consigned every morning till the report arrives from the Colonel. I had obtained a verbal permission from our lieutenant to go out before the report; on descending to the gate I was stopped by the sentinel on duty, who referred me to the corporal of the guard; the latter refused to let me go without a written permission; but I felt strong in my right and tried to enforce it, when I was immediately seized by the corporal and taken to the sergeant-major, who having heard the case decided that I must see the inside of the *Salle de police*. I demanded to speak to the lieutenant as soon as he came, I was however left to my own reflections for two hours, to convince myself that I was really under military discipline, and that another time it would be better to obey first and reclaim afterwards. As severity was not necessary to convince a recruit of this truth, two hours were judged a sufficient punishment for the first time, and I was then liberated.

As discipline cannot be enforced without punishments, there are several kinds in vogue in our corps, the mildest form being *quatre corvées a l'œil*, *a corvée* consisting of some kind of fatigue duty; next comes consignment to quarters for one or more days, then *Salle de police*, and lastly, prison. The two latter differ in that the confinement is not strictly enforced in the former case; very often a man is not detained at all, or only during the night, in which case he takes his bed and sleeps there instead of in his usual place; he is, however, obliged to remain in barracks when not on duty. The punishment of prison is given for more serious breaches of discipline, and no petty officer has power to award it to any one; when in prison a man is strictly detained and not allowed to perform any military duty. As the Romans as a rule follow out the teaching of the old proverb, "Early to bed and early to rise make a man healthy, wealthy, and wise," our evening appel is made at eight now, and every one must be in for it, unless he has permission for ten o'clock, which can easily be obtained by every well conducted soldier.

May 20th.—You tell me to avoid the dangerous evening air; with ordinary care it is not dangerous, for I am out in it every night, and feel no ill effects from it, the truth is, there is less twilight here than in England, and the change from day to night is not so gradual, and therefore one requires to take a little more care. As to the *malaria* it is supposed to be an exhalation, arising from some parts of the site of ancient Rome and the Campagna, late in the summer. I hear nothing of it; it has not been particularly hot here yet, the weather having been rainy occasionally, and such rain falls here as we do not usually see in England; when it rains here there is no mistaking it, "*il tombe de l'eau*," as the French say; we have not had much drill in consequence, this morning, however, we had a military promenade, and we were on the march, *sac-à-dos*, at 4.45 a.m. The *réunion* of the companies took place at the Piazza del Pópolo, we then marched out of the gate near, in the order of our respective companies into the country, the rain fallen previously had made it dirty, otherwise it was a beautiful promenade. We went through vineyards and gardens for about two miles, then we followed the course of the Tiber for some distance, and wound round towards the Farnesine meadows, where we arrived at 6.45 a.m.; we pitched our tents there and stayed nearly an hour, and afterwards marched back to Rome another way, arriving there about 9 o'clock.

Cardinal D'Andrea was buried yesterday, the Pope officiated in person. I was present and heard him (being quite near) read part of the Office most firmly and distinctly.

CHAPTER VI.

FEAST OF CORPUS CHRISTI—AT MONTE ROTONDO—PROMENADE TO MONTE LIBRETTI—LIFE IN THE COMPANY AT CECCANO—PIPERNO.

June 12th.—On mentioning Corpus Christi I can fancy you will be on the "qui vive" to know all about the procession in Rome on that day, so I will describe it as well as space and time will permit. It commenced at half-past eight in the morning, starting from St. Peter's and going round the Piazza San Pietro and the Piazza Rusticucci. First came a band, next a long procession of the different orders of monks and religious congregations, a pretty train of innocents of seven years, the orphans of Rome from that age upwards, dressed in their costume of white, the clergy of the principal churches of Rome, the bishops, the cardinals with their attendants, after whom came the Holy Father borne on the *Sedia Gestatoria* and carrying the Most Holy Sacrament, and accompanied by the noble guard, dressed in their magnificent uniform of scarlet and gold; next followed in order the Palatine guard, and the other military corps with their bands, some of them playing beautifully, while the rear of the procession was brought up by the gendarmes. To give you some idea of the length of it, I have only to tell you that it took an hour in marching out of St. Peter's. I forgot to say that the whole length of the procession, excepting under the colonnade, was canopied, the walls were hung with tapestry, and the ground strewn with sand and box the whole way, giving a festal, as well as pleasant appearance to the route. I was able to see very nicely all the first part of the procession, including the Holy Father, the latter part I could not see so well on account of the crowd. You may imagine I was very pleased to be present. At half-past five in the afternoon, thirty-eight English, Irish, and Scotch Zouaves went to the Vatican for the presentation to the Holy Father of the Banner of Our Lady of Victories, given to them by the Hon. Mrs. Kavanagh. The Pope received us very kindly, and seemed pleased with the banner (it is a splendid one worked with beads), gave us all his blessing, and a medal of the Immaculate Conception; he noticed very kindly Mr. Vavasour, who accompanied us. I am still at the depôt, and in Rome the weather is pleasant, except when it rains, as it did yesterday after the procession.

I have three or four friends amongst the Frenchmen, one particularly named Mercier, with whom I came from Paris. I have made it a point to be friendly with them on purpose to learn the language, at the same time I could not give up entirely the society of Englishmen. We expect to have some fighting in the autumn, but it is very uncertain.

Monte Rotondo, July 7th.—We took our departure from the Torlonia barracks, Rome, on June 23rd, for Monte Rotondo, at two o'clock in the morning (sac-à-dos). I had not been well for some days before, but did not wish to give up, so started on the march; but, however, before we got outside the boundaries of Rome, I was obliged to stop, and in company with another (who could not continue the march), went to the railway station and came by train, arriving here a couple of hours before the others, who arrived about eleven o'clock, most of them fatigued with their first march of about eighteen Roman miles. We are quite near Mentana, but we are much better placed here than there as far as barracks go, our barracks here being an old palace built by Prince Barberini, many of the rooms are magnificent, and there are plenty of them, so that we are not crowded. The scenery around in the distance is magnificent. A tremendously abrupt transition from the quarters to the catacombs. As regards the catacombs, I think any one who has visited them and has read Canon Northcote's small work on them, would know they were exclusively Christian cemeteries. One of the catacombs, viz., St. Agnes, is entered from an old *sand pit* for the better security of its entrance; but the two things are quite distinct, the latter being always dug where the soil is exclusively sandy; the catacombs, never, for it would be impossible for a cemetery, with six or eight graves one above the other, to remain intact in a sandy soil. Again, they could not have been Pagan cemeteries, as we know the Pagans burned the dead and placed their ashes in urns, a trace of which practice is not seen in the catacombs: the oldest of which date back as far as the apostolic times.

The church of St. Sebastian is reckoned one of the seven ancient stationary churches of Rome; it is situated on the Via Appia, about a mile before arriving at the tomb of Cecilia Metella, it contains a beautiful statue of the Saint in a reclining posture; underneath it reposes the body of the great Christian soldier and martyr. In the church are also several interesting relics—amongst them the stone of the paving of the Appian Way, which received the impression of Our Lord's feet when He met St. Peter, and one of the arrows which wounded St. Sebastian. The catacomb is entered from the church; on descending one is surprised to find the air so clear and dry, and one cannot but be interested in examining and exploring the innumerable passages striking off in every direction, which once formed one of the great cemeteries of the early Christians, and where one finds on every side the tombs of saints and martyrs. The immense extent too of the catacombs is something astonishing; on every side of the walls of Rome have catacombs been found, or have been known to exist; and the extent of some of them is very great. San Calisto and Santa Agnese have passages so long as to give rise to the idea that the former had one passage reaching to Ostia and another to the Vatican. Murray estimated that there were at least sixty different catacombs.

While at Monte Rotondo, we made a military promenade to Monte Libretti, about twelve miles distant; it is the scene of a gallant stand made by ninety Zouaves against 1,200 Garibaldians, during the campaign of 1867; we saw the gate near which the fighting had taken place, and where Alfred Collingridge was mortally wounded before being carried away a prisoner at Nerola. He died at the latter place, but not before he had received all the consolations of religion, through the heroic conduct of Monsignor Stonor and Madame Stone, who were taken prisoners by the enemy on their way to aid him on his death bed; but having asked for an interview with Menotti Garibaldi (who commanded the enemy's forces at Nerola), they obtained permission to visit the gallant youth, who willingly gave up his life in defence of the rights of the Church. His brother also fought in that engagement, to drive back the enemies of religion from the Pontifical frontier.

At the battle of Monte Libretti, when the ninety Zouaves fell back to a position outside the town, before the immensely superior forces of the Garibaldian enemy, the latter refused to pursue them, so highly did they prize the courage of their foe.

The town of Monte Libretti is situated on a steep rock rising almost perpendicularly out of the surrounding country, which is pretty and undulating, and there are grand mountains for the background of the picture. We pitched our tents in the valley below, having arrived at 8 a.m., rested and enjoyed a pleasant stroll, and started to return about 3 p.m. Our lieutenant took us a different way back, all across the country, over hill and dale, field and brook; we were well tired on arriving, but no one was knocked up, as we did not carry our knapsacks, but only rifle, tent, sword, belt, and cartridge-box.

'Camp, Rocca di Papa,' August 4th.—You will be pleased to hear that I passed into the 2nd Company, 1st Battalion, on the 17th ult. We have a good Captain, who has a care for his men, and I have very pleasant companions. I am pleased with the change and now we are *all* in Camp, I have an opportunity of meeting again my old friends both French and English, whom I left in the depôt. Having passed into the company at Ceccano, I thus went there again, and was as well pleased with it the second time as the first. It is really a magnificent neighbourhood for scenery. Seeing as I did the grand and lofty mountains, I could not restrain my desire to mount one, and descend the other side, so just a fortnight since, after obtaining one day's permission from the Captain, we started at five a.m., and arrived at the foot of the mountain soon after seven; after taking a refreshment of pears, bread and *ricotta*, or sweet cheese, at a farm-house, we commenced to ascend and found it very difficult, in some places we were obliged to climb with our hands as well as our feet. The scenery was very beautiful and the horizon clear, so that we could enjoy it very much; it only wanted a view of the sea to complete the picture. After six or seven halts we reached the top, but we had to descend a short distance to obtain a good view of the other side, which was very grand indeed; opposite to us was another range of mountains, and beneath a well watered plain. There was a choice of towns to make for: at our feet was San Stefano, a small town; in the distance on the right was Piperno, a town of considerable importance; on the left was San Lorenzo.

We decided to descend to San Stefano first, and then to the river for a bath. After resting a short time, we accordingly descended the mountain—which occupied longer than I expected, viz., about two hours.

The mountain is about 3000 feet high, and the descent is excessively steep in some places. San Stefano is built on one of the lower slopes of the mountain, but we did not find it particularly interesting, however we found an 'Osteria' where we were able to get some dinner, consisting of eggs, bread and wine; afterwards we went on to the river, where we had a cooling bath, for it was a hot day; I then proposed to return as we were due at Ceccano at nine o'clock, but I gave way to my two companions, who wished to go on to Piperno.—I am forgetting to say that my two companions were Mandy and R. . . . After crossing a second river—a beautifully limpid stream, and a long walk we arrived at Piperno at seven, rather fatigued, as you may imagine.

On arriving, our first care was to go to the 'Gendarmeria' and explain the reason why three Pontifical Zouaves came to 'Piperno' with a permission marked 'San Lorenzo.' As the gendarmes generally exhibit the utmost confidence in the good faith of the Zouaves, we managed our business there pretty easily; in fact, the Brigadier was courteous enough to advise us not to attempt to return that night—as my two companions proposed doing, and he wrote a line on the permission, saying that we could not return until the next day, so that we had something with which to appease the Captain on our return. We found a good Albergo, where we were provided with some good wine with our supper and comfortable beds.

We reconnoitred the town, and started to return at eight, the next morning. On our way we had an opportunity of observing the beautiful scenery around. Piperno is situated on a steep hill, and there are fine olive groves near it as well as vineyards; on one side of it rises the mountain of Rocca Secca, and across the broad valley, a chain of the Volscian mountains, including Monte Cacume, Monte Lupino, and others. As our road lay along the valley for seven or eight miles, we had a good view of the mountain scenery on both sides of us.

We enjoyed another bath—in the *clear* river to-day, and had a little pistol shooting with our revolvers and pistols on the banks of the river. On leaving the valley and taking a turn to the left, we had to cross a very difficult country. The corn was cut and carried from the fields. We crossed some very deep ravines and the beds of mountain torrents, and went straight ahead for Giuliano, which is a lovely place on a lower slope of the mountains. We did not enter the town, but kept to the left, and crossed the mountains, there being here a break or immense defile in the range; here we saw a series of mountain scenes on a smaller scale, viz., hill and dell but covered with olives, vines, or greensward—the last is rather rarely seen in Italy in summer. We reached Ceccano, after walking hard in the hot sun, at about 4 p.m., and escaped all punishment by going to the Captain at once, making a clean breast of it, and by showing him the line written by the gendarme. The Captain asked us, however, how we came to go so far without rifles, but when he learned that we carried revolvers, he was satisfied, but wondered how we could walk so many miles merely to see the country, but he remembered that we were '*Anglais.*' In two days we had walked nearly forty miles, in a blazing sun in July—ascending and descending a mountain included.

Coming from Ceccano by rail to Rome, we slept two nights at the Termini Barracks, and from thence marched here.

There are clouds in Italy as elsewhere, and it rains too and no mistake, but the air is generally much clearer and lighter than in England, and in spring and summer the weather is usually fine.

CHAPTER VII.

MARCH TO THE CAMP OF ANNIBAL—ROCCA DI PAPA—LIFE IN CAMP—LAKE NEMI.

Two battalions, viz. the 1st and 2nd, started from Rome at eight o'clock at night, July 31st. Our company, the 2nd of the 1st battalion, being near the front, we had the pleasure of hearing the band, which preceded the regiment, and enlivened us with inspiriting airs. We left Rome by the Porta San Giovanni, and had not passed it an hour before we were overtaken by the most tremendous rain I have ever experienced. It was a heavy thunderstorm, in about three minutes we were wetted through to the skin, and the water ran out of our trousers. We continued our march, and my English comrades, Messrs. Bishop, Mandy, Vrain, R——, and I, kept up our spirits by singing all the tunes we could recollect that were suitable for marching. At the last halt before arriving at Grotta Ferrata, I gave up a tin *bidon* I was carrying outside my *sac* to Vrain, with the only cigar I had left, and my *sac* was much lighter afterwards. We arrived at Grotta Ferrata about 1 a.m., and rested there for our principal halt.

R—— and I made the best of our way into the town to get some wine and something to eat, to warm ourselves a little after our soaking; afterwards we joined our comrades in making a large fire near the town to warm and dry our clothes; for this purpose we both carried away the whole of a dead hedge we found near, and by this means made a capital bonfire, got up the circulation again, and dried our clothes. We did not scruple about taking the hedge, as the case was one of downright necessity, and soldiers are often obliged to take what they can lay hands on.

The rest of our comrades who had remained in or about the field where we had stacked arms outside the town, were obliged to content themselves with a small portion of wine served out to them, and with preparing to boil some coffee; the latter was interrupted by the order of the commandant to march ahead at once, without waiting for the coffee. After starting we missed Mandy and R—— for some distance, but they joined us before we commenced ascending the mountain up to the camp. We had been ascending gradually for some distance before making our grand halt; but when nearing Rocca di Papa, about 4 a.m., we began the steep ascent which leads up to that town, and to the table-land called the Camp of Hannibal; it was, indeed, trying to climb a steep mountain, carry rifle, sword, ammunition (sixty rounds), knapsack, blanket, overcoat, tent, and sticks, and walk in shoes so softened by the rain that we felt every stone we trod on; however we cheered ourselves by singing, by the prospect of the new life in camp we had before us, and by the delightful scenery we saw around us as morning dawned. The rain slackened before we arrived at Grotta Ferrata, and had ceased altogether by daybreak. My English comrades and I were proud to be able to march in at the head of our company. I was very pleased to have so well got through my first march under such difficult circumstances.

I ought to mention that the march was commanded to take place during the night, in order to avoid the great heat of the day, and that the rain was somewhat unusual. Thus, perhaps, the authorities were a little taken by surprise.

Camp, Rocca di Papa, Aug. 24th, 1868.—In your last letter you speak of having visited Oxford; the colleges there are without doubt noble buildings and monuments of the zeal for learning and sound education of our Catholic ancestors. I have seen the exterior of them, but have not yet visited the interior. A thought, however, strikes me, that they do not in some respects equal the Roman College or the Sapienza, both of which are magnificent buildings; the former bounds two very considerable streets, and while one end of the quadrangle faces one piazza, the other, comprising the fine church of St. Ignatius, forms a splendid façade to a second. This church contains several rich altars, but that of St. Aloysius is its chief attraction; underneath it is a small marble statue of the saint spurning the world, which is represented by a globe of lapis-lazuli; above the altar is a beautiful statue of the saint, and under it reposes his body. On the Feast and during the Octave it would be difficult to imagine anything more resplendent than the sight presented at this altar, so great is the devotion of the Romans to St. Aloysius, and such good taste displayed in the decorations, lighting up, &c. On the opposite side is the altar of B. John Berchmans, another youthful saint, and its beauty is second only to that of St. Aloysius. The rooms of both these saints are shown in the college, but I have not yet seen them. All instructions given in the college are gratuitous, books and paper being brought by the students themselves. A man might begin in elements, and go up as far as philosophy, theology, and astronomy, without paying a farthing for one of the lectures given.

I am sorry to hear you have had such very hot, dry weather in England this summer; it has not been so extremely hot here in camp. I must now tell you something about the camp. It is situated on a high plain, about one mile in diameter, nearly surrounded by the peaks of Monte Cavi, Monte Pila, and another lower mountain; there is an opening on the side of Rocca di Papa, and a very precipitous descent into the valleys below. We are about two thousand six hundred feet above the level of the sea; from the highest part of the camp above Rocca di Papa we have a beautiful view of the sea, the Campagna and city of Rome, about eighteen miles distant, and the lovely blue lake of Albano. We are on the crater of an immense volcano, although many ages extinct; the cinders are still to be seen compact and perfect, and forming the subsoil. The Lakes Albano and Nemi are two other craters of volcanos; they are surrounded by the steepest mountains, and the scenery around is as lovely as may be imagined. I have been able to bathe twice in Lake Albano, and I enjoyed it very much. The mountains round are principally wooded, the lower slope at one place is cultivated, and produces vines and olives. The descent is generally so steep, that there are but few places that one can possibly get down to the lake. It is two and a half miles long by about two broad, the depth is very great; at the shore, in one place, there is a more gradual slope, and here it is very suitable for bathing: this is on the Marino side, or north end of the lake. Castel Gandolfo is pleasantly situated above the lake on the west, and farther on are Albano and Ariccia, both fine old towns. Leading from Albano to Ariccia, is a fine viaduct of three tiers of arches, each sixty feet in height, spanning the deep ravine ; this must have cost a great sum, so great is its length and height above the valley. It is one of the many great works which Pius IX. has caused to be executed during his reign.

Rocca di Papa is undoubtedly one of the most healthy spots in the Pontifical States for a camp in the summer, the great height being available both for avoiding the great heat of the day, and the fogs of the Campagna at night; I find it much cooler here at midday than in Rome, and not so damp at night as at Monte Rotondo. We all, including officers, sleep under tents of canvas in our clothes on the ground—a little straw separating us from mother earth—with a small blanket wrapped over us. I have got quite used to the tent now, and have not felt the cold since the first three nights. We rise now at five, a.m., and are called into ranks at half-past, with knapsacks, carbine, sabre, &c. Our exercise lasts till eight, then we clean up carbines, sabres, belts, gaiters, etc., then walk to the fountain half a mile distant and take there a good wash, return, and make up our "*sac*" for the *appel propre*, *sac-à-dos*, at twelve o'clock. Amongst these duties we eat our soup at ten; if we are not on guard, picket, or *corvée*, we have the other part of the day to ourselves to sleep, mend our clothes, meet our friends, or do pretty much as we like till nine, when the evening appel is made. I cannot complain myself, but some of the men of the depôt say they found it hard work here in camp, and particularly at first, as there was a *corvée* every day called out for duty on the military road being made up to camp.

We had the Holy Father here on the 10th instant; there was a stage erected for his reception and for the celebration of Mass, which he said in the presence of the officers and men composing our brigade, he afterwards received the officers. The Holy Father appeared pleased to be amongst his soldiers; there were rejoicings in camp, for his soldiers are always pleased to see him amongst them, and he left for Rome in the course of the afternoon.

All the superior officers of our brigade are with us in camp, the brigade consisting of four batteries of artillery, two squadrons of Dragoons, one or two companies of engineers; the whole regiment of the Zouaves, excepting the company "*hors rang*," nearly five thousand strong, and the battalion of the Pontifical Cacciatori. The other brigade of the army encamped here before us. Rifle shooting formed part of our exercises lately, we fired ten rounds each; I did nothing, but Mandy fired very well. After plenty of drill, we have had two sham fights, one on the side of Albano over a very difficult country—this was a trying day for me as I was not well. After participating in all the movements and firing off all our ammunition, we took the town of Albano by storm, and marched victoriously through it. The other sham fight took place before Rocca Priora, and it was a great success, although our men were not victorious, and we did not succeed in taking the town, notwithstanding that our artillery kept up a heavy fire on it, but then the position was very strong, on a steep hill, which it tried us to mount at a quick pace. We were deployed as skirmishers, and carried all our kit, and the place was well defended by our own Zouave depôts, assisted by artillery placed in a commanding position. The fight over, we bivouacked a short distance below the town, and thoroughly enjoyed our soup, wine, &c., after our hard work, lasting several hours, in a difficult country.

We made (*i.e.* several English comrades and myself) two excursions to Monte Porzio, when the English College and the Oblates of St. Charles were staying for their *Villegiatura*. The English College received us as usual most kindly, and accompanied us part of the way back. We passed the ruins of Tusculum, once an important city of ancient times, down to the middle ages, and in some respects a rival of the Eternal City, but afterwards entirely destroyed by the Romans in A.D. 1191.

On the site of the ruined city a cross has been erected by the College, and it is visible for some miles. We also passed the fine monastery of Camaldoli, and not far off we saw the Jesuit college of Mondragoni. The modern Frascati is built on the side of the hill of Tusculum, and it possesses some fine olive groves, and produces good oil and wine. While in camp, Mandy, R—— and I descended for a bath to Lake Nemi, after crossing part of Monte Cavi. We commenced to descend over a very broken country to the rocky mountain in which the lake—like an immense basin of untold depths—is situated; this lake is, indeed, very beautiful, though with a beauty different to that of Albano, for Albano is beautifully blue, while Nemi is a deep green. After descending somewhat, we pass through the town of Nemi, and then commences the difficult part of the road, for the precipitous rocks are nearly perpendicular, and it is only by following the tortuous path, bending first to the right and then to the left, that one can descend at all. Near the shore of the lake on this side is a most productive soil, in which peaches, apricots, and vines grow with wonderful luxuriance. We found the bath very refreshing after our hot walk, and much enjoyed it; and afterwards, before ascending, we were enabled to taste some of the fruit grown in this most delightful spot. In the town we tasted some of the wine of Nemi, and pronounced it *excellent*, and we enjoyed it as we sat in a kind of balcony outside the Albergo, and then discussed the possibilities and probabilities as to the nature of certain craft we saw passing at sea in the far-off distance. The shades of evening were closing over us as we left Nemi, and then dawned upon us the thought that we had a difficult path to find, an arduous road to walk, and an ascent of some fifteen hundred feet to mount, about eight miles in length, a great part of it through woods, where it was very easy to lose oneself, and, added to this, the prospect of " *Salle de police*" and "*corvée de quartier*" on the morrow if we missed the nine o'clock appel. Under these circumstances there was no time to be lost, that was certain, so after reaching the ledge of the mountain cliff, Mandy led the way through the woods at about the rate of five miles an hour, and fortunately he remembered the turnings, and we got out all right, for as we descended Monte Cavi to the camp, we saw the depôts going through the illuminated figures of the Lieutenant-Colonel—this was an amusement got up by him in honour of the visit of the Holy Father to camp, and the depôts were then rehearsing it. They carried lamps of various colours, and the effect was certainly very pretty, and we then knew we were in time for the appel.

One of the adjuncts of the camp was a military hospital, and it was necessary enough too, for a good number of men were ill from the effects of the soaking they got on the march out, and the dampness of the ground consequent on the tremendous thunderstorm; for the first three nights we found it cold lying on the ground, but afterwards we slept comfortably enough. I may mention that it was very unusual for the ground to be so damp in the summer, as the weather is generally fine and dry throughout; however, the greater part of those ill recovered, but we lost two Irishmen, and poor Mitchell died in hospital in Rome, of Roman fever caught at Ceccano: he was never very strong, and had suffered from fever soon after arriving. *Requiescat in pace!* Our chaplains were with us, and were very attentive to the patients, one of them taking his turn of guard every night. There were services in French, English, and Flemish, and confessions heard in these languages in the church of Rocca di Papa. The Dutch were conspicuous for their good attendance. Fr. Gurdon, our chaplain, got up a tea-fight for the English and Irishmen; it took place near the edge of the precipitous rocks hard by the camp fountain, most of the fellows came, and we spent a very pleasant social evening together.

CHAPTER VIII.

RETURN TO ROME—LIFE AT THE SORA—MONTI AND TOQNETTI.

September 14th.—THE first four companies of the first battalion of Zouaves are quartered at the Sora Barracks, the head quarters of the Zouaves. On the whole, it is the cleanest and most comfortable barracks I have been stationed at yet; in the way of lodging it is a very pleasant change from the camp, and as the weather is not, on the whole, so remarkably hot in Rome now (though Sunday was rather hot in the afternoon), I enjoy the change. Unless there is a campaign, which is altogether uncertain, we expect to remain here at least four months. The second and third battalion are gone, or going into the country. After they are all gone out I expect we shall have a good share of service in the way of guard, picket, and patrol, otherwise I think we shall be rather comfortably situated here.

We returned from camp on Saturday, September 5th. We started at two, a.m., and arrived three miles outside of Rome by eight o'clock. We bivouacked in a field near an aqueduct at a point where the road passes under it; the day was exceedingly hot, and it was difficult to find a shady place in which to rest out of the sun, so that we were far more fatigued than if we had marched right into Rome without any long halt. In addition to our own kit, R—— and I both carried a bidon—a tin used either for carrying water or for boiling it—outside of our "*sacs.*" As we marched in between five and six in the evening, I felt very much inclined to fall out, for I was very tired, and we felt the heat very much before passing the Porta San Giovanni; however, I kept on. At the gate we were formed into double file, then four deep we marched into the city in regular order, preceded by the band. Crowds of people were collected at the gate and along our line of march, especially at the Piazza Colonna, where we were drawn up before separating for our different barracks. Every one who had any "*esprit de corps*," did not mind his fatigue, but marched with spirit to the sound of the music through the streets to the Piazza above mentioned. After waiting there a quarter of an hour we felt stiff on starting again, and were well tired by the time we got to barracks. I was much more fatigued after this march than after the march to the camp, although we then mounted such an ascent to Rocca di Papa.

Rome, September 27th.—Our military service consists principally of guard, picket, and patrol. Now we are in Rome we have no drill, at least we have had none as yet since we arrived from camp. The weather is occasionally varied with heavy thunderstorms, but is generally clear, pleasant, and much cooler. Although the storms here are very heavy—the rain is especially heavy—I have never heard of any damage being done to life or buildings by the lightning, all important buildings of great height being protected by conductors.

I have heard nothing further lately of a campaign, but of course here we are ready to defend Rome and the States in case they are attacked. In case of a campaign I will attend to your wishes, so that you shall know the result of any battle as soon as possible. I have visited St. Peter's once since our return from camp; the Vatican Palace is attached to St. Peter's. It is not that I am tired of St. Peter's that I visit it so seldom, but I am much farther off than before, and there are other churches near; for instance, the Chiesa Nuova of the Oratorians, where is the shrine of St. Philip, and the fine church of St. Augustine. The Chiesa Nuova contains many pictures of great merit, and the exterior façade is very imposing. The entrance to the shrine is covered with ex votos, offered in thanksgiving for favours received through St. Philip's intercession.

St. Philip's memory is held in great veneration here, and the title of "Apostle of Rome" has been accorded to him. His Feast is a holy day of obligation in the city, and the Holy Father goes in great state to this church for the High Mass, and to venerate his relics. When his tomb was last opened in the reign of the present Pope, his body was found to be incorrupt. St. Philip effected an immense amount of good in reforming the manners of the Romans of his day.

The Palazzo Massimo, which is near, contains a room which was the scene of one of the miracles wrought by St. Philip Neri. The nephew of the prince was here raised from death to life by the intercession of the saint. This fact is commemorated every year on the 16th of March, the day on which it took place, and the room is on that day thrown open to the public. The interior of the church of St. Augustine is very fine, and beautifully painted with the different scenes of the life of our Blessed Lady, and the mysteries of the Holy Rosary. Below these paintings are the holy women of the old law, who were her types. The high altar and tabernacle are both very rich; above is an ancient painting of the Madonna, which is not often exposed.

The beautiful statue of the Blessed Virgin—La Madonna del Parto—is very much venerated by the people, and is enriched by a large number of ex-voto offerings. This is the Mother Church of the Augustinians, is much frequented by all classes of the Romans, and is a favourite church of the Zouaves. I have also visited lately Sant' Andrea delle Fratte; it was here that Alphonse Ratisbonne was miraculously converted in 1842, by an apparition of the Blessed Virgin. As the inscription in one of the chapels tells us "he went into the church an obstinate Jew, and came out soon after a Christian," a living miracle of the mercy of God and the powerful intercession of our Blessed Lady, which cannot be disputed by any one willing to believe the evidence of his senses. I have also visited the tomb of St. Cecily, in the Trastevere, and admired the beautiful statue of white marble over it representing the martyred Saint; she shares with St. Agnes the honour of being the most famous Virgin Martyrs of Rome.

As at present there is no *cercle*, or club, for the English and Irish Zouaves, I go to the Belgian *Cercle* to write my letters, to read the newspapers, and to get a beefsteak when I want one. None of the Zouave *cercles* are exclusively opened to one nationality; thus, every Zouave is at perfect liberty to enter the French *Cercle* and play at billiards, chess, cards, read, write, attend the Italian class, or take his dinner at the *restaurant*. I often go there, and sometimes to the Canadian *Cercle* also, but as every'one feels most at home in the company of his own countrymen, I oftener spend my evenings with my own particular English friends, R——, Mandy, Bishop, and others, either in the Caffè Luigi, when we go in for ten o'clock permission, or else we hold a "parliament" (thus named by Mr. Bishop), after the appel, the seats being furnished by the beds of R—— and mine own, which are side by side. The evening appel is now made at eight, but the silence is not sounded till ten, so that we have two hours for our discussions. We often muster to the number of five, including the three above-named, Mr. Thornton, of the third company, and myself. The subjects are various, the discussion generally interesting and very animated, but the conclusions not always unanimously accepted. Mr. Bishop is an excellent disputant, as his education and former profession necessarily make him.

Rome, October 30.—You think I must have a pleasant life of it in Rome, attending all the grand services, &c. I must admit I like the life on the whole, but you must not imagine it to be very smooth and easy, for it is not, as we have a great deal of service or work, which often prevents us from attending the Festas, or from seeing as much of Rome as we would wish to do; but as it is all for the Holy Father, and as we are able to have Mass three or four times a week, besides on the Sunday, and can often visit the Quarant' Ore in the evenings, we ought not to complain. The Forty Hours' Exposition of the Blessed Sacrament goes on perpetually in Rome, excepting from Good Friday morning till

Holy Saturday after Mass, continuing generally two days in every church named in a list in its turn. As there are about three hundred and sixty-five churches in the city, there are double the number required, in order that every one be taken in turn once a year.

There are trials and difficulties in our life as in every other, and I am sorry to have to mention that some of the Englishmen—some on account of ill health, and some for other causes—have lately felt the barrack life too hard for them, and have gone, or are going, home; amongst them are, I regret to say, M—— and B——; Mercier, my French friend and instructor in his language, is also going for the same cause. On the whole our numbers are not diminishing, as a good many recruits have come out; I know also that many who have already served in the Zouaves would return, were there any prospect of a campaign against the Garibaldians. It is not that they fear to meet the enemy, but they dislike the monotony of every-day life and work in the barracks.

The *tir*, or rifle practice, has lately been added to our other duties, our company going out one day in the week. We are mustered into ranks by daybreak, and then march out to the Farnesine Meadows, which are near the Ponte Molle—the ancient " Pons Milvius," the scene of the celebrated victory of Constantine the Great over Maxentius. It takes two hours at least for the whole company to fire the requisite number of shots. If the day be fine I rather enjoy the practice, but if it should be cold it is not so very agreeable— more as to the results next time. W. R—— has lately passed into our company, so we are now three Englishmen together, two having left.

At present I do not often see an English paper, but I make up by reading the French and Italian. However, we look forward to seeing them regularly as soon as our new English Library is opened; the arrangements are delayed in consequence of Mgr. Stonor's absence.

The Sora barracks is near the Chiesa Nuova and the Piazza Navona, and the English College is not far off, in the Via Monserrata. Although I lost two friends last month, as

I told you, I have still two left, and we continue to hold our "parliaments" after the appel, the members mustering still to the number of five. W. R——, R——, and I are nearly always together, and we are always talking English, so that I do not improve in French so much as I could wish. As my friend and instructor in that language has returned to France, and it would be hard, and even unwise, to give up altogether the companionship of Englishmen for others, it cannot be helped.

You are rather mistaken in supposing there are never any frosts in Rome; during this month the weather has not been so agreeable—it being now the rainy season here—and there have been a good many wet days, or days on which rain fell; and when it has been clear the nights and mornings have been cold, with slight frosts. We are exempt from fog during the day—one blessing.

Although our Library is not yet opened, we have been able lately to see most of the English Catholic newspapers, through the kindness of Fr. Gurdon, one of our chaplains. My own opinion as to the decease of the old *Tablet* is, that the editor made a mistake in supporting Mr. Disraeli, after the latter refused to do justice to Catholic Ireland, by disestablishing the Irish Church. The manifesto of Dr. Vaughan, the editor of the new *Tablet*, was, I thought, a very good one.

You wish to know the difference between guard and picket. The difference is this: when a soldier goes on guard, he takes his arms, and at least twelve rounds of cartridges, his knapsack with overcoat and rug rolled and placed round it; with this he has to pass the parade or inspection of the Captain Adjutant Major, who sees that he has everything clean and bright, otherwise he (the Captain Adjutant) inflicts some punishment. The parade finished, the private marches off under the conduct of his *chef de poste*, to relieve his comrades who have mounted guard the day before; arrived at their destination, the requisite number of sentinels are conducted to their posts, where they receive the consign, *i.e.*, the nature of the things or circumstances they have to watch over, from those they relieve. The sentinel remains standing, or walking about within twenty yards of his sentry-box for two hours, during which time it is forbidden to sit down, to talk without necessity, to read, or smoke; but he must keep a sharp look-out for anything which may happen in the neighbourhood of his post. At the end of two hours the sentinels are relieved by others of their comrades who have come with them, and who have been reposing meanwhile in the guard-room, or within call of the bugle. Of the twenty-four hours of the day and night, a man gets from four to eight hours as sentinel, though far oftener the latter than the former number; his meals are brought to the guard-room from the barracks by one of his comrades, and he remains on or near the spot for the twenty-four hours, ready to defend it against all attacks, and even to pursue an enemy who might venture to attack the post.

The business of a picket is to strengthen the guard, and to be ready in case of any attack being attempted; but the duty is generally much less arduous than that of guard; for instance, there is always a picket named for the *Sora Caserne*, but it often happens that a man on this duty has nothing whatever to do excepting to be present in some part of the barracks, in case the sergeant of the guard takes it into his head to call the picket down. Sometimes a picket is a guard of honour to the Holy Father, stationed at different parts of the line of route he takes when he goes in state to some church, and there is then also a picket inside the church; sometimes pickets have to be furnished to the theatres to prevent any disturbance, but then the duty only lasts during the performance.

You desire to know what kind of work we have to do. The following will give you an idea. Suppose that on Monday I am named for the *Garde Royale*; the parade being at eleven, the morning would be occupied in preparation. Tuesday, I finish my guard, arriving at barracks at one. Wednesday morning occupied by target practice, the afternoon in cleaning carbine, &c. Thursday, *corvée de soupe*, the duty consisting in taking the meals to the men on guard. Friday, patrol through the streets in the evening, either from six till ten, or in the night from ten till two. Saturday morning partly occupied in preparation for inspection of some sort in the rooms, this taking place between twelve and two, during which hours on Saturdays we are usually consigned to barracks and the care of the guard—sometimes it is an inspection of arms, sometimes of all our military effects; in either case it is necessary to have everything in order, and clean. Sunday, *planton* at the Ministry of War, a service I sometimes get instead of guard, and it does not involve so much preparation. If to the above you add the stitching that must be done occasionally, and recollect that we have always to keep ourselves clean and tidy, you will be able to imagine that *sometimes* at least we are fully occupied.

It should be mentioned, however, that anyone who chooses to pay an "ordonnance," (as a private who does the clearing up for a comrade or superior is called), can easily find a Dutchman who will be only too glad to save him some of the above work for a recompense of a few sous a day, and the ration of bread. I have chosen to do my own work as yet, as it is best for every one to know how to do it, in case he may be obliged to fall back upon himself; however, I occasionally pay a man to take my place for some of the service, such as *corvées*; and, as I have not been very well lately, I shall get myself replaced for my guard tomorrow, for our doctor here will not often give one exemption, unless one is seriously ill.

I saw the two conspirators, who blew up the Serristori Barracks last year, executed on Tuesday last. I was on picket to keep order, in case of any attempt being made by the Garibaldians to get up any demonstration in their favour. It passed off very quietly, at 7 a.m., the criminals, Monti and Tognetti, having previously begged pardon, for the offence of blowing up the barracks of their comrades and killing thirty Zouaves in cold blood, begged their prayers, and showed signs of great penitence.

This conspiracy of Monti, Tognetti, and others, fostered by the secret societies, was a most cowardly and diabolical one, its object being to destroy simultaneously the chief barracks of the Zouaves, and the whole of the military hospital of Santo Spirito, and thus annihilate in cold blood the soldiers whom they had been unable to conquer in the field. This deeply laid design was, however, frustrated by an over-ruling Providence, as the following circumstances will prove. The trains were laid underneath the Serristori Barracks, with ramifications under the very extensive hospital of Santo Spirito, and the quarters of the "*Garde Royale*" in the Piazza San Pietro, as well as under the Sora, and other Zouave barracks. The ringing of a certain bell at an understood hour was to be the signal for the different conspirators to fire the trains, and blow to atoms the hated *forestieri* (foreigners,) including the wounded in hospital with the Sisters of Charity, and their other attendants; but for some unexplained cause the bell was rung an hour too soon, before all the arrangements were complete, only the train under the Serristori exploded, and blew up the place with thirty *Italian* Zouaves of the band, the other men having been called out for some duty; thus the conspirators were entirely baulked in their purpose, and only destroyed their own countrymen, for not one of the *forestieri* perished.

Monti and Tognetti, although guilty, as they themselves admitted, were not the ringleaders of this conspiracy; these latter managed to keep clear of the Roman police. Their design will be ever held in universal abhorrence, especially as in case of its being successfully carried out, it would not only have cost the lives of the soldiers and Sisters of Charity of the military hospital, but probably also of a large number of civilians, principally women and children, inmates of another hospital, immediately opposite the former one.

CHAPTER IX.

IN HOSPITAL—LIFE IN ROME AT THE CASERMA DEL GESU—
THE VATICAN—ST. PETER'S.

Nov. 30th.—WENT into the hospital of Santo Spirito, suffering from an attack of pleurisy, which had been coming on for some time, but which I had not paid much attention to.

Dec. 5th.—R—— wrote a few lines for me, saying that I was ill in hospital.

18th.—I am now much better, though still at Santo Spirito. I have been bled once, and had leeches applied twice. The doctor ordered me to be bled a second time, but as I demurred to this, he acquiesced, and next day he found I was perfectly right in remonstrating, for I was better without having been bled. We have Mass said every morning in the room in which I am, and the Rosary and Litany of Loretto in Latin every evening. The chaplains of all the different nationalities come round very often, so that we have all spiritual advantages to avail ourselves of here.

The Sisters of Charity superintend the management, they are very kind, but there are very few of them in comparison with the number of sick. Under them is an infirmary corps of attendants, all soldiers. I have been comfortable here on the whole, having had plenty of friends to see me, and plenty of books and newspapers to read. R—— has come several times. As regards the farm which H—— has written about, I do not see how I can break my two years' engagement here for a chance of getting that, nor do I wish to break it; having enrolled myself as a defender of the Holy Father, I should like to carry out my engagement, and to be as good as my word.

25th, Christmas Day.—We had Midnight Mass and Holy Communion, the Mass being said in the large room in which I am, the other two Masses of the day being said at half-past six and seven o'clock. Altogether, very nice for Christmas Day in hospital. I enjoyed very much hearing the bells rung during the early morning. In the evening we had a grand Benediction in the other large room above our own; the Canadian Zouaves, came in to sing for us; some beautiful flowers, both natural and artificial, adorned the altar.

Dec. 31st.—I am glad to say I came out of hospital on the 29th, and came out cured, too, only of course slightly weak after being there a month, and the greater part of the time in bed. At present I am staying at a room in town kindly lent me by a comrade, having for this purpose the permission of my captain; I expect, however, to return to the *Caserne* and my duty very soon.

Jan. 23rd, 1869.—Our company has changed its number and battalion. It is now the 1st company of the 3rd Battalion, and we are quartered at the Gesù. You are not far wrong in your supposition of the duties of a *planton*, although the duties vary with the different posts—for instance, at the Ministry of War, the principal part of the duties consists in delivering some letters, and for the rest of the day remaining about one's post, where one can read, talk, or smoke, and take a look at the Dragoons, who are stationed close by. The duty finishes at four p.m., and commences next day at nine. At the hospital the duty consists in attending a sick man twenty-four hours, and it is more or less arduous, according to the nature of the disease and the disposition of the patient. The danger of contagion is slight, as I have never yet heard of a Zouave catching any disease from attending a sick man in hospital; indeed, the Roman fever and the majority of hospital cases are not contagious. I may add that I do not see any prospect of my having this latter duty to perform.

Some time ago I promised you a description of what I saw on the Feast of St. Cecily, November 22nd. I attended the Vespers at the Basilica of the Saint, in the Trastevere.

As St. Cecily is the patroness of music, the very highest talent of Rome is engaged to do honour to her Feast, and very splendid indeed is the result. The Basilica dates from the time of the Saint herself, viz., the commencement of the third century, and was formed out of her own house, after her martyrdom, which took place in it. It consists of a nave and two aisles, and is of the form called Basilica— i.e., the nave is completed by a semi-circular tribune or apse, the floor of which is raised several steps above the nave, and forms the choir: the high altar immediately over the shrine of the Saint is placed at the intersection of the nave and the choir, so that when the priest celebrates Mass he faces the people in the nave. On the ceiling of the apse are interesting mosaics of the time of Pope St. Pascal. The recumbent statue of the martyr underneath the high altar is very beautiful. Outside of the aisles are several chapels: into one of these one descends by a few steps from the church. This is the "*sudatorium*" of the bath in which St. Cecily was shut up for three days to be suffocated for her faith. She however survived, and was afterwards clumsily beheaded. This spot was most interesting to me, and I could see that the arrangements for heating the room were the same as I had seen in the ancient Roman villas discovered at Chedworth, Gloucestershire.

This Virgin Martyr's history is most interesting, on account of the numerous conversions to Christianity she caused by the influence of her example and prayers, the most remarkable of these being the conversion of Valerian, to whom she was betrothed, he being an officer of the Emperor Alexander Severus, of his brother Tiburtius, and of the centurion Maximus, who was leading the two former to execution, but was converted by their courage and readiness to die for their faith. All three suffered together about the same time as St. Cecily. As is usual on all festas in Rome the Basilica was tastefully decorated and illuminated.

The English Zouave Library, situated at 91, Piazza della Valle, and opened last month, is a great boon to us. It is open every day till ten p.m. It consists of a library of instructive and amusing books, of a reading-room, writing ditto, with materials supplied. Of others—one of which is to be a billiard-room, and another to be a refreshment-room, while a third will be used as a small chapel, in which we can assemble occasionally for a Novena. Father Gurdon lives here also, and occupies one room, Mr. Johnson, the Zouave secretary, one, and there is one spare bed-room for any one or two Zouaves who may be spending a few days in Rome, on permission from their company in detachment in the country.

We have a fire in the reading-room—quite a luxury in Rome,—a piano, chess, draughts, cards, and the English Catholic newspapers, as well as *L'Univers* and *Galignani*, provided for our amusement and reading. Opposite the Library is the fine old church of Sant' Andrea della Valle, the façade of which is one of the finest in Rome. During the octave of the Epiphany I had an opportunity of seeing the fine group of the "Adoration of the Magi," which was erected above and behind the high altar. The different figures of the group were very good, and particularly those of our Blessed Lady and the Holy Child; and also the dress and attitude of the three kings offering their gifts. There were masses in the different Oriental rites, and every afternoon and evening there was a grand Benediction, with a Te Deum. After the last the figure of the Holy Child was taken round to be venerated by the people, who came up to the altar rails. The different services were every day well attended. The Archbishop of Westminster preached on the octave day, and he had a large audience of English visitors, both Catholic and Protestant.

Feb. 13th, 1869.—With the exception of abstinence from meat on Ash Wednesday and Good Friday, we have no difference made in our diet for Lent, as a soldier's profession exempts him from fasting, and we are specially dispensed from abstinence. The Carnival certainly made a difference to us, as we had more work to do. It came to the turn of our battalion to do duty as a picket every alternate day, or nearly so. The carnival out of doors is brought to a close every day by a horse race, and the duty of a picket is to preserve order and to keep the Corso clear during the race, the crowd being generally a very dense one. Zouaves in *uniform*—like all the other soldiers—are supposed not to take part in the carnival in the Corso, *i.e.*, not to throw *confetti* or bouquets. W. R.—— and R—— managed, however, to enjoy themselves by throwing a few *confetti* occasionally, on the last day. They received several bouquets from the ladies in the balconies, and threw others in return. I was on guard, so did not see any of the fun on that day; but I suppose I must give you a little description of it. The carnival takes place in the Corso—one mile long—every house of which has several projecting balconies, one above the other, filled with ladies and gentlemen, who choose to hire them for the occasion. Many of these take an active part in the fun by showering down *confetti* on the passers-by—tall hats are considered fair game, and generally come in for a full share of peppering. These compliments are returned by those below, and regular battles of *confetti* ensue. If the gentlemen in the streets fight well they are generally rewarded by bouquets from the ladies above. All kinds of costumes are seen in the streets made up of a variety of colours. The *confetti* used are made of flour, and resemble sugar plums in appearance and size.

The Carnival commences on the Saturday week before Ash Wednesday, and is observed in the Corso on five other days, the two days immediately preceding the commencement of Lent are generally the days on which the most fun is enjoyed; it opens from two to three o'clock in the afternoon; soon after five, eight dragoons ride at a gallop up and down the Corso, to clear the way for the horse-race then about to take place; six horses without riders are then started from the Piazza del Popolo, and being frightened by the strangeness of the spectacle which meets their eyes on every side, gallop off at full speed down the Corso—the only avenue open to them—the spectators on both sides do their best to increase the speed of the animals to the utmost, the pace is generally pretty fast. The horses are caught and stopped after passing the Piazza di Venezia by canvas hung across the streets, and the winning horse is led off with musical honours. This race concludes the outdoor carnival of each day, except the last, when the whole Corso is illuminated, and a great number of people rush about with *moccoletti*—candles, and the fun consists in blowing out other people's candles, and in keeping one's own lit. The two friends above-mentioned enjoyed this last very much.

March 5th, 1869.—At present the whole regiment of the Zouaves is attending a spiritual retreat; there are preachers for the different nationalities at the different churches. The retreat for the English, Irish, and Scotch is being given by Father Vincent, a Maltese Passionist. He has done a great deal of good in England, where he resided eighteen years. I do not know whether it was at Broadway that he stayed. We have Mass and a sermon at eight a.m., and another sermon and Benediction at four p.m. I hope it will do us good, as we want rousing a little.

I have taken part in two sham fights lately, the first of which took place beyond the Tre Fontane, on the Via Ostia. The most remarkable feature of this field-day was a magnificent cavalry charge, executed by the Dragoons in prime style; the other took place on the Via Aurelia, or Civita Vecchia road. Although the fighting up and down hill was preciously hard work, there was of course no opportunity for any great feats of bravery; but in this engagement we were victorious, and what more could be asked of us? Mr. Vavasour has left the Dragoons, and is now a Zouave again in Captain D'Arcy's company. I see him at the Library occasionally.

The Holy Father resides at the Vatican now, he has not resided at the Quirinal since he was driven from it by the Revolution of 1849. I have seen part of the Palace of the Vatican; although the exterior is not particularly imposing. It is the most interesting, if not the largest palace in the world, and its interior is one of the most splendid; the galleries of monumental inscriptions are full of interest, the most ancient being Pagan inscriptions, the Christian have been taken from the Catacombs. Then there are courts of sculpture containing some of the finest works of the ancients, such as the famous Apollo Belvedere, the Laocoon, the Antinous, the Egyptian Museum containing the celebrated mummies and embalmed bodies of individuals who lived some thousands of years ago. There are two splendid sarcophagi of red porphyry of immense size, which have occupied twenty-five years in being restored. I went yesterday to see the picture-gallery, and saw there the very choice collection by many of the most renowned painters the world has produced. Here are the famous " Transfiguration " of Raffaele, the " Madonna di Foligno," the " Coronation of the Blessed Virgin," by the same master. The " Transfiguration" is considered to be the first in order of merit of any painting in the world. Near the picture-gallery are the rooms which contain the tapestry made after the twelve cartoons of Raffaele. The stanza of Raffaele contains a series of historical paintings in fresco of sacred subjects from the Creation of the world to the Redemption. The Sistine Chapel is not open to the public. It is in the Vatican, not in St. Peter's. There is also a large garden and several open courts within the precincts. The Belvedere is a very fine portion of the palace, and, as its name implies, commands a splendid view of the Campagna, the city, and the snow-capped Apennines. I also visited St. Peter's, and saw the place marked out, and seats being erected for the General Council, which is to be held in the north transept, that being sufficiently large to furnish several hundreds of seats.

ST. PETER'S.

"But lo! the dome, the vast and wondrous dome,
To which Diana's marvel was a cell,
Christ's mighty shrine above His martyr's tomb.

. . . .

But thou of temples old, or altars new,
Standest alone, with nothing like to thee,
Worthiest of God, the holy and the true.
Since Zion's desolation, when that He
Forsook His former city, what could be

Of earthly structures, in His honour piled,
Of a sublimer aspect? Majesty,
Power, glory, strength, and beauty all are aisled
In this eternal ark of worship undefiled.

Enter: its grandeur overwhelms thee not;
And why? it is not lessened; but thy mind,
Expanded by the genius of the spot,
Has grown colossal, and can only find
A fit abode, wherein appear enshrined
Thy hopes of immortality; and thou
Shalt one day, if found worthy, so defined
See thy God face to face, as thou dost now
His Holy of Holies, nor be blasted by His blow.

Not by its fault, but thine. Our outward sense
Is but of gradual grasp, and as it is
That what we have of feeling most intense
Outstrips our faint expression, even so this
Outshining and o'erwhelming edifice
Fools our fond gaze, and greatest of the great
Defies at first our nature's littleness,
Till, growing with its growth, we thus dilate
Our spirits to the size of that they contemplate."

CHILDE HAROLD.

As I have not yet given you my impressions about St. Peter's, I will say a few words about this, the finest Christian temple of the world. Viewed from the Piazza San Pietro, the façade is very grand and imposing, the height is so great as to hide somewhat the view of the dome, which is such a striking feature of the edifice. The farther, however, we recede from it, the more this splendid feature is unfolded to our view. On ascending to the Porta Cavaleggieri, the proportions of the dome and the Basilica are seen to great advantage. In the far off distance, the first object which will meet the eye of the pilgrim or traveller to distinguish the Eternal City is the cross surmounting the fine cupola of St. Peter's.

The portico is worthy of the fine temple to which it is the entrance. A story is told of an American tourist who, seeing its magnificent proportions, fancied it must be the Basilica itself, and said, "Oh, yes, 'tis a very fine church," and went home satisfied that he had seen St. Peter's. On passing into the interior we are at once impressed by a feeling of wonder at its colossal proportions; and whatever we may have thought previously, we cannot but admit the magnificence of what we see before us. At first we cannot think of details: it is the grand *whole* that strikes us. We approach and kneel, with deep feelings of veneration, at that shrine which has been the object and term of so many pilgrimages, the confession or tomb of the glorious apostles SS. Peter and Paul. We then take a glance at the principal features of the interior. The high altar—placed as explained before in the case of the Basilica—is immediately over the tomb of the Apostles, under the centre of the dome. Over the altar is a splendid baldachino, or canopy, made from the bronze taken from the Pantheon. It is about ninety feet high: the confession is partly surrounded by a marble balustrade on the side facing the nave: inside of this a great number of lamps are always kept burning. The dome which surmounts the whole is one of the greatest wonders which Christian art has ever produced. Any one who has visited the Pantheon or Rotondo, and reflects that this dome represents the Rotondo, raised about 200 feet into the air, will have some idea of its immensity, in fact the area covered by it is that of a fair sized church. Its interior magnificence is of the first order, and it would be difficult to imagine greater beauty of ornamentation. Above each of the pillars is a superb mosaic of one of the four Evangelists. The proportions of these four mosaics can be imagined from the fact that the pen in the hand of each is six feet in length.

These few words will give but a very imperfect idea of this, the great triumph of the skill of Michael Angelo, and of the energy of the great Pope Sixtus V., under whom it was carried out and completed.

Of the four statues which ornament the pillars of the dome I was struck more particularly by those of St. Helen and St. Veronica. The celebrated lions, too, of Canova, are marvellous triumphs of the chisel. The copies in mosaic of the most celebrated paintings in the world which we see forming the altar-pieces at so many points in the Basilica, are marvellously executed, so faithful are they to the original, that an unpractised eye would not discover that they were not the paintings themselves. The plan of the Basilica is that of a cross; the nave, the choir, and the aisles forming the longer portion, and the transepts the shorter one. The dome is placed at the intersection of the nave and the transepts.

The building of the present Basilica was commenced in 1450 : it was consecrated in 1626. Thus it appears that 176 years were spent in building it, at a cost which shows how Rome honours her apostles. The diameter of the dome is 195 feet; from the pavement to the top of the cross is 434 feet; from the entrance to the chair of St. Peter is 613 feet. At the transept the width is 450 feet; the nave is 88 feet wide, and 146 feet high; the aisles are 24 feet wide. The holy water vases are supported by angels six feet high, though, on first beholding them, you will suppose them to be of the ordinary height of little children, so great is the size of the building.

In the choir, at the extreme end, is the chair of St. Peter, placed on high, and enclosed in a beautiful bronze chair. This is the same chair which the apostle used in the house of Pudens the senator. It is supported by four colossal figures in bronze, which represent the four doctors of the church. From the gallery over the statue of St. Veronica are shown, on Easter Sunday and other festivals, a relic of the true cross, part of the spear which pierced our Lord's side, and the handkerchief of St. Veronica.

The tabernacle of the altar of the chapel of the blessed Sacrament is in the form of a round temple, decorated with twelve pillars of lapis lazuli. It is twenty feet high, and was executed from the designs of Bernini.

CHAPTER X.

SANTA SABINA—FEAST OF ST. JOSEPH—JUBILEE OF THE HOLY
FATHER—ST. GEORGE.

WE have a very good opportunity of knowing how things are going on in England when we choose to read the newspapers which remain here (at the library) from Thursday till Monday, when they are sent to the Zouaves in the country.

On the 24th ult. four of us visited the convent and church of Santa Sabina, which is situated on the Aventine—a strong position, now fortified, on the south side of Rome. We were introduced by Father Sadoc Sylvester, a friend of R—— and myself, from the Minerva. In the church we saw the splendid painting of Our Lady giving the Holy Rosary to St. Dominic, and to St. Catherine of Sienna, by Sasso ferrata. Under the high altar are the bodies of several martyrs; among them that of St. Sabina. The room of St. Dominic, now converted into a small chapel, is shown in the convent; and an orange tree in the garden, planted by this Saint himself, from which I send you a leaf. From the balcony of the convent one can enjoy a splendid panorama of Rome and the neighbourhood.

Close to Santa Sabina is Sant' Alessio. The body of this Saint reposes under the high altar; and the stairs under which he lived are kept in the church as a relic. In the underground church of San Clemente are several interesting pictures describing different phases in the life of this Saint. His father lived on this spot on the Aventine, and was a wealthy patrician. St. Alexius went to the Holy Land as a pilgrim, and when he returned to his home his parents no longer recognized him, but consigned him to the "stairs," and the care of the servants, at whose hands he received some ill-treatment. This he suffered patiently, and died a holy death, after revealing his history to his parents.

The church and establishment of the Gesù occupies an irregular quadrangular site of considerable extent, each side of the quadrangle bounding a street; our barracks forms one side, and is entirely cut off from the part occupied by the Jesuits. We are able, however, from some of our windows, to obtain a view of their orange garden, which was a beautiful sight before the severe frost of this winter destroyed the oranges. This garden is amongst the different buildings, and this, as well as several open courts—like the "atria" of the ancients—form part of the arrangements of every considerable building in the city, and every part of the whole is by this means furnished with light and air.

My friends and I are pleased that we are likely to remain in Rome for the present; and we are pleased, also, for many reasons, to be so well placed as we are here at the Gesù.

Low Sunday, April, 1869.—The Feast of St. Joseph is always a grand one in Rome. I enjoyed it very much this time, as I was not on duty except for the military Mass. Afterwards we visited San Stefano Rotondo for the stations. Round the walls of the church—which is circular—are a large number of fresco paintings, illustrating in a very remarkable and life-like manner the different kinds of torture inflicted on the martyrs and the death they suffered for the faith. The paintings are arranged in chronological order, which is very convenient. On the same day were commemorated the Seven Dolours of our Blessed Lady at the church of Santa Maria in Via, near the Corso, where there is a statue—Santa Maria Addolorata. This statue was carried in procession through several streets, including a part of a Corso, preceded by members of the Confraternity, carrying banners, the Cross, &c., by religious of different orders, the Bishop carrying a relic, and followed by a military band, playing appropriate music. We were able to fall in with the procession at several different points, and were much pleased and edified by it.

There are two churches in Rome, the interiors of which are principally of the Gothic style, viz., Santa Maria sopra Minerva, and the Redemptorist Church of our Lady of Perpetual Succour, on the Esquiline; the latter is, in my opinion, a very pretty church. I like the nave, chancel, and side-aisles of the Minerva; but the effect of the Gothic here is marred by the Roman of the other part of the church. In my humble opinion, the two styles never do well mixed, as the solidity and the heaviness of the one destroy the lightness and elegance of the other. You ask if I admire the Roman style. I certainly do; and I think it very well suited to Rome. I do not think any one can deny its grandeur and beauty when well carried out, and ornamented with beautiful marbles, porphyries, alabaster, lapis lazuli, mosaics, frescoes, &c., as we see it here. For example, take St. Peter's, justly acknowledged to be the most magnificent church of the universe.

On Good Friday we visited Santa Croce in Gerusalemme, in order to see and venerate the sacred relics of the true Cross:—one of the nails with which Our Lord was crucified, two thorns of the crown of thorns, the finger of St. Thomas, which he placed into the sacred wounds, a large portion of the cross of the good thief, and the title of the true Cross. All these precious relics are preserved with the greatest care in the monastery attached to the church, and it was a great privilege to see them, to venerate them, and to be able to touch some of them with our sabres. This church is named "The Holy Cross in Jerusalem," because here is kept not only part of the Cross of Our Lord, but also part of the earth of Mount Calvary, which was brought here by St. Helen, the mother of Constantine the Great, and to contain which the church was built. These facts are well authenticated in history. We next visited the Scala Santa— holy staircase—the very same that Our Lord ascended to Pilate's house. We mounted them, as do all penitents, on our knees; then we entered St. John's Lateran for the Miserere, rendered magnificently by the splendid choir of the Basilica. While there I met Father Canty, who took me into one of the beautiful chapels—I think the Corsini. We descended into a crypt, and there saw the very finest *Pietà** which, in my opinion, I have ever seen, not even excepting the one by Michael Angelo in St. Peter's; the attitude of the whole group was perfect. In the evening we went to the church of SS. Vincent and Anastasius, at the fountain of Trevi, for the "Ora desolata" of the Blessed Virgin. The service consisted of sermons in Italian, interspersed by verses of the Stabat Mater and other appropriate music. The latter was very plaintive and good; but of the sermon I could understand but very little. I did not hear the Miserere in the Sistine, as private Zouaves, or other soldiers are not admitted; but I heard it sung in St. Peter's on the Wednesday, and I was told by a person who heard it sung in both places, that he preferred that sung in St. Peter's on Wednesday to that sung in the Sistine on one of the other days.

The singing of the Sistine choir is of a peculiar character, and every one does not appreciate it. Anyhow, the Wednesday Miserere of St. Peter's was very beautiful and plaintive, and to get in a good position to hear it, it was necessary to put up with the pushing and jostling of a very eager and anxious crowd, as well as to stand for more than two hours of the time a solemn Tenebræ requires. The Palm Sunday procession is a grand one, consisting of members of the different religious orders, parish priests, Monsignori, Cardinals with their attendants, the Holy Father borne aloft on the "Sedia Gestatoria," surrounded by the Noble Guard, and followed by some of the ambassadors in grand costume, by the officers of the different corps of the army in full dress, all carrying palms in honour of the triumphal entry of our Lord into Jerusalem. Amongst the visitors on that day, and on Easter Sunday, we noticed several English officers in uniform, which they are expected to wear on grand occasions, so as to be able to enter the

* A *Pietà* is the dead Body of Our Lord in His Blessed Mother's arms.

cordon of the military on duty in the Basilica of St. Peter. Amongst them was a General, but I do not know his name. There have been a great number of visitors this year for the ceremonies of Holy Week, amongst them a large proportion from our own country. May the sight of the splendour of the offices of Holy Church, as compared with the coldness of Protestant worship, have some effect on their minds and hearts!

On Easter Sunday all the troops available were assembled to receive and be present at the Apostolical Benediction, which takes place after the Mass; the Holy Father gives it from the balcony of the portico of St. Peter's, overlooking the Piazza. I suppose you know the Benediction conveys a plenary indulgence to all in a state of grace with the condition of Confession and Communion. The booming of the cannon of St. Angelo announced the conclusion of the solemn blessing. Cheering followed. The Holy Father stopped a few moments to look at the multitude of all nations there gathered together, and then the assemblage began slowly to disperse. Although the weather was stormy, it did not seem to have the effect of keeping many people away.

I had an opportunity of reading a summary of the case of "Saurin v. Starr." I can understand its causing a great sensation in England. Although for many reasons it would have been better if the parties could have settled their differences without coming before the public, I think there has been one good result of the trial, it has shown the Protestant world that when a convent was laid bare no real *scandal* could be found in it.

May 1st, 1869.—It was indeed a great day here on the 11th of April last, being the jubilee of our Holy Father, *i.e.*, the fiftieth year of his priesthood completed. The rejoicings lasted three days, commencing on the Saturday, when the city was all alive with carts and waggons loaded with presents of corn, wine, oil, flowers, besides many other things too numerous to mention, all to do honour to our Holy Father's jubilee. In the evening the Basilica of St. Peter, including the dome, was illuminated; first takes place the silver illumination—this lasts during the first hour—when suddenly, in the course of some few seconds, the design of the illumination is changed by the lighting up of 500 larger additional lights, which throw a "golden" shade over the whole—this is the golden illumination. The whole is a splendid thing, and I have heard no one say that they have seen anything better of its kind.

I was present in St. Peter's for the Mass of the Holy Father on the Sunday. There was assembled a remarkable and eager crowd almost entirely of Catholics, and it was necessary to put up with a considerable amount of pushing, and to elbow one's way through the closely-packed assemblage even to catch a sight of the Holy Father. I believe he was employed for a great part of the morning afterwards in receiving addresses of congratulation from the Diplomatic Corps. Even the Queen of England and Emperor of Russia sent him their felicitations. At four p.m. he appeared at the balcony overlooking the Piazza San Pietro, to hear the singing of some music, including Gounod's hymn, specially composed for the occasion. This was performed by a band and a large number of singers chosen from the different corps of the army; among them were a great many Zouaves. The singing was considered very good; the crowd assembled to hear it was considerable, and at its conclusion the Holy Father bestowed the Apostolical Benediction on all present. In the evening there was a grand display of fireworks, some of which were very pretty. On the Monday, which was the anniversary both of the Holy Father's return from Gaeta in 1849, and of his wonderful preservation from injury when the floor of the room gave way at Sant' Agnese in 1855, the whole city was beautifully illuminated in the evening, the crowds of people to be met with everywhere were enormous; the whole thing was a great success. But I need not enter into particulars, as I suppose you have seen it all described in the columns of the *Tablet*.

I am forgetting to mention the review of all the troops at present in Rome, which took place on Easter Monday in the Villa Borghese; the Commander-in-Chief, General

Kanzler, reviewed us. On the occasion several of the visitors—among them General Slade, an Englishman—expressed themselves much pleased to see the regularity with which the march past was performed. The Commander-in-Chief was accompanied by a brilliant staff, a Highland officer being one of those that composed it.

During the whole time we have remained at the Gesù, W. R——, R—— and I have continued our friendship. We spend a great part of our spare time together, either at the Library or in visiting any of the monuments, churches or other points of interest in the City. When off duty, we make it a point to ask for ten o'clock permission every night, as we do not care to spend any unnecessary time in barracks.

On the eve of the Feast of St. George—the day itself falling on a Friday—all the English Zouaves were entertained to dinner at the Restaurant de Paris by Mgr. Stonor, who, as well as Father Gurdon, Mr. Loughnan, Father Canty, and Mr. Vavasour, dined with us. After the dinner had been done justice to, Mgr. Stonor proposed the health of the Holy Father in an appropriate speech. It was drunk with cheers of three times three. Next followed the health of the Queen and royal family, also drunk enthusiastically. Next Mgr. Stonor proposed the health of Father Gurdon, praising him for his devotion to the Zouaves, and mentioning the regret he felt in losing him. Father Gurdon is about to leave for a mission in England. Father Gurdon, in his reply, spoke of the great pleasure he had felt in being in Rome, so much so, that it seemed as if he had been spending a long holiday here. Mgr. Stonor's health was then proposed, and received with many a cheer, and then the party broke up.

On the Feast itself Father Gurdon said Mass for us in the Church of St. George, where we saw exposed his standard and spear head. At five in the afternoon we had, through the kindness of Mgr. Stonor, an audience of the Holy Father, who was most affable and kind to us, and gave us the apostolic benediction for ourselves and our families. He presented us all with a medal of the Immaculate Conception. After the audience we were able to see the presents of jewelled monstrances, chalices, vases, missals, chasubles, rosaries, the beautiful statue of the Immaculate Conception, the splendid vase given by the King of Prussia, and many other beautiful things. These constituted—not including money gifts—the more valuable portion of the presents made to the Holy Father. All the more bulky portion, including some works of art, we had seen on the 10th of April, arranged in the court-yard of the Vatican. Truly one may say, that whatever triumphs other popes have witnessed, never has there been *greater or more universal enthusiasm* shown than for Pius the Ninth.

To return to the Feast of St. George, at seven we had a tea-party at the Library. The refreshments were kindly provided by two ladies resident in Rome. After tea we had an Ethiopian entertainment, consisting of songs, jokes by Bones and Pompey, and concluding by a farce of the "Sublime and Ridiculous." Every one present, I think, enjoyed the evening. I certainly did for one. The Ethiopians were Zouaves, and the entertainment was got up by them, and it was certainly a success. Messrs. M'Guinness and Burchett were the two principal actors.

CHAPTER XI.

MARCH TO MONTEFIASCONE — LAGO DI VICO — BEAUTIFUL SCENERY—FEAST OF SS. PETER AND PAUL IN ROME—LIFE AT MONTEFIASCONE.

June 3rd, 1869.—I OUGHT to have mentioned, that while at the Gesù we were all armed with the Remington rifle, having given up the carbines we carried before. The Remington rifle is very simple, light, and a breech-loader, and we are able to fire very rapidly with it.

On our march out here from Rome we passed through a very interesting country, including some very lovely scenery. Thus I dare say a few words about the march may not be unacceptable. We started from Rome at four a.m., on Tuesday, May 17th, passed through the Porta del Popolo, and marched on the Via Cassia, through the Campagna, during that day, resting at La Storta from eight a.m. till three p.m. during the heat of the day; about half-past six we arrived at Baccano, a small place, and rested there that night. This first day I was one of the advance guard, which always precedes by one or two miles, but is supposed never to be out of sight of the main body, otherwise in time of war it might be cut off from it. The men on this service have also to mount guard over the baggage at the principal halts; I had three hours on "*faction*"—as sentinel—over two hours in the sun, and half an hour at night.

Wednesday we rose at two, started at half-past three a.m., arriving at Monte Rosi at half-past seven. This morning we left the Campagna proper, and as we approached Monte Rosi we got into a slightly mountainous district, in the midst of the northern portion of the Campagna. Near Monte Rosi is a small lake, in which R—— and I took a refreshing bath. We got into marching order about half-past three, and arrived at Ronciglione in three hours: we were now more than half-way to our destination, and had marched nineteen miles the first day, and seventeen the second. The scenery round Ronciglione is very picturesque, the town being built at the head of a very steep ravine, and quite amongst pretty hills, and only one mile from the calm Lake Vico. This lake was the scene of a swimming feat, performed here shortly before our march by an English Zouave, Sergeant Collingridge. This sergeant went down with his lieutenant to the lake for a bath; after they had been in the water a short time, the lieutenant missed Mr. Collingridge, and thought he must have gone down. He got out and dressed, but fancied he saw something moving in the middle of the lake—it might be him struggling for his life. The lieutenant immediately posted off to the barracks, to find some men to come and drag the lake for the body. All these movements occupied some considerable time, for as the lieutenant and his men went down to the lake, what was their astonishment when they met Mr. Collingridge all alive riding to barracks, after swimming across the lake and back! *a swim of about four miles*, the Lago di Vico being about two miles broad. The lieutenant was somewhat chagrined, as might be supposed.

We met Sergeant Collingridge and several other comrades at Ronciglione, and passed a pleasant evening with them.

I should have mentioned that on our first day's march we passed near the site of Veii, once a celebrated Etruscan city, and an ancient rival of Rome, and that on the second day before reaching Ronciglione, we passed the sites of two other cities famous in ancient history, viz., Nepete, to the north of the Via Cassia, and Sutrium, to the south, nearer Ronciglione; the latter, now Sutri, we observed peacefully nestled on a pretty hill-side, as we neared our evening destination.

The Lago di Vico, though not of great extent, is marked by features of calm, peaceful loveliness; it is nearly surrounded by very steep mountains of the Ciminian range, the highest point of which, Mons Ciminius, now Monte Soriano, overlooks the country of ancient Etruria. On the third day of our march we descended first for about a mile to the level of the lake, and then commenced the long, gradual ascent of eight miles, leading to the Gendarmeria della Montagna, which is near the summit of Monte Cimino, or Soriano.

We left Ronciglione before sunrise, but had not mounted sufficiently high at that identical moment to obtain the unequalled pleasure of viewing the glorious scene, first in deep shadow, and then gradually but swiftly lit up by the rays of the mighty orb. When we had attained a considerable height, the sun had risen perhaps ten minutes; but what a scene of beauty and magnificence burst upon our dazzled eyes as we looked upon the view! On our left was the peaceful lake and its mountain boundary; on our right we beheld four, if not five, ranges, one behind the other, of the bold, rugged Apennines, the highest peaks covered with snow; farther on to the south-east, the famous Sabines; at right angles to these, but separated from them by the plain of Latium, the Alban hills; behind us were the lower mountains we had crossed the two previous days — the Campagna, now covered, as every morning, with its *winding-sheet* of fog, white as snow, and Monte Soracte rising proudly defiant, and alone in its midst; then add to this the aid of an Italian sun gently rising higher every moment, and diffusing his glorious rays over the whole, and remember that nothing in England can adequately compare with this charming scene, and you will have perhaps some faint idea of its effect on our enraptured gaze. Now we pass some deep ravines and pretty wooded glens on the side of the Campagna, where, nearer to us than Monte Soracte, is Civita Castellana and the site of the classic Falerii. As we mount higher we catch sight of the beautiful blue Mediterranean, and the islands to the west of the Tuscan shore; we reach the Gendarmeria, and halt there several hours; we ascend a height near, and take our soup together, W. R——, R——, and I. The Majors of the 1st and 2nd company select the same spot; here we had a view of Montefiascone, with part of Lake Bolsena, which were so soon to become such familiar scenes to us, and the former our home during the approaching summer. In the afternoon we descended the mountain, and after a hot, dusty walk of six miles, we arrived in Viterbo.

Viterbo is a clean, respectable-looking town, and stands next in importance to Rome. The Emperor Napoleon's troops are in garrison there, and they appear soldier-like men. We rested there the whole of Friday, and we had then the opportunity of visiting the shrine and church of St. Rose of Viterbo and the Madonna della Quercia; the latter is now enclosed in a church, but is not always exposed: we entered the church, but did not see the Madonna. We arrived at Montefiascone on Saturday at eight a.m., having marched the twelve miles from Viterbo in four hours.

Montefiascone—Mons Faliscus of the ancients—is situated on a mountain 1700 feet above the sea level, at the south end of the splendid lake of Bolsena. From the side looking down on the lake is a very beautiful view; first, stretching out at a great depth below one, are vineyards and fruit gardens from the slopes of the mountains down to the lake; then there is the lake itself with its two islands—Martana and Bisentina—the latter containing seven ruined chapels; beyond, in the distance, the mountains of Tuscany; far off, on the left, is the sea and the island of Gianuti, and the rocky promontory of Argentario, the former about seventy miles distant in a straight line; on the right is a pretty country reaching from Bagnorea to Acquapendente, including a portion over the frontier.

The town is celebrated for its white wine, and although the wine in this part of Italy is neither considered good nor cheap this year, yet at Montefiascone we can buy a fiaschetto—containing about two pints—of wine for six sous, or threepence; earlier in the season it was cheaper still. Since we have been here we have had some very hot sultry days, but now it is much cooler; this morning was quite cold, the wind blowing off the Apennines. On the whole, it will be much cooler here than in Rome for the summer.

Rome, July 2nd, 1869.—It is about sixty English miles from Rome to Montefiascone the way we marched out; it was well arranged, and with the help of tallow—very good for the poor feet—the most of us were not over fatigued or footsore. You will be perhaps surprised to find me writing from Rome. I came in, on permission for eight days, for the Feast of SS. Peter and Paul, as I was not in Rome for it last year. I started on Saturday last, accompanied by R—— as far as Toscanella, and a Spanish Zouave of our company, Count Alvarez de Toledo, leaving the barracks at three a.m. in a carriage, in order to meet the train at Corneto, thirty-five miles distant. We passed through Marta and Toscanella, where we stopped to rest a short time; there did not appear to be anything very remarkable about these places as far as we could see from a passing visit, but I believe, as *Toscania* was one of the principal cities of Etruria, that there are some remains to be explored another day. We passed Corneto before arriving at the station, which is situated between that town and the Mediterranean. Corneto appeared to be a pretty town, strongly situated on a high hill, but we did not enter it, as my companion and I preferred to go down to the sea for a bath, during the time we waited for the train. We found a nice shore, and had a most delightful swim, and picked up on the coast a few shells to bring home. I found my companion very pleasant, and it was through his kindness that I rode to Corneto, for I had previously intended to walk. We conversed in French, and got on very well, although I am very far as yet from speaking that language fluently. The Count speaks French and Italian beautifully.

The railway fares are reduced two-thirds for the military who may be travelling.

On the Feast of SS. Peter and Paul, the Holy Father said Mass in St. Peter's at the high altar. I saw the procession return from the Basilica to the Vatican; although grand as are all processions in which the Holy Father takes part, it was not so brilliant as that of Palm Sundey or Easter. The Pope appeared in very good health, but looked very sad before reading the Excommunication against the robbers of the States of the Church, which he does on returning, when about half-way down the nave.

The whole of the crypt under the dome being open, I took the opportunity of visiting it, and saw there the tombs of a great many popes, among them those of Adrian IV., an Englishman, and Alexander VI., also those of the Stuart princes, descendants of James II. There were also inscriptions taken from the catacombs of the Vatican, mosaics, and other interesting objects from the ancient Basilica of St. Peter. On the evening preceding the feast the Basilica was illuminated, and partially so on the feast itself; there were also fireworks at San Pietro in Montorio; the display was splendid, the best I have yet seen. On the 30th I went, accompanied by two comrades, to St. Paul's, and saw there again the Holy Father, got his blessing, and examined again this splendid Basilica; here are collected the most beautiful semi-precious stones the world can produce. The baldachino is supported by four alabaster columns, the bases of which are formed of marble, malachite, and the centre panels of a beautiful purplish lapis-lazuli; but I forget that you have a book describing "Rome, its Churches," &c., better than I can do. I can only add that most of them well repay a second visit, as one at first sight does not take in all their grandeur and beauty. The chain of St. Paul being exposed, I was able to kiss it, a priest holding it, and taking it round the group of the kneeling crowd who came to venerate it. I afterwards visited the Tre Fontane, where this holy apostle was beheaded, and saw there also the pillar to which he was bound. The history of the Tre Fontane, *i.e.*, three fountains, is this: St. Paul was beheaded at this spot on the Ostian Way; as his head was severed from the body it was seen to make three bounds, and at each spot where it touched the ground, there issued forth a spring of water. These three springs can be seen inside the church, which was built to contain them.

To-day I visited the room of St. Philip Neri, at the Chiesa Nuova, and I saw there his bed, confessional, the altar at which he said Mass, and the crucifix he held in his hand when he died.

You hope I shall try my hand at sketching, but do not expect any results; my attempts will be *rough* enough without being *ready*. I am sadly in want of a master to teach me the elements of drawing from nature.

We are living at Montefiascone, in a part of a Franciscan monastery, which is used as a barrack, and we are certainly well situated for the summer. We have not been to the islands yet, although we went to Capo di Monte for the express purpose of going to Bisentina; but the boatmen asked too much money, and said it would take too long to go, as there was a little wind. We have exercise three times a week, *reveil* at 4 a.m., *appel* at 4.45; we are then taken to the fields and exercised in skirmishing drill, a great deal of it at the "*pas gymnastique*,"—a slow running step —until about 7.45, when we return to barracks.

The following are a few of our commands in the field: "*Seconde section en tirailleurs à vingt pas, prenez vos intervalles!* MARCHE!" After we are deployed in line at five paces distance we hear: "*En avant! Commencez le feu! En retraite! Cessez le feu! Par le flanc droit pas gymnastique!* MARCHE! HALTE! *Rassemblement!*" and at last, "*Peloton par le flanc droit,* DROITE!" "*Peloton en avant!* MARCHE!" "*Peloton!* HALTE!" "*A droite alignement! Fixe!*" "*Presentez arme!*" "*Rompez vos rangs!* MARCHE!" On hearing the last we are at our barrack's door, and there separate after three hours' healthy exercise. We mount guard about once in twelve days; we have inspection of all our effects twice a week, and are consigned to barracks from one o'clock till four every day except Sunday—this is to avoid the heat, and for the *siesta*,* if we choose to take it—then we have an *appel propre* inspection in the ranks as to cleanliness of dress, sabre, &c. Every day when there is no exercise, we have plenty of

* The afternoon repose.

time to smoke and take our *café* with our friends on the Piazza of Montefiascone, and to bathe in the lake three times a week.

Montefiascone, July 12th, 1869.—I returned from Rome on Saturday week, by way of Corneto and Toscanella, having walked most of the way to Montefiascone from the station. At Toscanella I met my two friends, W. R—— and R——; we stayed there the night. Toscanella appears to have been an important town in the middle ages, as well as in the time of the ancient Etruscans. Besides a strong wall surrounding the place, there are a good many towers built for its defence, and also two very fine old churches of the twelfth century; the doorway, ornaments, and arches very much resemble the Norman doorways we see in England. These last three days we have had very hot weather, with a strong sirocco blowing.

We have occasionally opportunities of speaking and learning Italian. When we go on patrol with the Gendarmes we talk to them. I do not understand enough Italian to carry on a conversation, but merely to ask and answer a few plain questions.

The history of *La Madonna della Quercia*, i.e., Our Lady of the Oak, is very interesting. Some hundreds of years ago some pious person put up a picture of Our Blessed Lady into an oak tree in a forest near Viterbo. There gradually arose great devotion for the place; miracles were wrought through the intercession of Our Blessed Lady. Some one took the picture to his house, in order to have it always near him; but next day, to his surprise, he found it transferred to the original place. Next time he placed it under lock and key, but no matter, it was taken back again to the original oak, and there it has remained to this day. It is now enclosed in a church in the charge of the Order of St. Dominic. A full description will be found in "Sanctuaries of the Madonna," by the Very Rev. S. Northcote, D.D.

Sunstrokes are very uncommon here. When we walk out in the heat we sometimes tie a white handkerchief on our "kepi." Marching with all our effects is very hard work while it lasts, but the actual march with us lasted only seven or eight hours per day.

Most of the orange trees I have seen are in gardens in Rome, where they present a very pretty sight in winter laden with their golden fruit; as do the lemon trees during the same season. The olives do not grow very high here, and are generally planted amongst the vines, or on the declivities of mountains. I have seen very fine olives at Frascati and other places. The wild flowers of this neighbourhood are few, and much the same as in England. The acacia trees were beautifully in blossom when we came here.

CHAPTER XII.

THEORY—BOLSENA, AND THE MIRACLE OF MOST HOLY SACRA-
MENT—ACQUAPENDENTE—FEAST OF SANTA CHRISTINA—
LIFE IN DETACHMENT AT BOLSENA.

Montefiascone, August 30th, 1869.—I HAVE been very busy lately studying the new "Theory of Rifle-shooting," which has just been published here for our instruction in the use of our new arm. My comrade and friend, W. R——, and I are amongst those who have been chosen to learn it with the corporals and sergeants of the two companies stationed here in detachment. As we do all our service of guard, patrol, attending appels, &c., the same as others, we have not had much spare time for writing. We are told that all those who learn the "Theory" will pass corporals the first, so we are anxious to do our best to master it.

The "Theory" teaches the manner of executing the different movements with the rifle, and the part the instructor has to play in teaching them.

On the 13th, four of us—one being a Canadian—started for a trip, on permission, to Acquapendente and other places. We arrived at Bolsena at seven a.m. There is a church—Santa Christina—which contains some precious relics, and our first care, after we had heard Mass, was to ask permission of the archpriest to see them. The archpriest was very kind and polite. He showed us first the relic of the patroness of the church, St. Christina, Virgin and Martyr. It consists of a stone which was attached with a cord to the neck of the saint when she was thrown into the lake to be drowned for the profession of the Christian faith. By a miracle the cord was broken, and the stone swam and carried the saint on its surface several miles to the island of Bisentina, where she was saved, but only in order to suffer still more, and to be at last beheaded. The stone has retained the marks of the feet of the saint which it received at the time of the miracle, and it now forms the front of an altar.

Later on another miracle took place at this altar. This was in the twelfth century, when a German priest who had doubted the Real Presence of Our Lord in the Blessed Sacrament, came to Bolsena, and begged the intercession of Saint Christina for the removal of his doubts. He said Mass, and at the moment of the Consecration he perceived the chalice filled with the Precious Blood of our Lord, and some drops of It stained the corporal and three stones of the pavement. These stones have been preserved with great care till the present time, and we were able to see them after the ceremony of offering incense, and the recitation of the "Tantum Ergo." The stains of blood were distinctly visible, and we perceived the apparent outlines of an infant countenance in two of them.

Bolsena is pleasantly situate near the lake to which it gives the name. It is near the present frontier. The soil here is very rich, producing vines, peaches, nectarines, apricots, cherries, figs, pears, and other fruits in the greatest abundance. W. R—— was stationed here for a time along with nine others, thus making a small detachment to assist the Gendarmes in patrolling the neighbourhood in search of brigands and other marauders; the men composing the detachment had a fine time of it, for as a great part of their business consisted in guarding the vineyards, they were often invited by the proprietors to help themselves and to partake of their hospitality, which they enjoyed thoroughly.

Before leaving the lake we enjoyed a cooling bath near the delightful coast beyond the town. We then pursued our way, and saw, before reaching San Lorenzo, some interesting Etruscan remains under the ruins of an old castle. The day was delightful; we thoroughly enjoyed our walk, conversing sometimes in French with Varin, the Canadian—

a very intelligent comrade—and at other times in English. We reached Acquapendente in the afternoon, and in the evening the Canadians—who were very numerous in the company in detachment, the 5ieme du 3—invited us to their rooms in town, and we passed there a very social evening with them, and next morning we breakfasted at the Pension des Sous Officiers, M. Desilé, the serjeant-major, having invited us.

Acquapendente is pleasantly situated among low hills, within a few miles of the most northern point of the present Pontifical States. The frontier here bounds Tuscany, and there is a fine view of the far-off mountains, as well as of the surrounding hills and valleys.

On the 14th R——, Weetman, and I left Acquapendente, Varin staying three days with his friends there, and visited Onano, Le Grotte, San Lorenzo, and passing Gradoli and Latera, arrived at Valentano in the evening. This day we came in sight of the lake of Bolsena again. Our walk lay through a pretty country, though not containing any more striking features than have been already enumerated. At Valentano we went to High Mass, as it was the feast of the Assumption. We did not observe anything very remarkable about Valentano, except that we saw in a small chapel some promising sketches of sacred subjects which were the work of a Zouave who had been formerly stationed here in detachment.

In the afternoon we returned through Capo di Monte and Marta, to Montefiascone. Before reaching our destination we were overtaken by a heavy rain, which wetted us well. Thus we completed the circuit of Lake Bolsena.

Sunday, Aug. 22nd.—We visited Celleno, a village to the east of Montefiascone, in charming country, surrounded by smiling vineyards and beautiful valleys—and Rocca al Vecce and Sant' Angelo. The latter is situated a short distance above the valley of the Tiber, and the vicinity of both these places consists entirely of steep hills and ravines.

Bagnoreà is situated near the last-mentioned places, at a

BAGNOREA.

short distance from the Italian frontier, and overlooks the valley of the Tiber. The aspect of the country about Bagnorea, Lubriano, and Civitella d'Agliano is most remarkable and peculiar. It gives one the impression that an earthquake has at some time split up the surface into all kinds of fantastically shaped hills and ravines, and thrown the pre-existing order into confusion. The result may be compared to the sight presented immediately after an immense landslip on the coast of Devon and Dorset, near Lyme Regis. Bagnorea, the ancient Balneum Regium, is built on an isolated rock, cut off from the surrounding hills and steep clay cones by deep ravines. Here is the grotto of St. Bonaventure, the patron of Bagnorea. There is but one approach to the ancient town, and it is by a narrow neck of land, in some places barely the width of the road. The larger portion of the modern town is situated near, on another perpendicular rock, almost as isolated as the former.

A friend and comrade contributes the rest of this chapter as follows:— On our march out to Montefiascone from Rome we halted for the night at Ronciglione, where we slept in a desecrated church, on straw. After dining on some meat and artichokes at a trattoria, we adjourned in a body—six or seven of us together—to a café, where we called for some coffee and rum. On tasting some of the latter we found it was rum mixed with that innocent liquid, water. Whereon one of our number—Sergeant Collingridge—called to the padrone of the café, and bluntly told him, "We want rum, not rum and water." Thereon the man tasted it, and with the greatest coolness remarked, "E vero!" ('Tis true), and entering his shop—outside the door of which we were seated—fetched us another bottle, this time true rum, not the exquisite mixture he had at first attempted to palm off. And all this he did without a blush. Such is the cool impudence and want of uprightness too common among some of the tradespeople of Italy. They scruple not to cheat, and if discovered they are not ashamed, but own their error quietly, and wonder at the purchaser's sagacity in discovering their underhand dealings. I remember, on one occasion, going to a certain photographer's shop in the Corso, with an English friend, I, like him, being dressed at the time *en pekin*, or in civilians' clothes. I inquired the price of a certain panoramic photograph, and was asked ten francs for it, which I thought too much, and not being anxious, at the time, to buy it, I did not bargain further about it. But some time later, wishing to purchase the photograph, I went to the shop, and the same man who served me before, now I was in uniform, and as he concluded up to their tricks, sold me the photograph for three and a half francs.

It may interest some of our readers to contrast the prices they pay for articles of food with what we paid in the barrack canteen at Mentana.

A beefsteak, with potatoes	5½d. a plate.
Stewed beef	4d. ditto.
An omelette of four eggs	4d.
A boiled fresh egg	1d.
Three sausages cooked (rather smaller than English ones)	2d.
Veal (a plateful)	4d.

Besides these things we eat a great amount of honey, which we bought at 2d. a tumbler, in a pure, liquid state. Also we bought *polenta*, and had it cooked with sugar as a pudding, or sometimes done with meat. Mutton is not to be had here, curiously enough. The wine was good, although it was rather dear for a country place like Mentana. Red wine, something like *Vin Ordinaire*, is threepence the foglietta, which is a bottle of about two smallish tumblers. Speaking of wine measures, an amusing story is told concerning them and the spirited Sixtus the Fifth. Up to his reign the vendors of wine, which is, with bread, the chief sustenance of the poorer classes in Italy, refused to sell to the latter a smaller quantity than a foglietta. Wherefore Sixtus issued an edict commanding all wine sellers to supply half this quantity to those who demanded it. It was the custom of this Pope to visit different quarters of the city in disguise, to see that the laws were enforced and observed. So one day, as a poor peasant, he entered into a wine shop, and demanded a "mezza-foglietta," or the half measure. The host refused to sell so small a quantity. Next day a scaffold was erected before the house, and mine host was congratulating himself, because at an execution he thought to sell much wine; but his joy was changed into horror when the officers of justice, entering his house, bound him, and led him off to be executed. Such is the tale, which, though I doubt its authenticity, illustrates the importance of the poor in Italy being able to purchase a small amount of wine, and also pictures to us the anxiety and conscientious strictness with which the falsely abused Sixtus the Fifth enforced the laws he made.

FEAST OF SAINT CHRISTINA AT BOLSENA.—Bolsena is a town situated on the lake of the same name, and consists of a long street built on a level with the lake, with a piazza near where the Orvieto road enters the town, in which stands a large church, dedicated to Saint Christina, with a lofty *campanile*, with a few excellent toned bells belonging to it. Adjoining the church is a chapel where are venerated the relics of the miracle of the Blessed Sacrament that was wrought here. Part of the town likewise is situated on a spur of the hills which are behind the town, and from the remains of a mediæval castle in it is called the Castello. From the Castle is a splendid view of the lake and its two islands and neighbouring country, with a distant glimpse of the Mediterranean. In this upper town is also a small collegiate church, dedicated, if I remember right, to St. Isidore. Bolsena, under the name of *Volsinii*, was one of the chief towns of Etruria. The upper town covers the site of the old Etruscan, and the lower town the site of the Roman town. Some Etruscan remains are visible in the neighbourhood—one an ancient cave, used, I think, as a place of sepulchre by the Etruscans, was shown me near the town, and is called the Robbers' Cave, it having been the chief rendezvous of the many brigands that formerly infested the roads around. Remains of a temple and its altar—now used as a Christian altar in the large church—are still visible.

On July 23, the eve of St. Christina's Feast, a detachment of about twenty men, with a sergeant and two corporals, were ordered off to this pleasant little town to do duty during the feast. No duty during my service in the Zouaves was pleasanter than this. A *festa*, in a country town of the Papal States, was always so full of hearty, innocent enjoyment. The people, while bent on pleasure, do not forget that the cause of the mirth is a Saint's feast; and thus it begins generally by a solemn High Mass veneration of the relics of the Saint. The temporal rejoicing follows. There is the *tombola* where for three sous you have a chance of gaining as many hundred francs. There is the horse race, sometimes with and sometimes without riders. There is the band, good or bad, for they differ much in quality, parading the streets all the livelong day, dressed in a semi-military attire; there is the pig roasted whole, without which the feast is never complete; there are itinerant vendors of hardware who live by going from town to town to the various feasts; and then the feast ends by a display of fireworks, and the ascent of a few fire-balloons. And let us not forget the hearty welcome, be you who you may, Zouave or civilian, resident or stranger, that you are sure to meet with in every house you enter.

But two features of this Bolsena festival are worthy of record, as they are not common to most other feasts, namely, the boat-race on the lake, and the torchlight procession on the eve.

The race consisted of five or six rickety boats, made of a few planks clumsily nailed together, being placed at a distance of 200 yards from the shore in a line, and then being started off, they strove who first should gain the strand and the prize, a fat pig! The amusing thing about the race was the difficulty of keeping the boats in a straight line, for they are rowed by one man standing up face to the bow, pulling an oar fastened by a small rope to the starboard gunwale, while another man in the stern steers against him with another oar, and thus the boats make a most zigzag course, which resulted during this race in many a collision, and a little, but certainly good-humoured, disputing.

The torchlight procession of the statue of St. Christina from her church to the college church was most picturesque. The burning torches, made of the old houses of the town, formed a beautiful background of strong lights and shadows to the various groups of priests, choristers, soldiers, men, women, and children composing the procession. And at intervals along the way we went were placed *tableaux vivants* done in exquisite taste. This one represents the Saint, a mere child, being dragged bound with cords before the stern Roman governor of the town, her own father, who asks her to sacrifice to the gods, but in vain. Next we see her tormented by horrible serpents. Here a soldier is sent to her with a drawn sword, to threaten her with death if she still persists in being true to the faith. Others exhibit her trials, her sufferings, and her martyrdom. One representing the Saint combating the devil, pictured as a hideous fiery monster, excited much the feeling of the people, who loudly cried, " Look, see, the devil, the devil!"

The Saint was the only and youthful child of the pagan governor of the town, and was put to death at Tyro, a city that is supposed to have stood on an island in the lake, but which has now entirely disappeared. A stone is shown in the church bearing the marks of a child's feet, which was fastened to the Saint when thrown into the lake, but which miraculously floated, and bore her in safety to the shore. Her relics are not here, but at Palermo.

LIFE IN DETACHMENT AT BOLSENA.—On Wednesday, August 18th, 1869, I left Montefiascone in the afternoon, and after a *sac-à-dos* march, part of the way through a severe thunderstorm, we arrived at Bolsena in the evening. The detachment to which I belonged numbered ten men, a lance-corporal and nine privates. We did the duty of Gendarmes, and were paid accordingly, receiving twenty-one sous a-day, which we divided thus:—ten sous for the *ordinaire* (daily meals), four for bread, and seven to put in our pockets. The first few days after our arrival we had to sleep on straw, for which we were paid five sous a night. Our duties were not very severe. We provided men for four patrols a day. The first patrol began at six a.m., and lasted till ten a.m.; the second from 3.30 p.m. till 7.30 p.m.; the third from 8.30 p.m. till 12.30 a.m.; and the fourth from then till four o'clock in the morning. The two night patrols were for the town, the other two were for the surrounding country, and especially along the road to Montefiascone, to protect the mails on their journey thither. Each patrol consisted of two Gendarmes and two Zouaves, armed with their rifles. We had no *corvées* except one, which was to buy the meat and other provisions in the town, and we mounted no guards, one man staying in turn at the barracks to see no civilians or suspicious characters entered. We were quartered in the house where the municipality held their meetings. The latter consisted of the doctor, the lawyer, the chemist, and two or three *signori* of independent means.

Five of the Gendarmes quartered in the town with us tried one night, dressed in civilian clothes, to surprise a well-known brigand in the neighbourhood, who had robbed several houses and harmless peasants. They found out where he was hid, and were about to capture him, when he took fright, and made off towards the frontier. The Gendarmes could not get up to him as the ground was full of ditches and holes, and they did not, as he did, know the country. He at last got clear away by leaping down a deep ravine, down which one of the Gendarmes fell and severely sprained his leg. They had their rifles with them, but could not use them, for, according to the law here, firearms cannot be used against an unarmed man, no matter what his crime may be.

Our lance-corporal was a nice young Canadian, Varin by name, and he and I became great friends with the Gendarmes. They were fine fellows those with us, and had nearly all fought at Castelfidardo. They all, without exception, came from the Pope's invaded provinces, from the Marches and Umbria. One of them had been twenty years in the Pope's services, and was close to General de Pimodan when the latter fell on the glorious but disastrous field of Castelfidardo. Another one of our Gendarmes was a native of the Holy Father's birthplace, Sinigaglia.

The wine of Bolsena was considered the best in the Pontifical States, being very pure, nourishing, and strengthening. The natives live almost entirely on it and a little bread and fruit. Some of the fish caught in the lake were very good.

Sometimes we made patrols into the hills among the vineyards, and the owners of them often asked us to taste their grapes. It was delicious work, plucking off large bunches of big ripe grapes, eating them fresh with the dew on them, such grapes as would at home cost three to four shillings a pound, and perhaps not even then equal them in flavour.

On one occasion, some of our detachment conducted two young men to the frontier; they were agents of the Revolution, arrested in Rome, and after a month or so spent in prison, were sent hither to be taken across the frontier. They were brought here in custody of two Gendarmes, and some Zouaves from Montefiascone, and were locked up for the night in the Gendarmerie. Next day they were taken along the Orvieto road, and at the boundary were set at liberty, and told not to venture into the Papal States again. One was a coarse, common-looking jail-bird, but his companion was a handsome young Italian, well dressed, and apparently of good family, and seemed quite ashamed to find himself manacled to such a low villain as his comrade. He told our lance-corporal that he had been surprised at the leniency of the Pope in so soon granting him his liberty, and that while in prison he had been treated with all the kindness compatible with prison discipline, that he had endured no special rigours or severities, as, for instance, the handcuffs had only been put on him while he was being conveyed from one town to another. So much for the rigours, severities, cruelties, dungeons, and chains with which the Pope is said to torture his prisoners!

Occasionally during our night patrols in the town amusing incidents would occur. On one occasion, when all the town was buried in slumber, two old women set up a hideous row, abusing each other in good round terms. In a moment all the neighbourhood was aroused, and heads with and without nightcaps were poked out from the windows of the houses round, abusing the disturbers of their rest, and striving by more noise to quiet the first uproar. It was as much as two Gendarmes and four of us Zouaves could do to get the originators of the hubbub to go to bed, and to induce their would-be pacifiers to close their windows, and hold their tongues, and return to rest.

Many of the inhabitants on hot nights often slept outside their house, but this was forbidden by the authorities, as injurious to the people's health, and dangerous to their purses, if evil-doers were about, so the Gendarmes had orders to wake them up and send them to their homes. One worthy who had been indulging in strong liquors, had betaken himself to rest near the gate of the town. On being awaken by a Gendarme, he was too sleepy and stupid to comprehend the questions asked him, but kept on repeating them over as the Gendarme spoke them. At length the latter, impatient, gave our good friend a box on the ears, which at once cleared his brain, whereon our worthy citizen betook himself to his home and his bed.

After near six weeks of detachment duty, we were replaced by another party, and returned once more to Montifiascone.

CHAPTER XIII.

FEAST OF ST. ROSE AT VITERBO — BOATING EXCURSION ON LAKE BOLSENA—EXCURSION TO ORTE, CIVITA CASTELLANA, SORIANO.

Montefiascone, Sept. 14th, 1869.—SINCE writing last, I have been with my friends to Viterbo for the Feast of St. Rose—Sept. 4th—but as on account of the "Theory" our commandant would give but twenty-four hours' permission, we were only able to see the grand procession which took place on the eve of the feast; the *macchina*, a kind of triumphal car, forty feet high, beautifully executed in the Gothic style, containing representations of different passages in the life of St. Rose, was carried by sixty men. As it was entirely illuminated, as well as the streets, the whole was very beautiful; the streets were thronged with visitors, who had come to see the procession, and to visit the shrine of St. Rose; a picket of French troops attended.

In the church, the body of the Saint can be seen under an altar; it appears to be incorrupt and perfect.

Next morning we had just time to visit La Madonna della Quercia, and to hear Mass there. This time we saw the veritable Madonna of the Oak, with the part of the tree in which it is placed; it appeared to be well executed, and showed appearance of great age; it is kept carefully in a large case or shrine at the back of the high altar, which is formed of beautiful marbles; the church—a new one—is very fine, and is served by the Dominican Fathers, who have a large convent adjoining it.

On Sunday last, after Mass, a party of six started by boat to visit the two islands of Martana and Bisentina. We placed ourselves under the care of R——, who has had some experience in boating; after getting out from shore, our first movements consisted of a series of zigzags, arising from the peculiar nature of the boat, and the manner in which the oars were placed, one on the bow, and the other astern. These were succeeded by misgivings as to the propriety of having left the boatmen behind, the boat commencing to make a straighter though slow course, a consequence of the different arrangement of the men and oars, abandonment of the design of three of the party, swimming from the nearest point of the coast to the first island, followed by the boat—the consequence of loss of time occasioned by badly constructed boat—then change of course, and pointing the bow towards Martana, where we arrived after an hour and a half's rowing. Then followed examination of the ruined monastery on the island, ascent of the steep cliff, bird's eye view of the ruined mediæval castle thereon, and of the lake therefrom, descent, cutting names on a fig-tree—this was the cause of a serious inconvenience to two of the party, viz.: R—— and Woodburn, who in cutting freely through the bark of this wild fig-tree, allowed the milky sap to flow on their arms and feet; this afterwards caused severe irritation of the skin to both, and one of them did not get rid of it for more than six weeks. Refreshments succeeded, consisting of bread, ham, figs, and grapes. No inhabitants were seen, though a cow and a donkey were. We re-embarked at 1.40 p.m., enjoyed a lovely row, intermingled with some misgivings as to the possibility of returning to Montefiascone that night, and arrived at Bisentina at 3.25, reconnoitred the island, the seven ruined chapels at different points on the rocky coast, the almost ruined church, and the old English boat—this was the property of an Englishman, a former owner of the island of the time of Napoleon I. Re-embarkation at 5.40; damages done to an oar, thereupon ensued reparation, afterwards comparatively good run to the Montefiascone shore, where we arrived at 8.5 all right, and in time to be in barracks before ten.

Montefiascone, Sept. 30th, 1869.—The weather has been somewhat variable, but in general very good for the grapes,

LAKE OF BOLSENA.

the crop of which is good. Some snow has fallen on the Apennines, although it is at present as warm here during the day as in England in the middle of summer. We shall return to Rome probably in the month of October, and our company will be there—as will the whole regiment—for the opening of the Œcumenical Council.

Last Monday a party of four—one being M. Desnoyers, who assists me in learning French—started for the Grotte San Stefano. This village of San Stefano is about nine miles from here. We entered an albergo to take some refreshment, and met there a Gendarme, whom we asked to take some wine with us, and to smoke some of our English tobacco; this he did, and became very sociable, and afterwards showed us the "grottoes," and told us that they were excavated by some refugees, who were driven out of Florence some centuries ago. I forget to describe a grotto as seen in Italy. Generally speaking it is a kind of cave, excavated out of the volcanic subsoil to store and preserve wine; but in [this mountainous country grottoes are often dug out in the shape of a house of one or more rooms, on the side of hills and mountains, to be inhabited. At San Stefano there is a population of about 2000 souls, the vast majority of whom live in grottoes.

The inhabitants of this and other mountainous districts round Montefiascone, and other country parts of the States which I have visited, are generally simple and industrious in their habits, polite and obliging to strangers, and the women modest and retiring, and their dress very picturesque; red, green, and white are generally the prevailing colours.

After visiting the village of Mugnano, and admiring the valley of the Tiber, we returned to Montefiascone, having passed a very agreeable day.

The vintage has already commenced here, and promises to be a very abundant one, so we may hope to taste the new wine in a short time: we expect it to be better than that of last season, when the vintage and wine were by no means good. Figs and grapes have both been abundant this year.

Saturday, Oct. 9th.—R—— and I started to Orte and Civita Castellana, having a permission of absence for three days. We left at eleven a.m., and after passing Grotte San Stefano, we made the best of our way to Bomarzo across the open country; we could see the place before us on a steep hill, but before we could reach it we encountered four deep ravines, in one of which was a river, and in two others tiny brooks. On the top of one of the rocky hills we crossed we found some grottoes and peculiar excavations, apparently of Etruscan origin. The vicinity of Bomarzo is very pretty, the town being on a steep declivity, the lower slopes of which were covered with vines and olives. Before mounting the hill into the town, we discovered an ancient Roman villa and gardens, in which were terraces, a bath, statuary, &c.; it is now called Villa Antica Borghese, belonging, I suppose, to the Borghese family. We passed through Bassano, and arrived, well soaked with rain, at Orte at eight p.m.

Orte was so called because in ancient times there were here very splendid gardens; we saw the town and neighbourhood to advantage, as the Sunday was a very fine day. The town is placed on a steep rock rising directly from the Tiber, and the scenery around, including its valley and that of the Nera, was magnificent; it included also the bold Apennines in the distance, pretty vineyards below us, and rocky precipitous hills near us, on the opposite side to the mountains. The junction of the Nera with the Tiber takes place below the town near the railway station. Orte, like Montefiascone, Soriano, Civita Castellana, Corciano, Vignanello, and many other Roman towns, occupies a strong and commanding position, and is capable of being defended by a small body of men. Two reasons may be assigned for the position of these places and others in Italy: not only were they capable of being easily defended in the troubles and wars of ancient times and of the middle ages, but their situation, removed above the fogs and mists of the valleys during the night, was and is more healthy.

After hearing Mass in the cathedral, and seeing the

Zouaves of the detachment at Orte, we left for Borghetto by train, passing quite near the frontier of Umbria, formed here by the Tiber; we saw several Italian towns on the tops of high hills on the opposite side of the river; walked from Borghetto to Civita Castellana, met our Zouave friends there, who were not a little surprised as well as pleased to see us. Civita Castellana is a finer town than Montefiascone, possesses two fine churches, besides several smaller ones, and also a fort in which there are a company of discipline, some civil prisoners, and some brigands—among them a celebrated brigand chief named Gasparoni. Next morning we started to return at half-past eight, and passed Corciano, Vignanello, Soriano, and Viterbo, arriving at Montefiascone about eleven p.m. On the way we saw the peasants very busy carrying the grapes from the vineyards to the towns to make the wine. If we asked them to sell us some they would generally give them without being willing to accept anything in return. I have generally found the peasants who lived away from the garrison towns very generous in this way. Near Vignanello the vineyards extend for miles, and the roads were swarming with donkeys carrying the grapes in tubs strapped on like panniers.

At Soriano we met with Sergeant Mohr, a friend of ours, who showed us the tower of Soriano surmounting his barracks. We had there a splendid and extensive view of the whole country round for miles; placed on the declivity of Monte Soriano, one obtains here a beautiful panorama of immense extent, including the valley of the Tiber, the mountains, Montefiascone, &c. No description can convey an adequate idea of the beauty, the striking features, and the variety of the scene before us. This, like so many others in Italy, must be visited to be appreciated. We walked forty-two Roman miles this day, and eighty in the three days, but I was not so tired as from the march back from camp last year.

Just before leaving Montefiascone we had a High Mass there for the six Zouaves who died the year before, and a procession of Zouaves and priests to the cemetery, carrying a cross to be there erected to their memory. This cross was purchased from the proceeds of a subscription among the two companies of the detachment.

The country about Montefiascone was part of the territory of the ancient Etruscans, and Bolsena, Tuscanella, and Corneto were formerly important cities of Etruria. A cemetery in very good preservation has been discovered at Turchina, near Corneto. Cervetri was also an Etruscan city, and interesting remains have been discovered there also. In an old church at Montefiascone are traces of a style resembling the Norman and Gothic; also the tomb of the celebrated Canon who is said to have travelled to find out the best wine in that part of the world. He was so well satisfied with that of Montefiascone, that he settled and died there. On his tomb is the inscription "Est, est, mortuus est."

Between Viterbo and Montefiascone are remains of the ancient Via Cassia.

CHAPTER XIV.

RETURN TO ROME—AT SAN MICHELE—TARGET FIRING.

Rome, Nov. 3rd, 1869.—OUR company arrived here just a week ago. Father Bowen and Father Duckett arrived on Sunday. I saw them on Tuesday, and was very pleased to make their acquaintance. They have very good rooms in the Via Sistina. We marched in by way of Valentano and Montalto, then came from the latter place by train to Rome, thus we had only two days' march, instead of four viâ Viterbo and Ronciglione. The second day we marched twenty-four Roman miles, viz., from Valentano to Montalto, passing through Canino; this was the longest day's march, *sac-à-dos*, that I have ever done: beyond being foot-sore, we were not over fatigued, and not a man was laid up from its effects. After resting a night at Montalto we came in quite fresh on the Friday morning. At Montalto we enjoyed a fine view of the sea and the two islands, one of which is off the Pontifical coast, and the other off that of Tuscany; the former is Gianuti, and the latter Giglio.

As regards your apprehensions on the subject of our boating excursion on Lake Bolsena they were quite unfounded, as the worst that was likely to happen was our being detained for some hours on the lake, and consequent "*salle de police*" on the morrow, for not being in barracks by ten p.m. Even this did not happen, thanks to the aquatic skill of Mr. R——. I am sorry that my account of the trip, written off-hand, should have led you to suppose that I and my friends rush madly into rash enterprises; such, however, is not really the case.

Immediately before leaving Montefiascone I was named

functionary corporal, which is equal to lance-corporal in the English army, except that here one is innocent of, as well as exempt from, the *stripes;* one is exempt from all services, patrols, and all the work of a private soldier.

I mounted my first guard as functionary on Wednesday at Santa Balbina, there being a sergeant above me as "*chef-de-poste.*" I got through it pretty well, barring a little confusion in reconnoitring the "*Ronde d'Officier,*" consequent on being aroused at eleven p.m., from a deep sleep by a cry of "*Caporal de garde!*" "*Ronde d'Officier!*" I had to go out with an escort of two armed men, a third carrying a lantern, and advance within fifteen paces of the officer, and cry out, "*Qui vive?*" Answer—"*Ronde d'Officier!*" Then I cried, "*Avance à l'ordre!*"

The officer then advanced, touched my bayonet, gave me the "*Mot d'ordre;*" in reply I gave him the "*Mot de ralliement;*" all right so far, and I then commanded, "*Portez arme,*" &c. The officer then walked into the Corps de Garde and wrote down in the sergeant's report as to the fact of everything being quiet and all right at, and in the neighbourhood of the post. A functionary does no duty as sentinel; but when he is corporal of the guard he has to relieve the sentinels every two hours, by conducting others to replace them.

We are pleased at the prospect of being in Rome for such a great and momentous event in the history of the Church as the opening of the Œcumenical Council of the Vatican. We consider it quite a privilege. We are stationed at San Michele, with two other companies of our battalion—in all the first, second, and third of the third battalion. San Michele is at once an hospital, barrack, orphanage, prison, as well as an institution for the encouragement of useful arts, such as tapestry, sculpture, &c., situated in the Trastevere, near the island of the Tiber. There is one inconvenience which we have here. We are some distance from the heart of the city. We are also very high in the world—about one hundred steps above mother Earth.

The whole establishment is a very fine one, and the

institutions named above are in full working order, although parts of the building which were founded to encourage and assist all the different mechanical arts, are not now used for that purpose. The different parts are of course separate from each other. The area of the whole comprises sufficient ground for a moderate sized village at the very least.

Nov. 26th.—Although there are a great number of visitors arriving and about to arrive in this city, I believe there will be plenty of accommodation for them, and plenty of provisions, which are not dearer than last year, owing to a good harvest and vintage. The arrangements for the accommodation of the bishops will make no difference to us in any way, as I believe there is enough room for the bishops and ecclesiastics in the palaces and convents which are not used as barracks. Some will, no doubt, take private apartments in the city. Already a good number of bishops have arrived. One meets them everywhere now. There are also a good number of English visitors.

On the 5th inst. there was a grand Requiem Mass for the souls of all those who fell in defence of the Church at Mentana. All the different corps were there represented. The music, both of the choir and the band, was beautiful and appropriate. I have seen, lately, the great relics of the Gesù, viz., the incorrupt hand of St. Francis Xavier in its splendid shrine; also some others tastefully arranged in rich reliquaries. I also had the happiness of receiving Holy Communion, in another of the rooms of St. Ignatius, from the hands of Father Duckett.

On the Feast of St. Stanislaus Kostka, we visited the Church of Sant' Andrea at the Quirinal, where his feast is kept, and heard Mass there. Saw his room in the house attached to the church, and in it the beautiful statue of the Saint, said to have been sculptured by a Protestant, who was very much struck by the beauty of his work, and was afterwards converted to Catholicity. On Sunday last the first vespers of St. Cecily were sung in the Basilica, in the Trastevere, a Cardinal pontificating. I made a point of being there for the commencement. The singing was exquisite;

one solo, accompanied by the harp and flute, was particularly admired. I was very pleased with the whole. At first one does not fully appreciate the grand singing here, or the beautiful churches; but now, after being away for a time, I see the beauty of both far more than at first.

Next day, the 23rd, we visited the interesting Basilica of St. Clement, which is situated between the Coliseum and St. John Lateran. The ancient church situated under the present one is supposed to have been built in the fourth century, and the frescoes on the walls are the most ancient known, next to those of the Catacombs. They are supposed by competent judges to have been executed at different periods between the fourth and the ninth century. One painting represents our Blessed Lady and Child, another the Crucifixion; a third St. Clement, enthroned Pope, assisted by St. Linus and St. Cletus; and as all, more or less, represent Catholic doctrine and practices, there are here historical monuments which show to any unprejudiced observer that the Catholic religion *has been in all ages the same*; and that its doctrines are not novelties, as is asserted by most Protestants. I do not know whether you are aware that the ancient church was buried for 800 years, as the ground around had risen greatly. The present Basilica of the eleventh century was built above the ancient one, on the same spot, on the level of the ground then existing. It is now many feet below the present level; and the ancient church, filled up with rubbish to sustain the foundations of its successor, was lost sight of for many ages, until it was re-discovered by the present Prior, the Very Rev. Father Mullooly, Superior of the Irish Dominicans, to whom San Clemente belongs.

This day being the Feast of St. Clement, the subterranean church was illuminated, and it appeared to excite the interest of a great number of visitors, who were attentively observing and examining the ancient paintings and the recent excavations. Besides the paintings before mentioned, here are to be seen a series describing the exceptional life of St. Alexius, before alluded to, and also a portion of a pagan altar, found in the lower excavations, under the subterranean church. These lower excavations have resulted in discovering a portion of the Palace of St. Clement and some brickwork of the Republican period, as well as masonry of immense blocks of stone, forming part of the city wall of Servius Tullius, sixth king of Rome.

The Rev. Father Mullooly has exhibited great energy in carrying on these excavations, and the expense of them has been very considerable, as before all the rubbish could be cleared away from the subterranean church, supports had to be built to carry the weight of the present Basilica. The excavations are still being carried on, even to the depth of two floors, or levels, *below the subterranean church*.

The rifle-shooting in the Farnesine meadows must not be passed over. I mentioned before that we were all armed at the beginning of the present year with the Remington rifle, and that we studied the new theory on it at Montefiascone, in the summer, after which several of us passed a satisfactory examination.

R—— would never be bothered with it, but used to poke fun at those who studied their theory so assiduously, and say, during the three weeks we were learning it by heart, that "all the roads about Montefiascone were to be seen diversified here and there with single Zouaves, Theory book in hand, from morning till noon and night." Nevertheless, I have never regretted the time I gave to it, for besides improvement in the French language, it gave us an interest in our drill; and those who were proficient in it were soon named functionary corporals, and were thus saved the most trying part of our work; and I feel sure that it was an assistance to me in target-firing. Thus we had our quiet revenge for all the fun poked at us.

Our targets for distance up to 400 metres—about 440 yards—are round, and marked off in five circular zones, commencing from the rose or centre, each succeeding zone being larger than the one preceding. For every bullet that strikes the rose we score 5; for the succeeding, 4; for the

3rd, 4th, and 5th larger zones, we score 3, 2, 1, respectively —the farther from the centre, the smaller the score.

The position of every shot that hits the target is immediately pointed out by a long rod, held in the hand of one of the men in the pits below the targets, so thus every one sees directly the effect of his shot, and he is able to calculate the symmetrical point at which to aim on either side of the rose, in case there is any disturbing cause, such as wind, to turn the balls out of their direct course.

For longer distances than 400 metres, there is a different target, having only two zones, viz., the rose, and the rest of the target, the scores of which are respectively 2 and 1.

There was not sufficient time for our battalion to go through the whole course before the winter came on, so we only fired 30 rounds each man—10 rounds each on three separate days—of these six were fired from the upright position, two from the knee, and two from the ground, couché, *i.e.*, the man lying flat on the earth, and all at distances less than 400 metres..

The English and Irishmen of the corps sustained our reputation very well; Shee and O'Donnell fired very well. I made about 56 points, with 20 balls in the target, and 5 in the rose, out of the 30 rounds. I am well satisfied, considering that I never did anything the year before with the muzzle-loaders, and that R—— was far ahead of me then; this time, however, I have beaten him by a good number of points, and balls in the target: *so much for Theory!* and breech-loaders. There were many in the company who made more points and hits than I.

I called on the Right Rev. Dr. Clifford immediately he arrived here; he appeared very pleased to see me, as being one of the Zouaves from his diocese. I have also been introduced to the Bishops of Northampton and Hexham, both of whom were most affable and agreeable.

I have visited the hospital, tapestry manufactory, and school of sculpture of San Michele, accompanying Father Bowen and Father Duckett. In the hospital, the old men and other inmates seemed to be well cared for, and to be very contented—quite a contrast in the latter respect to the inmates of the English workhouses. The manufacture of tapestry has here attained to great perfection, very beautiful specimens being shown to us, and prizes for San Michele tapestry have been awarded at the London, Paris, and Dublin Exhibitions. Young women are employed in the manufacture, and also in repairing the ancient tapestry of the Vatican. Taken altogether, San Michele is a wonderful establishment, exhibiting, as it does, the munificence of different popes, the care they have taken in promoting industry and the fine arts, the provision made—as everywhere throughout Rome—for the aged and infirm poor.

We afterwards visited the Franciscan Monastery of San Francesco, near San Michele, and were able to see the number of precious relics there collected, particularly the portion of the purple with which our Lord was clothed, the sponge of our Lord, and the stone used by St. Francis as a pillow. Round the cloisters are to be seen some very old paintings relating to events which happened to Saints, and other members of this great Order. The church is a favourite one with the inhabitants of the Trastevere, and is also frequented considerably by the Zouaves of the barracks of San Francesco and San Michele.

CHAPTER XV.

THE OPENING OF THE COUNCIL OF THE VATICAN.

I WAS unfortunately on guard at Sant' Andrea on the 8th inst., so I was unable to be present at the opening of the Council of the Vatican. I tried very hard to find some one to take my place on this great day, but it was quite out of the question, so great was the interest felt in this momentous event. I had no other resource left but to perform my duty, and remain at my post. There was another Open Council on the Feast of the Epiphany, at which I was present; but I must make use of the assistance of a comrade and friend to describe the ceremony of the great day: the 8th of December, 1869, the Feast of the Immaculate Conception of the Blessed Virgin, on which took place, in St. Peter's, the Opening of the Œcumenical Council of the Vatican.

" If you can only realise Byron's superb and elegant description, you will then have some inadequate idea of the immensity, magnificence, and sublimity of the Basilica of St. Peter. The Council was held in the transept on the right as you enter and approach the tomb of the Apostles. A person entering from the vast lobby, and looking over the immense prospect before him, could see to the extreme end of the tribune, where the identical chair in which St. Peter sat is preserved in a superb monument of bronze; yet, while seeing to the extreme end of the unequalled edifice, he would not have been aware, although the Council may have been sitting, that there were upwards of 2000 bishops, theologians, and chaplains then engaged in one part of this wondrous pile. When, however, you arrive at the shrine of the Apostles, where repose the bones of St. Peter and St. Paul, under the matchless baldachino of Pope Urban, of which the magnificent one over Napoleon the Great in the church of the Invalides, Paris, is only a faint imitation, and under the still more matchless cupola of Michael Angelo, under which the dome of St. Paul's, London, may be placed, and yet leave a space of sixty feet between its top and that of St. Peter's:—when we arrive here, we have the transepts branching right and left. In the right transept, running as it were into the Vatican Palace, was held this last and greatest of Councils, hence called the Vatican Council. During the private sittings of the Council, this transept was cut off from the church by a screen some forty feet high, which was painted to represent the façade of a temple. At the top our Saviour appears as though emerging from a cloud, with his hands extended to bless the sacred conclave deliberating beneath, and just by was inscribed (in such a manner as to give the idea that He was actually speaking) the promise: 'I am with you all days, even to the consummation of the world.' In the four panels of the imaginary door of this façade, which was painted to represent bronze, are the representations of our Saviour in the right hand panel, our Blessed Lady in the left, and in the under panels, St. Peter in the right, and St. Paul in the left. During the open sessions of the Council, this screen was altogether removed, so that the Pope and the whole of the bishops could be seen; the Pope on his throne at the extreme end of the transept, the cardinals on seats near him, and the bishops on benches arranged in rows, according to the manner of the old Roman amphitheatres, where the seats rise one above the other.

"The Council Hall, thus formed, was decorated, like the other parts of the church, with magnificent pictures. . . .

"On the opening day the bishops had assembled in one of the Vatican chapels as early as seven o'clock, where they proceeded to robe themselves, the western bishops wearing white mitres and rich copes, and the eastern bishops wearing magnificent crowns sparkling with jewels, while their copes were of the richest materials. Here the bishops fraternized with each other until the arrival of the Pope. You may ask how men of all nations could talk and confer with each other in this great Council, as their languages must necessarily have been so different and so many. The Latin, the language of the Church, which they all knew and could speak, at once obviated that difficulty.

"The Holy Father, after having said his usual Mass, and breakfasted, appeared at eight o'clock in the chapel where all the bishops were assembled. As he entered the chapel he intoned the 'Veni Creator,' which was then taken up by the Papal choir, the finest in all the world.

"In passing through the assembled bishops, he gave them his blessing. After a short time the bishops formed in procession. First of all came the various officials of the Council; next to them the generals of religious orders, and the mitred abbots; the bishops, according to their dates of consecration; the archbishops, the primates, and the patriarchs: next the cardinals in their order, cardinal deacons first, cardinal priests next, and cardinal bishops following; and last of all the Pope, on his 'sedia gestatoria,' or chair of state, on which he is always carried in every grand procession. In this order the procession wound its way through the halls of the Vatican, and down the 'Scala Regia,' or grand stairs, the masterpiece of the great Bernini. A grander scene than this Rome itself never saw, much less any other city in the world. After descending the 'Scala Regia,' the procession entered the lobby of St. Peter's, and on entering the immense bronze door of the cathedral, each bishop's mitre was taken off by his chaplain, in honour of the Blessed Sacrament. The procession took about an hour winding its way from the starting point in the Vatican to the Council Hall, as it was past nine o'clock before the head of the procession entered St. Peter's. The bishops walked two and two, with their chaplains by their side. When the Pope came to the great door of St. Peter's, he descended from his chair, and walked into the church bareheaded, in honour of the Blessed Sacrament, which was exposed on the high altar of St. Peter's. As soon as the procession appeared at the great door, the famous Papal choir commenced the 'Veni Creator,' the bishops singing the alternate verses.

"A prie-Dieu had been placed in front of the tomb of the Apostles, before the high altar, over which the Blessed Sacrament was exposed. When the bishops reached the prie-Dieu, each in succession knelt, then turned to the right, and walked to the place allotted to him in the Council Hall. When the Pope arrived at the prie-Dieu he knelt down and remained for a considerable time, doubtless imploring the Divine aid and benediction on the undertaking. that day commenced.

"The procession, thanks to my own regiment of Zouaves, notwithstanding the immense pressure of people on every side, was never once broken through, for the space appropriated to the passage of the bishops was firmly held by a close line of that celebrated corps. The bishops fell into their allotted places, without the slightest confusion; and when they were placed, and the Pope had taken his throne, the spectacle was magnificent beyond description. I saw it, and I shall never forget it. The tribune to the right of the Pope was reserved for the Empress of Austria, the King and Queen of Naples, the Grand Duke of Tuscany, and other illustrious princes. The tribune on the opposite side was reserved for the ambassadors of the different powers represented at Rome, and the élite of the Roman and foreign nobility.

"When the Pope had taken his place, the Mass, 'Coram Summo Pontifice' was commenced by one of the cardinals, the music being sung by the Papal choir, unaccompanied by organ or instrument of any kind, thus displaying, in all its marvellous capacity, that best and finest of all instruments, the human voice. When the Mass was over, a sermon of forty minutes' duration was preached by one of the bishops in Latin, robed in cope and mitre. After the sermon was over, the Pope was vested by his attendants, as if for Mass. When thus attired, wearing his golden mitre, he received the obedience, or homage, of all the bishops in succession, the cardinals kneeling and kissing his hand, the patriarchs, primates, archbishops and bishops kissing the cross on his stole, which generally rests on his knee. The Pope, however, held it up to each of his venerable brethren as they came forward to kiss it. This imposing ceremony took an hour and a quarter. At its conclusion, the cardinal deacon on the right of the throne, in a loud voice sang the word 'Orate,' whereupon all knelt, the Pope, at his faldstool, saying aloud the prayer, 'Adsumus Domine Sancte Spiritus.' Nearly a thousand voices answered 'Amen.' This prayer was the invocation of the Third Person of the Blessed Trinity to shed upon the Council His sacred illuminating influence.

"The cardinal deacon at the left of the throne sang, 'Surgite vos,' addressing the bishops, who then arose *en masse*, and the cantors intoned the Antiphon, 'Exaudi nos Domine.'

"The cardinal deacon at the right of the throne again repeated 'Orate,' and all prostrated themselves in prayer for some time. After a while, the cardinal deacon on the left again summoned the assembled fathers to rise, which they did; whereupon his Holiness, the Supreme Pontiff, with head uncovered, said the prayer 'Mentes nostras.' This ended, all again knelt, and the two cantors commenced the Litany of the Saints, the responses being given by the bishops, in which the many thousands of spectators of all countries joined, with the most thrilling effect. Such a scene could only remind one of heaven, and create a wish in each heart to be there. Near the end of the Litany the Pope rose, and with mitre on, and a most magnificent cross in his left hand, blessed the bishops before him with his right hand, praying that Almighty God would bless this, His holy Synod, and all ecclesiastical orders. This most solemn blessing was three times invoked, each time differently; the difference, however, consisting only in the addition, each time, of a new word, viz., to 'bless' in the first, to 'direct' in the second, and to 'preserve' in the third. The Pope sang this triple blessing in a voice wonderful for its power, fulness, clearness, and sweetness. It struck me, as I stood beneath the mighty dome of St. Peter's and heard it, as being sound as a bell, clear as a trumpet, and indescribably sweet and musical. Many times afterwards, such as when he blessed the world from the balcony of St. Peter, and from the balcony of St. John Lateran, and on various other occasions, I heard that grand old voice, and at hundreds of yards distance, and heard each word distinctly, *but never was I more affected by it than when I first heard it under the matchless dome of the world's greatest basilica.* Not even when he addressed me and others in one of the rooms of the Vatican, on St. George's Day, April 23rd, 1870, when we had the honour of being personally presented to his Holiness, and kissing his sacred hand. Whilst this blessing was being pronounced over the heads of the bishops they all knelt. When the Litany of the Saints was finished, the Pope turned to the altar to pray—the cardinal deacon on his right saying, 'Flectamus genua,' when all knelt for a time, and rose again when called by the cardinal deacon on the right.

"The tenth chapter of St. Luke being the Gospel of the day, was then sung by the cardinal deacon. At the conclusion of the Gospel, the bishops put on their mitres and resumed their seats.

"At this stage the Pope delivered an allocution with an energy and strength surprising in a man of his years. At times he displayed great emotion, and throughout its delivery the solemnity and impressiveness of his manner was most striking. In it he expatiated on the motives which had induced him to convene the Council, on its objects, and on the marvellous devotion displayed by the whole Episcopate to the Holy See, on their union with each other, and on the great consolation which these facts afforded him. He delivered the allocution sitting. At its conclusion he rose, as did also all the bishops. He then prostrated himself in prayer, and intoned the ' Veni Creator Spiritus.' During the first verse the bishops knelt uncovered. It was sung as before, alternately, by the choir and the bishops, joined by the 20,000 spectators. After the first verse all the bishops stood without their mitres. When ended, His Holiness offered up to the Holy Ghost the prayer, 'Deus qui corda fidelium.' After this the first decree of the Council was read by the secretary, with a view to its adoption by a unanimous and most enthusiastic 'Placet.' The decree publishing the second solemn session for the 6th of January, 1870, was adopted in the same manner. The first session of the Vatican Council was then closed by the Pope grandly intoning the first verse of the 'Te Deum.' The remaining verses were sung alternately by the choir and the bishops—the thunder of the voices of the 20,000 spectators combined with those of the bishops as before. A prayer of thanksgiving, and the first session of the most illustrious Council in history was ended. This session lasted nearly seven hours. The second session was somewhat similar, but it had not the *eclat* of the first. The Knights of St. John of Jerusalem, of which Sir George Bowyer is a distinguished member, had the honour of mounting guard over the Council of the Vatican, as they also had 300 years ago over the Council of Trent."*

As to myself, the first opportunity I had of seeing the Bishops assembled was on the occasion of the Papal Chapel, on the third Sunday of Advent. I was much pleased to see such a fine, intellectual body of men, the representatives of the Church, from all parts of the world.

Any one who reads attentively the foregoing description of the opening of the Œcumenical Council must observe a character of solemnity, of earnestness, of a spirit of prayer, about the whole proceedings, and must, I think, be struck with a feeling of the *reality* of the great event.

Every true Catholic will not only feel the reality of the event, but will also experience a sense of consolation in beholding the clearest evidence of the energy and vitality of the Church in the nineteenth century.

As Mr. Jacob says :—" Neither age nor infirmity, nor dis-

---

* "Personal Recollections of Rome," by W. J. Jacob, Esq.

tance, prevented the bishops from responding cheerfully to the call of the Chief Pastor, while the laity, on their part, not only supplied those of their bishops who required it with their travelling expenses and means of support while in Rome, but also forwarded by them from all parts of the world the most costly gifts and presents to our Holy Father the Pope.

"Some bishops spent six months and upwards in travelling from their dioceses to the centre of unity—the eternal city of Rome. One bishop from a remote part of Asia actually travelled fifty days on horseback to the nearest seaport, before he could embark for Europe. Over how many thousands of miles of sea and land, of desert and prairie, did those devoted men travel at the call of an aged man standing on the brink of the grave? But who is that man? That man is Peter, the Prince of the Apostles, and the representative and successor of Christ in all His spiritual power in the Church which He has purchased with His Most Precious Blood. From all parts of the vast continent of America, from the frozen North to the Brazils-(I had the honour, indeed, of living under the same roof with an excellent bishop from the latter country, a member of the Institute of Charity, who died a martyr to his devotion to the Vicar of Christ); from the cities of California to the cities of New England; from the land of the pyramids, of Cheops, and the Ptolemies; from the land of which Homer sang; from the shadow of the Greek schism and the Mahometan delusion; from Turkey in Europe and Asia; from Africa, ancient and modern; from the land trod by our Saviour;

"'From Greenland's icy mountains,
From India's coral strands;'

from celestial China; from the then beautiful France—now haggard from starvation, and disfigured by burnt villages and towns and ruined cities;—from sunny Italy; from the now victorious Prussia; from Catholic Spain; from Austria and the other parts of Germany; from Holland; from

Switzerland; from England, and Scotland, and Catholic Ireland; and from the fifth quarter of the globe, Oceania; in fact from every clime, from every country, and from every race, the successors of the Apostles came at the call of the successor of St. Peter.

"The number of bishops in the Council of the Vatican trebled the number of prelates at the Council of Trent, for three hundred was the utmost number that ever attended the Council of Trent during its eighteen years' sitting. This Council of the Vatican was beyond all comparison the grandest and most numerous in the history of the Church of Christ, and proves the existence in the Catholic Church of the nineteenth century of an energy and vitality unequalled in any period of her history.*"

* "Personal Recollections."

CHAPTER XVI.

CHRISTMAS—PASTORAL MUSIC—A FEW WORDS ABOUT LEAVING THE CORPS—SANT' ANDREA DELLA VALLE—CONFESSION IN ST. PETER'S.

Dec. 28, 1869.—You are going on at a gallop in the matter of the corporal business, whereas events and nominations take their time, and don't usually hurry themselves. I cannot be addressed as "corporal" yet, except when on duty.

My Zouave friends, Messrs. Robinson, R——, Burchett, Thornson, and I, were fortunate enough to obtain four days permission for Christmas. We first visited the battle-field of Mentana, accompanied by a civilian friend, and afterwards saw the grand ceremonies of Christmas. On Christmas eve we went to Santa Maria Maggiore for the first Vespers. There we saw and venerated the relic of the Holy Crib of Bethlehem. Later, we visited the Santa Scala and the celebrated painting of our Lord, by St. Luke. At midnight we went to *St. Louis des Français* for the midnight Mass, where was also the Quarant' Ore, and the illumination was very beautiful. At half-past three we went to St. Peter's for the pastoral music, the service consisting of matins sung by the choir of the Basilica, and afterwards of the Mass of the Aurora.

The music called pastoral is very peculiar, and consists of music arranged to resemble the singing and instruments of the shepherds of Bethlehem praising their new-born King, and the music of birds sounding forth the praises of their Infant Creator. The variety and beauty of the composition is well calculated to express and to convey to the mind the circumstances attending the birth of Our Lord. I was thoroughly delighted, and so was R——, as well as our friend from London. We stayed till the end of the Mass, but were not at all fatigued, although we were standing three hours. After taking breakfast, we returned to St. Peter's for the Holy Father's Mass at nine. The singing of the Sistine choir was as beautiful as usual, as also was the music of the dome, the silver-like trumpets. The Apostolical Benediction was given by the Holy Father from the High Altar. In the afternoon we visited the Bambino of Ara Cœli, and there saw a beautiful sight—the preaching of little children. There was a small stage erected before the chapel of the Crib, and the children stood up in twos and spoke the praises of the Holy Bambino. First one commenced, and made an eloquent little speech, then the other took up the subject, the two vying with each other to speak the best of their Infant Lord. The action of some of them was very good, particularly of the girls. There was quite a crowd to listen to them. This Bambino is very much venerated in Rome, on account of the favours that have been obtained of God by means of it. The Crib was arranged with very good taste.

In an old tower in the Trastevere there is arranged a crib in a grotto, or stable, and with houses and rockwork adjoining; and so placed that through an opening in the tower a view is obtained of the mountains in the distance. This gives an air of picturesqueness and reality to the imaged scene; and the idea is certainly a very happy one.

On the 26th came off the Christmas dinner of the English Zouaves at the Caffè Nuovo, and it was a great success. We had seventy-three to dinner. Amongst the visitors were Lord Denbigh, the Marquis of Bute, Lieutenant-Colonel de Charette, Colonel Patterson, Captain de Fabbri, Captain D'Arcy, Lieutenant Coombs, Major Lewis, Captain Stourton, Mr. Bodenham, Mr. Greenhalgh, and several others. The healths of the Holy Father, the Queen, the Lieut.-Col., Lord Denbigh, and Mgr. Stonor were proposed and received with great enthusiasm. Mgr. Stonor was present, of course. As chaplain he always considers himself one of the Zouaves. After dinner we all adjourned to the Mausoleum of Augustus, in order to be photographed, but the group was a failure, as some of the party could not keep sufficiently still for its success.

At present there does not appear to be any prospect of war, but the Holy Father wishes the Corps of the Zouaves to be kept up, and has asked some men who were going home after two years' service to re-engage. Already we are much diminished in numbers, and I do not like the idea of giving up the life next spring, especially as it suits me very well, as it is a great privilege to be in Rome, and as I should not like to be absent if there were any upset here, or any means of obtaining back for the Holy Father the States he has been deprived of; and there is no difficulty in obtaining leave of absence for two or three months to visit one's friends from time to time: nor again is there at any time any difficulty in leaving the service, in case one has a substantial reason.

Rome, Jan. 26th, 1870.—In accordance with your wishes I am prepared to return home after the expiration of my two years' engagement.

I was successful in my endeavour to be present for the opening of the second session of the Vatican Council on the Epiphany. I saw the Holy Father and the bishops very well. On this feast, and during the octave, there were grand services going on at Sant' Andrea della Valle. Besides the Latin Masses there was every morning a Mass in one of the Oriental rites, sermons in different languages four times a day, and every evening a grand benediction given by a cardinal. The Greek Melchite rite we found very interesting. The Mass at which we were present was a High Mass, and the choir of the Greek College sang with very good effect. It is in the commencement of the solemn sacrifice that the ceremonies differ from that of the Latin rite, as well as in the substitution of the Greek for the Latin language. After the Consecration the different rites—which

I have seen—all resemble each other, more or less. Several of the ceremonies, such as the joining of two and of three candles—the former representing the union of the two natures of Jesus Christ, the latter the doctrine of the Blessed Trinity—exhibit the union of belief of the faithful of the East and of the West. A very eloquent sermon was preached in French by Mgr. Mermillod, the Bishop of Geneva, on one day, as well as by Mgr. Manning and Mgr. Ullathorne on other days. For the nine days following the feast, the different services and sermons four times a day were attended by crowds of people, including Romans and visitors from various countries.

The beautiful group of the Adoration of the Magi was erected as usual.

The Confession of the Apostles in St. Peter's consists of their tomb, which is immediately under the High Altar, the latter being exactly under the centre of the dome. As one walks up the nave one comes to the marble balustrade surrounding the steps, and the entrance to the shrine, before reaching the High Altar. It is quite true that the congregation in the nave see the face of the officiating priest, because here, as in all the ancient Basilicas, the High Altar is isolated and placed at the junction of the nave and the tribune or choir—just the reverse to what we are usually accustomed to see. The priest looks towards the people, instead of away from them.

The confession is richly adorned with different coloured marbles, and ornamented with about one hundred lamps, kept continually burning. The present lamps are gilt; but formerly here were lamps of sterling metal, until the time of Napoleon I., when they were carried off to France, as were so many other precious things.

The Confession in Santa Maria Maggiore was erected by Pius IX. The very rich marbles intermingled with alabaster, are arranged with the most exquisite taste. Some prefer the design of this to that of St. Peter's. I certainly think it more beautiful. The Holy Father, it is said, intends to be buried here; but I cannot say whether this is true or not.

In this Basilica, besides the relic of the crib of Bethlehem, there are the bodies of St. Jerome and of St. Pius V. There are also very interesting mosaics round the walls of the nave. The Borghese chapel is quite a gem in its way. It contains many beautiful things; first, the very ancient picture of the Madonna—one of those ascribed to St. Luke—then there are beautiful reliefs describing the very interesting manner in which the Basilica was founded by Pope Liberius, and on account of which the Feast of *S. Maria ad nives*, "Our Lady of the snow," was instituted.* The pointed *campanile*, or bell tower, is one of the most conspicuous objects which meet the eye of the traveller as he enters the city by train, and it is the only one of any considerable height now remaining in it. Near, is the Church of St. Antony, remarkable for its Byzantine doorway. On the Feast of St. Antony takes place outside the church the ceremony of blessing the horses, and a great number of the Roman horses are annually brought here and blessed. Few things bring home to one more than this ceremony, how thoroughly in Rome religion enters into every detail of ordinary life. It is remarkable how very few accidents happen in the narrow streets, many of which are not protected by a raised pavement for foot passengers, notwithstanding there is great traffic through them. The church contains pictures representing the remarkable life of St. Antony, the first Hermit.

---

* See Butler's "Lives of the Saints," Vol. 8.

CHAPTER XVI.

THE "WEEK" IN THE ZOUAVES—PARADE—CORPORAL OF THE WEEK—THE EXHIBITION OF CHRISTIAN ART—SANT' ONOFRIO—SANTA PUDENTIANA AND SANTA PRASSEDE—PRÆTORIAN CAMP.

ROME, Feb. 26th, 1870.—As I have the "week," I am rather busy just now; though to-day being on guard, I have a little spare time. The word "week" will puzzle you, but in our army all our services are regulated by the "week," there being a commandant, captain-adjutant-major, and an adjutant of the week for every regiment, as well as a lieutenant, sergeant, and corporal of the week for each company. The commandant commands at parade; the captain-adjutant-major names the officers for guard at the most important posts in their different turns; the adjutant names the sergeants and corporals for guard, and gives the sergeant of the week the number of men required from his company (for the service of guard, picket, and patrol) at a certain hour fixed by himself; he also assists each day at the parade, accompanying the captain-adjutant-major at the inspection, which the latter passes of all the men then going on guard. This over, he commands: "*Division en masse, serrez la colonne!* MARCHE!" upon which command the first rank remains still, and all the others close in and form a compact column in the order of their respective battalions and companies. In the ranks the sergeants stand first, the corporals next, then the privates, and lastly the "corporal of the week." Another command: "*Division! par le flanc droit!*

DROITE!" and the whole division faces the adjutant, and listens to his reading out the different posts to which the men composing it are assigned. The first post to be guarded is the "*Garde Royale*" of the Vatican—this is composed of a captain, a lieutenant, two sergeants, four corporals, and forty privates, though sometimes only twenty-eight. As soon as the names of the sergeants, &c., are called out, they shoulder arms, and walk out to the head of the new division of a single file, which they then commence to form, and so on till all the posts are filled up, and the new division is completely formed in a long line. At the command of "*Chefs de poste, au centre!*" every head of a post walks out, and the whole form a ring round the adjutant, who then delivers to each a report to be filled up, accounting for anything which may happen in the neighbourhood of each post; he then gives to one the "*mot*," or password, consisting of the "*mot d'ordre*," and the "*mot de ralliement*," these two words are then passed all round the circle, and the adjutant enquires of the last the words; thus he is quite satisfied that every one knows them thoroughly; now all return to their places. The officers of the "week" stand in rank behind the commandant; the sergeants and corporals of the week stand together to the left, the "*trombe*," or buglers being to the right of the officers. The commandant commands: "*Division! par le flanc droit!* DROITE!" "*Pour defiler. Division en avant, à vos postes!* MARCHE!"

The division then defiles, or marches past, to the sound of the bugle, after which the men for the different posts are led off by their respective chiefs, to relieve the men who have been on guard twenty-four hours. The officials of the week then separate, and this concludes the parade which takes place every day, the inspection only being sometimes omitted to save time.

The sergeant of the week gives the names of the men whose turn it is to go on guard, picket, and patrol, to the corporal, as well as the names of the different posts to which they are assigned; the corporal then writes these down, and arranges the other service, he himself naming the men for *corvées* such as cleaning out barracks, assisting the cooks, taking the meals to men on guard, loading and unloading the bread, according to a list which he keeps. The corporal has to attend all *appels*, or roll calls, to answer to the sergeant for all men absent on duty or permission. I am up at six a.m. I first read out in the rooms the names of all men on duty that day, collect all permissions to be signed, take the names of any men reporting sick. I then drink my coffee, prepare myself for parade, and see that the men are also preparing themselves. At seven a.m. I have to be ready to accompany the sergeant to parade, which now, during the carnival, takes place at 7.30 a.m. After parade, I return to barracks, and remain there till after four, when I assemble the men on patrol, and conduct them to the gendarmeria. This patrol gives me the opportunity of having a few hours to myself: but I have to be back for the *appel* at 7.30 p.m. In barracks, during the day, I have to hold myself ready to answer the sound of the bugle at any moment, and have to accompany any men sick to the doctor, and to take down his report. I have sometimes to find men for some unforeseen service; to see that all men named for *corvée* are ready at the proper time; to attend *appels* for picket or exercise, and then to arrange the service for the next day. Thus you may imagine I have plenty to keep me alive, especially at a barracks like San Michele, where we have the adjutant of our battalion—the latter sometimes taking a fancy to shout to the bugler on guard, "*Tromba! Il corporale di settimana!*" which command being executed, I have suddenly to rush down a hundred steps to see who wants "*Il corporale di settimana.*" I find, perhaps, he wants to tell me something to the effect that if certain of the *trombe*—Italian buglers—do not behave themselves in the courtyard of the barracks, they are to be consigned to "*salle de police!*"

I do not find it very difficult to fulfil the duties, and have so far, escaped punishment; but I have been fortunate in one respect, viz., in not having any inspection on parade, as this takes place so early, on account of the carnival—sometimes at the later parade the captain-adjutant-major punishes the sergeant of the week for any fault he observes in the men; who, in turn, comes down on the corporal and the men themselves. I have been able to catch a glimpse of the carnival every evening till now. After I finish my guard to-morrow morning, I shall retake the week till Sunday morning.

I have visited the gardens and interior of the Quirinal Palace lately. The Palace I found most interesting, the state apartments being very fine, enriched with paintings by the best masters, with most beautiful tapestry, &c. We saw the room from which Pius VII. was taken prisoner by Napoleon I., and from which Pius IX. fled to Gaeta, and also the bed on which Pius VII. died. The arrangements of the gardens are rather formal, and not according to English taste. The plants in the greenhouses looked very well.

Rome, March 18th, 1870.—I have visited the Exhibition of Christian Art at Santa Maria degli Angeli, and was much pleased. There were so many beautiful pictures, statues, &c., that I hardly know what to choose as most to be admired. I may, however, mention a beautiful veiled statue, in which the features could be discerned under the marble veil, a veiled bust, and a model in wood of St. Peter's, beautifully executed, and very faithful to the original. On mid-Lent Sunday we visited the Exhibition for the second time. I was accompanied by R——. We noticed several objects which had arrived since our first visit, such as stained glass windows from Germany and France, and some Gobelins tapestry of exquisite workmanship, so beautifully executed that at a short distance it looked like a splendid painting. We admired again the beautiful pictures, the veiled statue and bust mentioned before, and the statues of St. Aloysius and St. Cecily. In the pentagon there were chasubles of various shapes, some of which were very ancient; sacred vessels in great variety; some fine crucifixes in ivory; the pastoral staff of St. Gregory the Great, in ivory; and some beautifully executed cameos. On our third visit we remarked the vestments and copes of the Vatican and Lateran. They are all very rich and magnificent. The monstrances in crystals and in precious stones are also the very finest possible; and there are beautiful chalices and missals, a very rich tiara of the Pope, set in diamonds, rubies, and emeralds; and a splendid illuminated manuscript missal, a gift of the Emperor of Austria to the Pope. The ancient illuminated manuscript missals are wonderful specimens of patient labour and perseverance.

Last week I visited Sant' Onofrio, with W. R——, Father Robinson and his cousin. In the church are some very ancient paintings, which pleased us very much; also the fine monument to Torquato Tasso, erected by Pius IX.

In the convent we saw the room and many of the objects formerly belonging to Tasso, as well as one of his last letters. In a vineyard we saw Tasso's oak, and the ruin of a kind of amphitheatre: seated on this amphitheatre we enjoyed the beautiful view there to be seen of the Eternal City. Seated in the midst of the Campagna, we inhaled the balmy air of spring, and drank in the beauty of the scene as we remarked the ascending and retreating snow-line on the distant mountains of the Apennines, as well as on the tops of the nearer Sabines. St. Onofrio is situated on the Janiculum, and it was there we obtained this fine view.

One day during this week we went to Santa Pudentiana, where were the Stations of Lent, and the Quarant 'Ore. We saw there the pavement of the house of St. Pudens, in which St. Peter lived nine years; a relic of the altar on which the Apostle celebrated the holy sacrifice of the Mass, and the well in which St. Pudentiana placed the bodies of the martyrs after their execution. This church is very ancient, and some portion of it, at least, dates from the time of Pope St. Pius I., in the second century, for on this site, and that of the church of Santa Prassede, which is near, it is known that some of the first Christian churches were erected.

The senator Pudens, his mother Priscilla, his sons Novatus and Timotheus, and his two daughters Praxedes and Pudentiana, were among the first converts of St. Peter the Apostle in the city of Rome. Their house was on this spot, and here the Apostle came and resided for the space of nine years. Here it was that he consecrated Linus and Cletus, both of whom were his successors as head of the Church on earth, and Vicar of Christ. The mosaics of the choir of St. Pudentiana are very ancient, and Bosio discovered under the floor the existence of a catacomb. It consists of a great number of arches, probably the remains of the baths of Timotheus. In this cemetery the illustrious Sixtus deposited nearly 3,000 martyrs who were slain in the early persecutions. The body of St. Pudentiana lies under the principal altar.

Near this church is the church of St. Praxedes. This church is built on the place where the baths of Novatus formerly stood. This asylum of the primitive Christians became an oratory in the second century, and in the year 822, through the instrumentality of Pascal I. it was made one of the most venerable churches of Rome. The mosaic in the apsis is a representation of heaven. In the centre is a city, towards which are seen coming several pilgrims, with their hands laden with presents. St. Peter and St. Paul, under the figure of two angels, are standing before the door. In the middle of the Eternal City is the King of Ages, holding in his hands a globe. The joyous inhabitants of the heavenly Jerusalem stand around their king with crowns on their heads and palms in their hands. Outside the city is an angel, who points out to the pilgrims the way. Above this is the monogram of Pope Pascal, the restorer of the church. Lower down is a hand coming forth from the heavens, and holding a crown and placing it on the head of our Saviour, who stands with his hands extended and surrounded by sheep at his feet, and by saints at either side.

At the right is St. Paul, and near him a young virgin,

St. Praxedes, dressed in a vestment of gold, ornamented with precious stones, and holding in her hand a crown, an emblem of the offerings which were made at the altars by the primitive Christians. Pope Pascal occupies a place next to St. Praxedes. He has a square nimbus on his head, showing that the mosaic was erected in his lifetime, and he holds in his hand a model of the church of St. Praxedes.

To the left of our Saviour is St. Peter, presenting to him a young virgin, St. Pudentiana, dressed like her sister. Beneath this mosaic is the high altar, under a baldachino, supported by four columns of porphyry, the gift of St. Charles Borromeo, who was Cardinal titular of this church. The fresco on the roof is the work of Julius Romanus. It represents St. Praxedes and St. Pudentiana gathering with sponges the blood of the martyrs, and squeezing it into a well.

Near this is the chapel of St. Charles Borromeo. In this chapel are preserved two precious relics of the Saint, his faldstool, and the table on which he fed the poor. In the centre of the nave is the well into which St. Praxedes poured the blood of the martyrs. In the aisle on the left of the high altar is the chapel of St. Henon, ornamented with beautiful mosaics. In this chapel is preserved the column of the flagellation. It was guarded by the primitive Christians with religious care, and was placed in this church by Cardinal Colonna, legate of the holy see. It is of oriental marble.

Three hundred thousand martyrs, the most remarkable of whom are named in a tablet erected by Pascal I., form the companions of our crucified Lord. Their relics are buried in the church. Attached to Santa Pudentiana and St. Prassede are two *campanili* or bell-towers, that of St. Prassede probably belonging to the ninth century, and in the court before the entrance to the former, remains of the house of Pudens have lately been brought to light.

Masks were allowed for the two last days of the Carnival, and there was far more life and animation displayed than I have seen before, particularly the last day. Six English Zouaves disguised as sailors, passed up and down the Corso in a large car, and profusely showered confetti and bouquets at the occupants of the balconies above and the streets below. They also received in return a fair share of bouquets, confetti, &c., from the ladies of the balconies. As the Zouaves were forbidden to take part in the Carnival in uniform, I put on my suit of *pekin*, or civilian, and a mask. I carried on a brisk fire for some time, but having got separated from Duke, with whom I started, and the war of confetti becoming rather too hot—the mask hindered me from seeing all my assailants in the streets, and its very prominent nose was a great object of attack—I found it better to unmask. I was thus better able to reply to my assailants, and to find my friend again.

I cannot say I obtained many bouquets to reward my exertions; but then they are not so easily got, and buying them is rather expensive. We finished off the Carnival of 1870 by going to the grand benediction at the Gesù, which is attended by the Senator, and was crowded to excess.

On Ash Wednesday I was present in St. Peter's at the Papal Chapel, and got the Holy Father's blessing, and we visited again with much interest the three churches appointed for the stations of Lent on that day, viz., St. Maria in Cosmedin—where we saw exposed the relics of a great number of martyrs—Santa Sabina and Sant' Alessio.

On the feast of St. Frances of Rome I visited the rooms which she inhabited near San Michele, and the church in the Roman forum. There is a beautiful statue of the Saint underneath the high altar, over her tomb, which is ornamented with rare marbles and bronzes, after the design of Bernini.

Monsignor Stonor is anxious to get up some active amusements for the English Zouaves. We have lately been practising cricket in the Villa Borghese, and there is a match to come off to-morrow morning between the English Zouave eleven and eleven English visitors. I have been practising with the others, but do not expect to be amongst the eleven.

On Wednesday last we had the sham-fight or field-day that has been so many times proposed and put off on account of the bad weather. Now at last it has come off, but I do not think it was a very brilliant affair, at least as far as our part of the field was concerned. After a wet winter for this climate spring has now set in, and we have had some beautifully genial weather. However, during two days of this week we have experienced a piercing *tramontana*.* To-day is dull and mild. The early trees are just now budding.

On Tuesday R——, W. R——, and I went to see the Villa Albani, now belonging to Prince Torlonia. It is situated a short distance outside the Porta Salara, and there is a splendid view from it of the Campagna, and the Apennines covered with snow. This day being one of those before mentioned on which was blowing a cutting *tramontana* we were unable to enjoy the view much. Even the villa had a somewhat cheerless aspect from the same cause. The grounds are nicely arranged, but the contents of this villa are not equal to those of the Villa Borghese.

In the Villa Borghese are many rare and beautiful marbles and pictures, but the statuary, both ancient and modern, is exceedingly fine. "David in the act of slaying Goliath," is a very fine work of Canova's, executed while he was yet a boy. The first hall contains fine ancient statues and reliefs.

The Prætorian camp, or the ruins of it, which can still be seen, is situated between the Porta Pia and the Porta San Lorenzo, and immediately within the Aurelian wall. The ruins are at present partly used as stables for the horses of the dragoons, who as well as the artillery, are quartered at Macao barracks, which are built on this site, and are the finest in Rome.

* A wind blowing from the mountains.

The Prætorian camp was built by Sejanus, minister of Tiberius, outside the walls of Servius Tullius. The camp was dismantled by Constantine, and three sides of the enclosure—the length of which is over a mile—were included by Aurelian in his wall.

CHAPTER XVII.

LIFE AT SANTA GALLA AS CORPORAL—CHURCH OF SAN MARTINO AI MONTI—OF SANT' AGNESE—"VERSEMENT."

MARCH 20th.—W. R—— and I have both passed as corporals to-day into the 5ieme du 3, and we are now quartered at Santa Galla, in the Via Montanara.

Rome, April 7th.—W. R—— and I both like our new company very much. Our sergeant-major Desilé, and *sergent-fourrier* Beaulieu, are both Canadians. They both appear very pleased that we have passed into their company, and we are on the most friendly terms with them and the other Canadians, and also with the French and Germans. In fact the fellows of the company altogether seem a very nice lot.

The Captain of the company, M. Talman, is a German, and a very pleasant man to deal with. Corporal the Baron von Berlichingen is a Bavarian nobleman.* His manners are pleasing and gentlemanly. I feel very much at home in the company, and I feel quite sorry at the prospect of leaving it so soon.

I had to take the "week" soon after coming into it. I got through it again satisfactorily, although I had a strict sergeant above me. He, however, allowed me a few hours out every day after I had arranged all the service. W. R—— and I now mount guard as *chefs de poste* at the smaller posts

* This gentleman has been, I understand, unfortunately killed in battle during the late dreadful war in France. To do him justice, let me add, that he died, like so many others of our noble comrades, both French and German, a soldier's death, nobly doing his duty to his country. Requiescat in pace.

comprising a corporal and six men, or a corporal and three men. Sometimes, also, we are with a sergeant, though now we get named to more important posts than when we were only acting corporals. The new Theory which was brought out on the " Ecole du Soldat," " Ecole du Tirailleur," &c., in consequence of the substitution of the Remington for the carbine is a great improvement on the old Theory, especially as regards simplicity of movement. The *grades*, including sergeants, corporals, and acting corporals, have been studying it this spring, and the different companies have been exercised on it occasionally. For myself, of course, since I decided—in deference to the wishes of my friends—to return home before the summer, I have not very assiduously studied it.

Another of the reasons which contributes to make us enjoy our sojourn at Santa Galla is that we have a great friend and pleasant companion in Sergeant Shee, of the 6th, which is quartered here together with our company. This brave man, whom I have always admired as a model soldier, greatly distinguished himself in 1867, and then obtained a gold medal and his rank of sergeant for being the first to enter a nest of Garibaldians in the Trastevere, they having fired upon the patrol as it passed down the street.* The well-known Mr. Woodward holds the rank of sergeant in our company.

This week we have been occupied with the Retreat for the Zouaves, which is being given by Father Walshe, S. J. for the English, Irish, and Scotch Zouaves. The general Communion will take place on Saturday at the church of St. John of the Florentines.

To-day I am finishing two consecutive days' guard at the Polvericra San Paolo, near the gate of St. Paul, whilst our corps is occupied with a field-day. We have here a powder magazine to guard, which is situated near the Protestant cemetery, close to the pyramid tomb of Caius Cestius. Very near is Monte Testaccio, a mountain on a small scale formed entirely of broken pottery, the continued

* See Chapter II.

accumulation of many ages. The sides are now excavated, and in them are formed very good caves for keeping wine. In fact, a great part of the supply of wine for the inhabitants of Rome is stored here.

We have now amongst the English Zouaves three sergeants, seven corporals, and several lance-corporals. There are two Irish captains, viz., Captain D'Arcy and Captain De la Hoyde, and one Irish corporal. The Irish Zouaves are now much reduced in numbers. At present our countrymen appear to be in very good favour with the authorities,— much better, I think, than when I first joined the corps. My old captain, M. Thomalé, told me that I ought to re-engage now I had passed corporal. I replied that I was very sorry to be unable to do so.

One day during my "week" I visited the church of San Martino ai Monti. I descended into the subterranean church which Pope St. Sylvester formed out of the baths of Titus in the time of Constantine the Great. I saw there a very ancient painting of our Blessed Lady, remains of ancient frescoes on the walls, and the tomb of Cardinal Tommasi. In this subterranean church two councils of the Catholic Church were held under Pope St. Sylvester, at which the Emperor Constantine was present.

In this church there are relics of a great many saints and martyrs. This church belongs to the Carmelites. The good taste with which its rich gildings, its marbles, its columns, and its paintings are arranged make it one of the most beautiful churches in Rome. The aisles are divided from the nave by twenty-four columns of the Corinthian order, of various kinds of marble.*

Under this church, so resplendent with marble and paintings, is another which shows the modest attire primitive poverty arrayed itself in. Christianity, which in early times hid itself in the caves and ruins of old buildings, concealed itself here in the ruins near the baths of Titus.

---

* The landscapes on the wall are by Poussin, and two paintings near the altar of St. Mary Magdalen are by Francesco. The paintings in the chapel of the Blessed Virgin are by Cavalieri.

There is in the subterranean church a beautiful mosaic, representing the mysterious Eve, to whom God promises the victory over the dragon. At her feet is Pope Sylvester, a happy witness of the result of this struggle. He is paying homage to the Blessed Virgin under the title of the Joy of Christians. St. Sylvester is surrounded by a noble army of martyrs, whose blood was shed for the faith for which he contended. A tablet, inserted in the wall, has the following inscription: " When Pope Sergius the younger occupied the pontifical throne, there were placed under this altar the bodies of Sylvester, pope, and Fabian and Soter, popes and martyrs, and of the holy martyrs, &c." All these bodies were brought from the catacombs of St. Priscilla on the Via Salara.

I visited some time since the Catacombs and church of Sant' Agnese,* situated about one mile and a half outside the Porta Pia, on the Via Nomentana. The Catacomb is most interesting, and the tombs are in a better state of preservation than in San Calisto. The mural paintings are very worthy of attention. The extent, too, of this Catacomb is very great, and it is said that the students of a college were once lost in its galleries through their having strayed from the guide.

The church is also very remarkable for its antiquity. It is of the Basilica form. It is now partly underground, and there are galleries built on, or rather supported by, pillars and arcades in the interior. On the feast of St. Agnes the two lambs are here blessed from whose wool the palliums of the archbishops are made. This ceremony usually attracts a great number of English and other visitors.

Near Sant' Agnese is the equally ancient church of Santa

* Regarding the church of St. Agnes we find the following note in the " Lives of the Saints," Vol. I. " A church was built on this spot in the time of Constantine the Great, and was repaired by Pope Honorius, in the seventh century. It is now in the hands of Canons Regular, standing without the walls of Rome, and is honoured with her relics (those of St. Agnes) in a very rich silver shrine, the gift of Pope Paul V., in whose time they were found in this church, together with those of St. Emerentiana."

Constanza, containing the bodies of several saints and martyrs and some ancient mural paintings.

On the Via Nomentana, about seven miles from Rome, are the newly discovered church and catacomb of St. Alexander. On our way to Mentana we were able to catch a passing glimpse of the ruins of the church. I believe it would have well repaid a visit, only that we then were pressed for time.

From Dr. Smith's "Ancient Geography" we learn that the inhabitants of ancient Nomentum once fought against Rome, and that it was afterwards the abode of Seneca, Martial, Ovid, and Nepos.

April 11th.—To-day R—— and I made our *versement* i.e., we gave up all our regulation effects, uniform, &c., at the magazine at Salviati. We received the account of the money due to us on our *masse*, less the deductions made for some slight dilapidations. We can hardly be said to have yet left the corps of the Zouaves, for we shall not get our *congés* until we are prepared to leave Rome, which we do not intend to do till the 28th. Thus we shall have Holy week and Easter week free, and be able to see once more the grand ceremonies of the Eternal City.

We visited Santa Prassede to-day. We saw and venerated there the column to which our Lord was bound during His scourging, and three thorns of His crown of thorns. We saw the well into which St. Praxedes put the blood of the holy martyrs which she collected after their execution, and the stone on which she sometimes slept.

CHAPTER XVIII.

DIARY DURING HOLY WEEK—BASILICA OF ST. JOHN LATERAN—
EASTER FESTIVITIES.

APRIL 12th, 1870.—R—— and I have now left barracks, and we have taken up our quarters at the *Pension*, Via Monserrata, where we have very comfortable beds. To-day we visited the baths of Caracalla, the magnificent ruins of which pleased us very much. In the course of our visit there a storm arose, with thunder and lightning, and we were obliged to take refuge for an hour or more in the Osteria del Carciofolo. To-day we dressed *en pekin*.

April 13th.—We visited to-day the library of the Vatican. We walked through the ante-chamber and the grand hall which is both beautiful and magnificent. We saw there the present of the King of Prussia to the Holy Father, in porcelain of Sevres, and those of Charles X. of France, in malachite—one being a splendid crucifix, and the other an immense vase or basin—as well as the present, in Scotch granite, of the Duke of Northumberland, made to Cardinal Antonelli, and a large, fine specimen of malachite. We had not time enough to see the other halls, and the fine illuminated books; but we hope to return another day to see them.

Afterwards we went into St. Peter's for the office of *Tenebræ*. The chant of the Lamentations was the most plaintive and mournful possible. In these, and the "Miserere" which follows, the Church bewails the sufferings of her beloved Spouse on Calvary, and the sins of men which caused them, and nowhere can her grief be found so well expressed as by the solemn chants of the choirs of the Sistine, St. Peter's, and St. John Lateran. This year the former choir sings all the offices of Holy Week in St. Peter's. This arrangement has been made in order to accommodate the bishops and others present in Rome during the Council, as in the Sistine chapel there is room only for a limited number.

14th, Holy Thursday.—Went first to St. Mark's and then to Saint Peter's, where we arrived in time to hear the "Gloria in excelsis," the joyous singing of which is an agreeable variety amidst the mourning of Holy Week. The "Benedictus" sung to-day was a very fine piece. The relics of the handkerchief of St. Veronica, which miraculously received the impression of Our Lord's countenance, of a portion of the true cross, of the spear with which Our Lord's side was opened, and of one of the nails with which He was crucified, were brought out to the front of the balcony over the statue of St. Veronica, to be venerated by the congregation, who kneel to receive the benediction. The Apostolic benediction bestowed from the balcony over the portico by the Holy Father is given in cope and mitre, while on Easter Sunday the Pope wears the triple crown.

Afterwards takes place the *Mandatum*, or washing of the feet by the Pope, and the *Cœna*, or repast, at which thirteen poor priests are waited on by him. After the example of our Blessed Lord, the Sovereign Pontiff here humbles himself to wash the feet of these thirteen pilgrims, and afterwards to wait upon them himself at table. I have never been able yet to see this remarkable ceremony performed by the Holy Father, the crowd being generally very great, and admission to the *Cœna* being granted only by ticket.

In the afternoon we visited St. John Lateran for the *Tenebræ*. The responses, etc., of the Lamentations were very beautiful; the "Miserere," too, was most striking. R—— preferred the singing of them here to that of the Sistine, but I cannot say that I agreed with him. We visited the Holy Sepulchre at the churches of St. Clement, La Trinità dei Pellegrini, and St. John's before mentioned. La Trinità dei Pellegrini is a very fine institution for the lodging and entertainment, free of charge, of pilgrims who come to Rome for the ceremonies of Holy Week. We saw here Cardinals, Princes, and other persons of high rank engaged in washing the feet of the pilgrims. After this was finished the latter were served by them at table. The number of pilgrims was very great, the institution being capable of holding a large number. The Cardinals and others waited on them and saw that they were properly entertained.

In the upper rooms of the "Trinità," Princesses and other ladies of rank were doing as much for the women, who were lodged in a separate part of the institution. The crowds of persons who came to witness these acts of humble charity were so great as to make it almost impossible to pass through some of the lower rooms.

15th, Good Friday.—Went to St. Peter's for the Mass of the Pre-sanctified; the reproaches commencing, "Populo meus, quid feci tibi ?" sung by the choir, are most plaintive, and full of tenderness and sorrow. The procession, in which the Holy Father carries back the Blessed Sacrament to the high altar from the altar where It had been laid the previous day, often called the Holy Sepulchre, is accompanied by the singing of the "Vexilla Regis," which was magnificently rendered by the choir. In the evening we went to San Marcello for the "*Ora desolata*," or "desolate hours" of our Blessed Lady, and heard the "*Stabat Mater*."

I copy the extracts below from the interesting account in "*Rome, its Churches, &c.*," commencing with Holy Thursday evening in St. Peter's :—" What a desolate appearance does the entire church present. No holy water in the fonts; no cross or candlestick on the altars; all seemed desolate, and reminding me much of those beautiful cathedrals in England, still preserving their Catholic appearance; but, alas ! their altars are desolate, for the glory of them has departed; but in St. Peter's one spot is yet radiant with light—the repository—whither all are hastening to pay their adorations. After the '*tenebræ*' in the chapel of the choir was concluded, a procession of the chapter was formed, and they proceeded to wash the high altar. Wine and honey were poured on it, and then each of the canons, with a small besom, went up and wiped the altar; the choir in the meantime sung the antiphon, 'Diviserunt vestimenta mea,' and the Psalm, 'Deus, Deus meus, respice in me.' When the chapter retire, the altar remains entirely uncovered, and the hundred and twenty-two lights round the confession of St. Peter's are extinguished; a shade of darkness hangs over the spirits, which seems to impart itself to all around, the proportions of the vast Basilica seem doubled, and the few lights which are placed in large candlesticks through the church, to direct the steps of the worshippers to the repository, serve only to show the mysterious darkness which on this day reigns through all the chapels and the transepts of this glorious temple. After leaving St. Peter's, we proceed to visit the repositories in the different churches. The most beautiful are those of St. Anthony of the Portuguese, the Gesù, SS. Dominico e Sisto, and St. Catherine of Sienna. Thus the pious Romans spend their evening, and the streets are crowded, for all Rome seems to go forth to visit the place where they had laid their Lord. In some of the churches a sermon is preached on the Passion, to which crowds hasten to prepare for the ceremonies of the coming day.

"How different the feelings with which these days are observed in the Holy City to what they are in other places —a feeling of the realities of the solemnity seems to pervade the entire masses of the people. But Good Friday has arrived, all Rome seems in mourning; the Bishops have laid aside their purple stockings, and the cardinals their silk cappas, and have assumed those of serge. Every church has its devotions in addition to the usual solemnities of the day. In some the three hours' agony of our Lord is preached; in others the desolation of the Blessed Virgin during these three hours.......The office commences at the Sistine amidst the appearance of sorrow, the Grand Penitentiary officiating; Moses and the Prophets have bewailed the death of the Just, who Himself has prayed for His murderers."

16th, Holy Saturday.—Went to St. John Lateran, where Cardinal Patrizi, the Pope's Vicar, officiated as usual. We arrived about eight, and found the ceremonies of the day already commenced. At first the Basilica presented the mournful appearance of the preceding days; we heard the prophecies read, and afterwards the Cardinal Vicar, the sacred ministers, and priests form in procession, the paschal candle being carried, and a chant sung by the choir, who also form part of the procession, which now wends its way to the Baptistery of Constantine, situated outside of the Basilica. After the blessing of the font, the Cardinal proceeded to baptize the Jews—the neophytes consisting this year of two Jews and one Jewess—who are clothed in white, emblematic of the baptismal robe of innocence. I was unable myself to see this ceremony performed, on account of the crowd, but R—— was more fortunate, and told me it was a very beautiful one. As the procession returned to the Basilica, I saw it very well; the calm, devout demeanour of the newly-made Christians, clothed in white, made it very edifying and interesting.

After returning to the Basilica the neophytes are confirmed; then the Litanies are recited, the candidates for Holy Orders, which are to-day administered by the Cardinal Vicar, being prostrate during them. At this time the Cardinal lays aside the purple cope and vests for Mass, the ministers take off their purple and put on white vestments, and the whole Basilica and assistants have suddenly assumed a festal appearance, and the aspect of mourning has as suddenly disappeared. At the commencement of Mass the scene is the expression of joy and gladness, for now the Church celebrates the eve of the great Paschal Feast of Easter, and the "Gloria in excelsis" is again sung. Anyone who has witnessed this expression of the change from the mourning of Holy Week to the joy of the Christian Church in the glorious resurrection of her Divine Spouse, cannot but have been moved to feelings of gladness, in sympathy with the mind of the Church in commencing and preparing for the great Feast of Easter. After the commencement of the Mass the ordinations are proceeded with by the Cardinal Vicar. He commences with the candidates for the tonsure;

then he ordains those for minor orders, next the subdeacons, then the deacons, and lastly the priests, who finish the celebration of the Mass with him.

This being the first time we had witnessed an ordination, we found it very interesting, and especially that of the priests. The ceremony lasted a very long time, the candidates for Holy Orders being very numerous; their devotion and recollection was very striking; very fine pieces of music were played and sung during the vesting of the different Orders, which is performed by the Cardinal himself. We did not wait till the end, as the ceremonies were not concluded till the afternoon.

The Basilica of St. John Lateran deserves more than a passing remark, for it takes precedence of every other in Rome and the world; it is the special Cathedral of the Sovereign Pontiff, as Bishop of Rome. On the walls near both its entrances its titles are inscribed, "Mater ecclesiarum et caput." The exterior façade is of great height and of beautiful proportions. It is ornamented at the top with colossal statues of our Blessed Saviour, St. John the Baptist, and St. John the Evangelist, to whom the Basilica is dedicated; the aspect of this façade is very chaste and imposing, and is preferred by many to that of St. Peter's.

Over the grand portico is a fine balcony, or loggia, from which the Holy Father gives the Benediction on the Feasts of the Ascension and of St. John the Baptist.

The top of the façade and its statues form one of three principal objects which stand out prominently in relief at various points from fifteen to twenty miles distance from the city. These are, the cupola of St. Peter's, the *campanile* and domes of St. Maria Maggiore, and the façade of St. John Lateran. Thus is modern Rome distinguished from every other city—by the beauty and variety of her Christian temples.

On the steps of the grand entrance a beautiful view of the bold scenery of the Sabines and of the pretty Alban mountains can be obtained.

On entering the majestic Basilica the principal features

we notice are the immense width of the nave, the beautiful roof, the Gothic canopy over the high altar erected or restored by Pius IX., the mosaics of the apse, and the gigantic statues of the Apostles on either side. In the left transept is the chapel of the Blessed Sacrament, in which is carefully preserved the table of the Last Supper, the tabernacle here being formed by rare and costly marbles and precious stones. In the right transept is preserved the flag of John Sobieski, recalling the victory of Vienna; and there is here an organ of such tremendous power as to give rise to a fear lest the full power of its deep notes should break the glass in the windows. The high altar contains part of the very altar which the Apostle St. Peter used for the celebration of the Holy Sacrifice. It has been covered with marble by Pius IX. It has been already mentioned that part of this same altar, used by St. Peter, is kept in Santa Pudentiana.

The history of the site of the Confession I have never been able to learn to a certainty, but it is said to have been the spot where St. John the Evangelist was imprisoned.

In the canopy over the high altar are kept the heads of St. Peter and St. Paul.

The Corsini chapel contains many beautiful and valuable objects. The *Pietà* in the subterranean chapel has been already mentioned as a beautiful work of art. The Torlonia chapel contains some fine monuments.

The museum in the Lateran Palace contains Christian inscriptions taken from the catacombs, sarcophagi, and a very fine mosaic floor found amongst the ruins of ancient Rome.

In the group of buildings of which the *Scala Santa* and *Sancta Sanctorum* form a part, a beautiful mosaic is seen on the exterior. This formerly was the apse of the *triclinium* of the ancient palace of the Lateran, built in the eighth century and afterwards destroyed by fire.

17th, Easter Sunday.—A great many details having been given already about this feast, I will only give here the few notes I put down at the time for this particular year.

We were present in St. Peter's for the Mass celebrated to-day by the Holy Father himself, and had a good place, where we were able to see the Holy Father and all the ceremony. The sound of the trumpets at the Elevation, the "Benedictus," and the "Sanctus," were extremely beautiful. The singing of the Sistine choir is always very striking, and I think so particularly now that I am so soon leaving the Eternal City, and can hardly hope to hear it again, at least for some years to come; and I cannot look on this matchless temple of the Apostles and its many beauties without feelings of sorrow and regret at being so soon obliged to quit the city of Rome, and to be no longer able to behold the familiar scenes so often appreciated and enjoyed in this grand Basilica.

There was to-day an enormous crowd assembled in the Piazza San Pietro to receive the Benediction "Urbis et Orbis" bestowed to-day by the Holy Father on the Universal Church, and whose members, from so many countries far and near, were there to be seen gathered together. The voice of the Holy Father was clear and loud, and his action while pronouncing the words of the benediction very energetic. The cannon of Castel Sant' Angelo announced the conclusion of the solemn act, and this was followed by the acclamations of the people resounding throughout the piazza.

In the evening took place the illumination of the façade and dome of the Basilica, in honour of the feast of the day. The first, or silver illumination was not a success on account of the wind, but the golden was as beautiful as usual.

April 18th.—Grand fireworks at the Piazza del Popolo, on the slope of the Pincio. The representation of Jerusalem and its temple was the principal design. The whole was very pretty.

19th.—This evening took place the amateur theatricals got up by the English Zouaves at the Teatro Argentina. It was a great success, as we have some comrades who are very clever in this way. We had a very select company of spectators, including some of the *élite* of English Catholic society in the city.

20th.—To-day took place the horse-races on the Via Appia, beyond the tomb of Cecilia Metella. These are got up by English gentlemen and others. As we were walking out on the Via Appia we turned somewhat out of our way to see a race. The horses went a very good pace, but we did not learn who was the fortunate winner. One of our comrades, who had been anxious not to miss seeing the race, had some little reason to regret going there, as in the very short time that we spent there he was robbed of his purse.

To-day there was a general illumination of the city, in honour of the return of Pius IX. from Gaeta, and of his deliverance from accident at Sant' Agnese, on the 12th inst. The anniversary of both these events fell this year in Holy Week. The Holy Father went to that church to-day, and on his return in the evening he received quite an ovation. The façade of St. Peter's was lighted up with Bengal fire, and presented a very fine appearance. Near the bridge of Sant' Angelo there was a Madonna placed in a niche surrounded by jets of gas. This had a fine effect. We admired the illuminated steamboats on the Tiber, at the Ripetta, and the illuminations of the Via della Scrofa, of the Piazza San Lorenzo in Lucina—also a Madonna,—of the Roman College, and of the Via Baullari, in front of the Farnese Palace.

CHAPTER XIX.

THE VIA APPIA, COLUMBARIA, AND CATACOMBS.

THE Via Appia, made B.C. 310 by Appius Claudius, connects Rome with Terracina and the south of Italy. This *regina viarum* is certainly one of the best routes one can take who is interested in either classic or Christian antiquities. Anticipating by half a mile the Way named above, we will start from the Piazza Bocca della Verità, so called from the popular tradition that the ancients were accustomed to place their hands in the mouth of a colossal statue when affirming anything in a solemn manner. If they told the truth they were able to withdraw their hands; if not, their hands remained immoveable as a punishment for their falsehood. The head of this statue is now in the vestibule of Sta. Maria in Cosmedin.

The first object of interest is the ruined palace of the Cæsars on the left, to which the words of the poet are so appropriate:

"Cypress and ivy, weed and wallflower grown
Matted and mass'd together—hillocks heaped
On what were chambers; arch crush'd, columns strown
In fragments, choked up vaults, and frescoes steeped,
In subterranean damps, where the owl peep'd,
Deeming it midnight. Temples, baths, or halls?
Pronounce who can; for all that learning reap'd
From her research hath been that these are walls—
Behold the Imperial mount! 'Tis thus the mighty falls.
There is the moral of all human tales;
'Tis but the same rehearsal of the past,

First freedom and then glory—when that fails
Wealth, vice, corruption,—barbarism at last.
And history with all her volumes vast,
Hath but *one* page—'tis better written here,
Where gorgeous Tyranny hath thus amass'd
All treasures, all delights that eye, or ear,
Heart, soul could seek, tongue ask——Away with words! draw near."
CHILDE HAROLD.

These magnificent ruins cannot fail to impress the thoughtful visitor with an idea of the greatness of the ancient Romans, as we wander through those massive substructions, admire the perpendicular lines as perfect as ever, and then ascend and view the remains of the spacious temples, halls, library, etc., once ornamented with the most rare marbles, statues of great beauty, richly coloured paintings; and if we then consider that the Palatine Hill was once one vast palace, we are struck with astonishment at the skill and energy of the people who produced such things; and, at the same time, the Christian will adore in silence the dispositions of the Providence of God, who decreed the overthrow of that Paganism, and its most splendid monuments, which had shown itself such a determined enemy to Christianity.

It should be mentioned that the excavations have been carried on with great energy of late years, and many portions of the finest part of the Palace have been brought to light; and the different halls, library, temples, etc., can now be distinguished. Immediately below the Palace of the Cæsars the road passes through the site of the *Circus Maximus,*" now partly occupied by the Roman Gasworks. After the churches of St. Gregory, and of SS. John and Paul, which we leave on our left on the Cœlian, we come to the site of the *Porta Capena,* of the Republican period, of which not a vestige now remains; immediately afterwards on the right we observe the prison and church of Santa Balbina, built from the ruins of the Baths of Caracalla. This is a reformatory for young prisoners, who are taken care of and instructed by a community of monks, by whom, they are taught the useful trades. A little farther on are the imposing remains of the Baths of Caracalla. The grand hall is of immense height and size, and the mosaic floors now remaining very beautiful; the massiveness of these ruins may be imagined from what has been related of the effect produced from the fall of a portion of the roof or arching—that the neighbours felt the shock as that of an earthquake. The present extent of the ruins is very great, but does not include a third of the whole of the original Thermæ, or baths. I have picked up remains of beautiful mosaics, mural paintings, serpentine marbles, and *rosso antico* in the vineyards adjoining, at some distance from the present ruins.

Next we come to the church of SS. Nereus and Achilles, on the same side, and then to that of San Sisto Vecchio, on the opposite side. There is a monastery adjoining this church which was rebuilt by St. Dominic himself, and in which he wrought the miracle of raising a dead man to life who had been killed by a fall from his horse; in one of the rooms we saw the painting representing this fact, and all the circumstances connected therewith. Before reaching this point the ancient Via Latina branched off from the Via Appia. At the Porta Latina—now walled up—we visit the church of St. John, and the chapel on the very spot where this holy Evangelist suffered martyrdom for the faith, in a cauldron of boiling oil, though miraculously preserved from death. Before reaching the Porta San Sebastiano we visit the tomb of the Scipios, and the *Columbaria*.

These *Columbaria* — so called from the apertures resembling dovecotes—probably formed the burial-place of some wealthy burial association of the ancients. We enter a door, and descend some twenty feet, and then behold the Columbarium, having recesses arranged in tiers, one above the other, and containing urns with the ashes of the dead. The form of the cemetery is square, about, I should suppose, eighteen feet by eighteen, and of equal height; the apertures are formed out of the wall, and in this small compass there was room to contain the ashes of more than a thousand persons.

The Arch of Drusus is reached before the gate of St. Sebastian. This fine old arch was built to support the aqueduct which conveyed the water to the baths of Caracalla, and the stones of which it is composed were originally clamped together with iron, as were those of the Coliseum and other imperial works. The iron, however, has long since disappeared; the masonry remains in all its solidity, notwithstanding the violence it must have suffered, when the iron clamps were forced out of it. On nearing the gate before-mentioned, we see two towers flanking it on either side, and we notice the immense thickness of the walls, originally wide enough to drive a carriage along the top of them. At the time the walls of Rome were built they must have been of great strength, the mode of warfare of that time considered; the present walls were built by the Emperor Aurelian, but they have been restored in many places since that period.

After passing the walls of the city, the Civita Vecchia Railway, and some ruins of ancient Roman tombs, we come to the chapel of "*Domine quo vadis?*" built on the spot where St. Peter, flying from Rome and persecution, met his Lord and Master going into the city, and there addressed to Him the question, "Domine quo vadis ?" ("Lord, whither goest Thou ?") He received the answer, "Venio iterum crucifigi" ("I come to be crucified again"), on which St. Peter immediately returned to Rome to receive the crown of martyrdom.

Farther on the same side branches off another road, leading for some distance towards the grotto of Egeria. There is a remnant of the ancient statue above the fountain of the grotto, which is a cool retreat in summer, and abounds in ferns.

Near the grotto of Egeria, towards the Via Appia, are the remains of a temple of Bacchus, now converted into a small chapel. Returning now to the Via Appia, we next pass the Catacomb of Pretextatus on the left, and then reach that of San Calisto opposite. On entering the vineyard under which the latter is excavated, we see the ruins of an ancient building, and near it some cypresses, and underneath the remains of a small cemetery; this building was used probably as a chapel, or as a place of assembly for the Christians on the occasion of their visiting the tombs of the martyrs in the Catacomb.

As the Catacombs cannot fail to interest every Christian, a few more remarks about them will not, I trust, be deemed out of place.

The early Christians, from the Apostolical age, were accustomed to take great care of their dead, and especially of their martyrs, and to bury them in their own cemeteries, which they excavated at great labour underneath their own property, so that the dead should not be profaned by Pagan hands. In Rome they had facilities for carrying out their desires, both in the customs of burial of their Pagan neighbours—for they were also accustomed to care for their departed friends, and to assemble at their tombs on the "dies natalis"*—as well as in the nature of the volcanic soil in the environs of Rome. The "*tufa granulare*" was a subsoil, admirably adapted for an excavation of the nature of a catacomb, easy to work, but yet of sufficient consistency to allow of passages, chambers, small chapels, graves, being cut out, and retaining their shape, sides, and roof, without any assistance of masonry or brickwork; not only this, but in many instances, there are several stories one above the other. The extent of many of the Catacombs was very great, some of the passages being of great length; then others branched off in every direction. As the graves were ranged one above the other the whole length of every passage, the number of faithful buried in that of San Calisto alone must have been very great; it is estimated there were 174,000 *martyrs* and forty-six Popes there interred, according to the inscription in the church of St. Sebastian, which is built over a portion of this cemetery. When we add to these figures the probable number of other Christians, not martyrs, buried in the cemetery, and then consider the great number of catacombs in the vicinity of Rome—estimated to be

* The birthday, or other anniversary of the departed.

from sixty to one hundred and sixty by different writers—the number of dead contained in the whole must amount to some millions. A Christian cannot visit these resting-places of so many martyrs and saints without feelings of veneration and awe; the paintings, too, will arrest attention, as showing forth in the language of Christian symbolism the doctrines believed in those early days of Christianity. Both San Calisto and Sant' Agnese contain many interesting paintings—those of the "*Good Shepherd*," "*Moses striking the Rock*," the "*Fish and the Loaf*" occur very frequently; I have also seen a small tabernacle—in Sant' Agnese, I believe—hewn out of the *tufa*, for the reception of the Blessed Sacrament. On traversing a catacomb one is surprised to find the air so pure and dry; the latter quality arises from the dry nature of the *tufa*, and the former from the ventilation produced by the *luminaria*, or shafts, constructed for that purpose, and for giving a certain amount of light.

A catacomb was often entered from an *Arenaria*, or sand-pit, and the earth excavated from the catacomb removed through it; this was for the better security of the entrance, and to prevent observation. In the chapels we see the *arcosolia*, or altar tombs, and in these the altar was placed over the body of a martyr. Thus in the catacombs we find the origin of the custom of the church, celebrating the Holy Sacrifice over the relics of the martyrs and saints. On the subject of the paintings of the catacombs, the Rev. W. H. Neligan writes—he is here speaking of the connection of these with the earliest professors of the Christian faith:—" That they made those paintings, which are to be seen in the subterranean chapels, will appear by comparing them with the paintings in the baths of Titus, and with those in Pompeii, which had been destroyed by an eruption of Vesuvius, A.D. 79. D. Agincourt, who had devoted thirty years of his life to a study of the fine arts, especially with respect to the different epochs in their history, having compared the paintings in the Catacombs with those in the baths of Titus, and those at Pompeii, which had been then but recently discovered, and extending his researches further by comparing them with the paintings of the tomb of the Nasones and of the Columbaria, came to the conclusion that they were the works of the primitive Christians. .... The Good Shepherd seems to have the most prominent place amongst those paintings. In this our Saviour is represented as bearing a sheep on his shoulders. In a very old painting in San Calisto, he is represented as standing between a sheep and a goat—the goat always representing the sinner in the catacombs, and being typified thus in the Scriptures. The goat is placed on the right hand, as a place of honour, and the sheep on the left. The heresy of the Montanists, one of the earliest which troubled the church, and which denied the power of the church to forgive some of the more heinous sins, gives us the reason for this arrangement being adopted, in order to show that such was not the teaching of the church. .... Our Lord's healing the paralytic is another subject of painting in the catacombs. The mystical meaning of this is sufficiently clear. The body of the sufferer was typical of the soul palsied by sin, and He who saw both the body and soul of the man with the palsy, said to him, 'Thy sins are forgiven thee.' The first Christians connected this with the Sacrament of Penance; for in the catacomb of Hermes, in immediate connection with this subject, we have a penitent kneeling on both knees before the priest, who is giving him absolution." The reverend author also explains the many figures and types representing the Blessed Eucharist, seen in the catacombs, and particularly the "*Fish and the bread,*" so often to be met with. On this head, he says: "Christ, from the very earliest times, was always represented under the figure of the fish, which was considered typical of him, and which in the Greek presents the initials of our Lord's name and office. Any one tolerably acquainted with the Fathers, must be familiar with instances of the fish being considered as representing our Lord. The fish and the bread, when taken together, are a suitable representation of the Eucharist, the one representing the outward form, or accidents; the other the hidden reality, or substance."

On the subject of the inscriptions taken from the Catacombs, the reverend author notices their character of brevity and simplicity, which will strike any one who has seen the collections in the Vatican, and Lateran Museums, and elsewhere. The words "in pace," in peace; "in Deo," in God; "depositum in pace," deposited in peace; "vivas in Deo," mayest thou live to God; with the name only of the deceased, constitute a great number of the inscriptions; "bene merenti," well deserving, is sometimes added. Husbands and wives are commended for having lived together in harmony and peace: "Semper concordes, sine lesione animi, sine ulla querela." Women are commended for their chastity and modesty, and children for amiability and innocence. "Anima dulcis," sweet soul; "Innocens parvulus," innocent child; "Innocens agnellus Dei," innocent little lamb of God; "Agnella innocens," little innocent lamb; "Palumba sine felle," dove without gall; "Palumbulus sine felle," little dove without anger. .... Nor are the catacombs silent with respect to the virgins and widows who were consecrated to God. We constantly meet with "Virgo devota," devout virgin; "Ancilla Dei," handmaid of God; "Virgo votis deposita," here is deposited a virgin consecrated by vow; and, "Matrona (vidua*) Dei," a widowed matron of God; "Vidua quæ ecclesiam nihil gravavit," a widow who troubled the church in nothing.

The reverend author before mentioned discusses the various interpretations given to the word "*pace*," and "*requiescat*," so often found amongst the inscriptions. He proves that sometimes it was used as a prayer for the departed, by its resemblance to the following inscriptions, often to be met with : "In pacem estote," may you be in peace ; "Quiescas in pace," mayst thou rest in peace ; " Vivas in pace," mayst thou live in peace. He then continues :—"Prayers for the dead are to be met with constantly. The following are specimens of the inscriptions. The originals are in Greek, and are taken from the Catacombs of SS. Nereus and Achilles: ' Aurelius Olianus, of Paphlagonia, a faithful servant of God ;

* Original, vidui.

he sleeps in peace; remember him, O God, for ever.' 'Demetrius and Leontia, to their well deserving daughter, Lyrica. Remember, Lord Jesus, our child.' The two following are taken from the Catacomb of St. Pretextatus. The first is in Greek and Latin; the second is in Latin. 'To my well-beloved sister, Bon——, who died on the 8 day before the kalends of November; may the Almighty God, Christ, refresh thy spirit in Christ.' 'Kalemina, may God refresh thy spirit, together with that of thy sister Hilara.'" The learned author remarks on the similarity of these prayers to that used in every age in the Canon of the Mass, which is as follows: "Remember, O Lord, Thy servants who have gone before us, and who sleep in the sleep of peace; give them a place of refreshment, blessedness of rest, and clearness of light." ..... There are instances also, in which the departed soul is commended to the care of some Saint who had already gone to glory. "Domina Basila," or, as it would have been written in after ages, "Sancta Basila, we, Crescentius and Micina, commend to thee our daughter, Crescentina, who lived ten months." Another taken from the same catacomb of Basila, called the catacomb of St. Hermes, is as follows: "Aurelius Gemellus, who lived — year and eight months, and eighteen days. A mother made this to her dearest, well-deserving son: In peace I commend to thee, O Basila, the innocence of Gemellus." In the catacomb of SS. Nereus and Achilles, is a fragment of a Latin epitaph. It says the person for whom it was written died in June, and then concludes: " Vibas in pace, et pete pro nobis," mayst thou live in peace, and pray for us. Instances of this description might be quoted without any limit.

In a work on the Catacombs, the Very Rev. S. Northcote conclusively proves that all those above mentioned were *exclusively* Christian cemeteries, if any further proofs were needed than the above inscriptions.*

* Any one, however, who may wish to have further information on this very interesting subject, I can recommend with confidence to read both the work from which the above quotations are taken, and also the interesting work on the "Catacombs," by the Very Rev. Canon Northcote.

Via Appia continued.—To continue our journey onwards, we pass the church of St. Sebastian, which has been described already. On the left, farther on, are the ruins of the immense circus of Caracalla, and near it are some ruins which I have not had time to determine—perhaps a palace or baths connected with the circus. A little further on is the tomb of Cecilia Metella, which is, like the Mausoleum of Adrian —now Fort Sant' Angelo—of the circular form, and of great size; on the top was added, in the middle ages, some solid masonry to form a castle; this was probably held by the Gaetani family, the ruins of whose palace and chapel can be seen on the opposite side. About half a mile farther on, we come in sight of a very interesting portion of the "Via Appia," here we see before us a regular street of tombs on either side of the way, extending for miles across the Campagna towards Albano. To the antiquarian and classical scholar this portion of the *Regina Viarum* will have the greatest attraction.

These tombs were all more or less of magnificent proportion, and many were ornamented by marble pillars, and many inscriptions are also to be seen; but sad havoc was made here in the many sackings of the city, since the Imperial times, and especially in that particular one of the Constable of Bourbon. On examining the interior, we find everywhere traces of the Pagan custom of burning the dead, and placing the ashes in urns, which are still remaining. One of these tombs, remarkable for solidity and size, now remains standing on a very small base, the other portion having been removed. Its shape now somewhat resembles an enormous mushroom.

In the Vatican Museum are collected a large number of ancient Pagan sepulchral inscriptions, and any one wishing to compare the Pagan and Christian inscriptions has every facility for doing so.

The classic scholar will feel interested in visiting the scene of the celebrated contest between the Romans and the Albans in the time of Tullus Hostilius, the third King of Rome. It was on this occasion that the Horatii and the

Curiatii fought as the champions of either side; the tragic end of the contest, and the sad subsequent act of the victor are well known.

There is very much more that could be said about the Via Appia; for myself I had not sufficient time to examine more, and will conclude this subject by a remark connected with the customs of the ancient Romans with regard to the dead. They often provided in their wills that a feast should be celebrated at their tombs on the *Dies Natalis* of the departed; for this purpose all the friends and relatives assembled at the tomb on this day, and this custom it was that made it so easy for the Christians also to assemble near *their* cemeteries, without making themselves a subject of observation and remark to their Pagan neighbours.

CHAPTER XX.

VISIT TO TIVOLI.

THE ancient name of this delightful spot was Tibur.* It was a favourite resort of Mæcenas, Catullus, Horace, Sallust, and Varus, who had villas there. Many remains are still visible, the chief being a periphral temple, dedicated to the Sibyl Albunea; an oblong temple of Vesta; part of a temple of the ancient forum; with two villas of Mæcenas and Varus.†

April 21st.—Walked from Rome to Tivoli, accompanied by R——. We enjoyed the view of the lovely mountains as we approached it; we turned somewhat out of our course to the left, to visit one of the sulphur lakes; we walked up to the head of it, where it takes its rise, rushing up from a depth of one hundred and eighty feet. The water is warm —over seventy degrees Fahr.—the sulphurated hydrogen

* In Dr. Smith's "Ancient Geography," we find the following notes in reference to it:—"Tibur, a town of Latium, on the Anio, founded by the Siculi, first noticed B.C. 446, when M. Claudius retired thither in exile. Taken by S. Camillus, B.C. 335, after many wars with Rome."

† In Murray we read:—"Tivoli, the ancient Tibur, a city of the Sicani, founded nearly five centuries before Rome, was one of the early rivals of the Eternal City. . . . The Roman historians tell us that the Sicani were expelled by Tiburtius, Corax, and Catillus, grandsons of Amphiaraus, who came from Greece with Evander, and that the settlement derived its name from the eldest of these brothers. . . . The classical associations of Tivoli have made it a memorable spot in the estimation of the scholar; its scenery inspired some of the most beautiful lyrics of Horace. . . . He tells us that he often composed his verses while wandering among the groves and cool pastures of the surrounding valleys."

arising from it, gives it a strong odour, rather unpleasant, but the taste is on the contrary soft and agreeable. We both plunged in at this spot; I was first in, and R—— was astonished at the effect produced by my plunge, for it created a surging and boiling in the water, caused by the contact of it with the skin; added to this it caused a slight irritation or unpleasant soreness. After seeing me in a few minutes, R—— followed, and experienced the same effects as myself. We found the water too strongly charged with sulphur, etc., to allow us to remain in it long at this point, but, however, it was long enough to give us both a fine dip. These lakes were once of great extent, but the petrifying effect of the water is so great, that it has created a travertine rock over the greater part of their former extent, the lakes thus gradually diminishing in area, till now they are reduced to very diminutive proportions. The water is celebrated for its power of curing diseases of the skin, and we saw the bathing establishment on the river below the lake. We both carried away some curiosities—petrifactions of rushes and grass. On our return next day we bathed in the river, where we found the water was not so strongly charged with sulphur as in the lake. Farther on we left the high road again, to visit the villa of Hadrian; this we found in a lovely situation in a pretty valley near a river, the higher part of the villa commanding a magnificent view of the Campagna, with the Eternal City in its midst, of Monte Soracte, the Sabines and Tivoli, of the Alban Hills, and Monte Cavi.

It is difficult to give an idea of the splendour this villa must have exhibited in the days of Hadrian; it must suffice to say that the ruins are magnificent. In one of the "*triclinia*," or grand halls, we saw some remains of beautiful mural decoration, executed with great skill. There were theatres for games, and we noticed one in very good preservation; this was used for aquatic sports, there being a lake in the centre, and seats arranged all round, and there were in addition fine gardens and groves.*

* " This villa was built from the Emperor Hadrian's designs, in order

We ascended the mountain rock behind Tivoli. Now we are amongst the Sabines at last, entirely surrounded by mountains; in the east are the highest, their snowy peaks standing out in the far distance beautifully white and dazzling; next follow chains of high mountains, dark and bleak, but beautifully sharp and bold in their outlines, and variegated with patches and lines of snow. Next I see three small towns, built on lower mountains, rising from the beautiful valleys, the most distant supposed to be Vicovaro, the nearest, Castel Madama; the valleys are diversified by undulations, ruined aqueducts, by mediæval castles, by lovely fields, now clothed with the verdure of spring, and by pretty brooks and torrents.

If I change places and look west, I see through an opening in the mountains, immediately beneath me, Tivoli and its lovely falls, surrounded by olive groves; to the right are the picturesque towns of Monticelli and Sant' Angelo; farther off, Monte St. Orestes, or Soracte, and, farther still, Monte Soriano and Monte Fojano; immediately before me is a beautiful plain, in the midst of which are three small lakes, the sources of the Sulphur Baths of Tivoli—the whole plain was once one fine lake; farther off I see the Eternal City, crowned by St. Peter's, and in the distance the beautiful blue Mediterranean.

This is indeed a sweet spot; here is Tivoli under my feet, built on a rock, cut off from the mountains by the force of the torrent; the sound of the rushing waters, and the song of the nightingale, make indeed music to the ears, while the bright sun of this climate, and the fresh pure air of the mountains, complete the harmony of the whole scene.

---

to include in one spot all he had seen most striking in the course of his travels. It covered a space said by the Roman antiquaries to be from eight to ten miles in circuit. When first built it must have been more like a town than a villa. Nothing in Italy can be compared to its imposing ruins. It contains a Lyceum, an Academy, a Pœcile, in imitation of that at Athens, a Vale of Tempe, a Serapion of Canopus, in imitation of that at Alexandria, Greek and Latin Libraries, Barracks for the Guards, a Tartarus, Elysian Fields, and numerous temples. . . . The villa is supposed to have been ruined during the siege of Tibur, by Totila."—Murray's Handbook.

The grand fall at Tivoli is partly artificial, the waters having been brought into one channel by engineers under Gregory XVI., for there was danger of their undermining the town had they continued to pour through the crevices of the rocks under the foundation of its walls. The waters are now brought through a tunnel to one spot, where they fall in a grand mass at least three hundred feet. The effect is very graceful and fine, and the spray is precipitated to a distance of a hundred yards. Formerly the whole water of the river flowed under the town, and broke forth from the rocks in innumerable tiny cascades; the effect of this must have been very picturesque and pretty, but the majestic effect of the grand fall was missing, and the town would in time have been washed away. The innumerable caverns and grottos, washed out of the face of the rock by the force of the water, look very pretty and interesting, and form a pleasing variety in the façade of the rocky precipice, when viewed from the road on the opposite side of the defile; there one sees at once the destructive effect of water—

"Not by force, but constancy alone,
Drop by drop, water will wear away a stone—"

and its petrifying power; while it wears away one rock it forms other tiny ones, in all kinds of fantastic shapes, by petrifaction. The Grotto of the Sibyl exhibits this fantastic effect on a large scale, and the interior of it is most strange and remarkable. Taken as a whole, I consider the scenery at and around Tivoli to be the most lovely I have ever yet beheld. We had not time to visit all the points of interest, but we very much enjoyed a stroll about the rocks near the cascade; we also visited with pleasure a pretty garden near the river side, above the falls, and from thence we were able to see the tunnel through which the waters are led, under the side of the mountain, to the grand cascade.

Besides the grand falls, *La Cascata*, there are two other series of smaller ones, *Le Cascatelle*, which present great features of beauty when viewed from the opposite side of

TIVOLI—LE CASCATELLE.

the deep ravine into which their waters are precipitated; the variety of scene here helps greatly in making up the different lights and shadows of a fine picture. The view here would, I dare say, be preferred by many to that of La Cascata; in loveliness Le Cascatelle may be equal to La Cascata, but, in my humble opinion, its feature of grandeur is wanting. The Villa d'Este is laid out and arranged with good taste, water being introduced with a very pleasing effect.

A TRIP TO SUBIACO.

Having sufficiently admired the falls of Tivoli and explored its neighbourhood, we started for Subiaco. It was a curious kind of carriage that carried us on our way rejoicing. A washing basket on two wheels with a board across it to sit upon is the best comparison I know of for our vehicle. As we were three, and there was only room on the board for two, one of us sat in the back part of the basket, his legs elegantly dangling over the side of the basket-like body of our conveyance. But whatever inconvenience we had to put up with in our ricketty carriage was well repaid by the beauty and grandeur of the mountain scenery through which we passed. The bright sunshine made the outlines of the mountains stand out in bold relief against their blue background, and ridged their sides with dark shadows, and made the Anio in its mountain bed dance joyously in the gladsome light.

A good road, a horse not so good, but yet fresh, jolly companions, and a decent cigar, would make the longest road seem short; but when that road wends its way amid noble mountains, through fresh, grass-clad valleys, past picturesque villages and romantic ruined mediæval castles, one soon seems to come to the journey's end. On our way we passed Vicovaro, famous for a picture of the Madonna, the eyes of which are believed occasionally to move miraculously.

Shortly after midday we entered the town of Subiaco, which is placed on a hill, and boasts a church built on the side of the hill, and so placed that one altar and half the church is above the other part of it. On the summit of the hill is a large building, very ugly. It is a convent of nuns.

After putting up our horse and having got some refreshment for man and beast, we began the ascent to the celebrated Benedictine monasteries outside the town. Passing through the gate of the town a venerable, white-bearded old man saluted us in military style. He was one of the first Napoleon's veterans, many of whom still are to be met in some parts of Italy.

The first monastery reached is that of St. Scholastica, about a mile and a quarter out of Subiaco, and situated on the side of a steep and almost perpendicular hill along the foot of which runs the Anio. In face of the monastery, across the Anio, rises a high, woody hill, on the top of which is planted a cross. The monastery is most interesting in its religious associations, and it also possesses some beautifully painted chapels built on the spot where St. Benedict and St. Scholastica were wont to walk together conversing on heavenly subjects.

The bodies of the two Saints lie here buried together in the church. In the crypt is a chapel called the English chapel, where is shown the resting place of St. Bede, commonly supposed to be the English Saint, but most likely is St. Bede of Genoa, as our Venerable Bede is supposed to be buried in Durham Cathedral.

Having visited this monastery we went on to the Sagro Speco, or Holy Cave, where St. Benedict lived for many years. It is much higher up, and is quite on the steep and almost perpendicular side of the hill. A small convent and Gothic church are built up over the cave in which the Saint passed so many nights and days, and which is still preserved just as it was in his time, and has in it a beautiful statue of St. Benedict at prayer when he first came to live there, being then only fourteen years of age. The chapels are beautifully painted with very old frescoes in a high state of preservation, the mountain air being so dry that they have not been injured by damp. The way to this cave, in the Saint's time, was by means of a rope hung from above, by which also he received his food. When he wanted anything he had a bell to ring, which is still preserved here.

There is another cave near, where his disciples and the shepherds used to come to see him and hear him preach; and near it is a bed of thorns on which the Saint threw himself when the devil assailed him with a great temptation, and which, when St. Francis of Assisi came here, he caused to bud forth with beautiful roses. There is in the chapel an old portrait of the latter saint said to have been done by a monk from life while the Saint was engaged in prayer.

In one of the chapels are three lamps, presented by the missions of Deal, Ramsgate, and Margate, and which are kept burning at the expense of those missions. One of the most curious and wonderful things is a large mass of rock, quite detached from the mountain's side, and which hangs in a most threatening position right over the monastery, and which has remained in this strange manner since St. Benedict's time. Beneath it is a statue of the saint holding up his hand towards it, and on the pedestal is inscribed, "Stay, O rock; thou shalt not harm my children!" It is said that he stood thus and spoke thus as the rock was about to fall on his disciples. A few years since a piece of rock fell on the roof of the chapel and bounded off into the valley below without doing any serious harm, although it was 2,000 pounds in weight.

In one of the small chapels here are numerous relics. One is exceedingly curious, being a measurement of St. Benedict's height, according to which he must have been full six feet eight inches. We were shown over the monastery by a monk, a Prussian by birth, but who spoke English fluently, and seemed much pleased when I mentioned knowing F——, of Ramsgate.

We met here two most amusing travellers, one a Mr. B——, an American Catholic, and a young Englishman, named T——, his travelling companion. B—— was most amusing, having been to almost all parts of our globe, and having visited nearly every battle-field of importance. We sat talking with them till near half-past nine in the evening, outside the gate of Subiaco, smoking our cigars and nearly worried to death by all the Italian peasants who passed asking us for a "mezzo baiocco," or the enormous sum of one farthing sterling.

Passing the night at a clean little inn, we left Subiaco early next morning for Tivoli, not forgetting on our way to call in at the half-way *osteria*, or wayside inn, to have a dish of poached new-laid eggs, country bread, and pure wine, the latter an article I would advise all to enjoy if they can get it, for it is a "rara avis," and if one only touched wine when to be got pure, one would be nearly as abstemious as a teetotaller.

CHAPTER XXI.

DIARY CONTINUED—BATHS OF DIOCLETIAN—SANTA CROCE—
CONGÉ.

April 23rd.—We returned last evening from Tivoli. To-day, being the Feast of St. George, the Patron Saint of England, and of the English Zouaves, all the latter were exempted from any military duty. Our comrades and ourselves commenced the day by attending Mass at San Giorgio in Velabro —several received Holy Communion there—the Bishop of Birmingham saying Mass for us. In the church were exposed the standard and spear-head of the Saint. In the afternoon the English Zouaves were admitted to an audience of the Holy Father, R—— and I being amongst the fifty-nine who were present. The Holy Father received us with his usual amiability and kindness, gave us the Apostolical Benediction for ourselves and families, and addressed us in French as follows :—" St. George rode on horseback, and hastened quickly from place to place; we ride in a manner also, for we are all hastening quickly towards death, for which I trust you are all well prepared. You have to-day received the Holy Sacraments, by means of which you have prepared yourselves to encounter all the anxieties and troubles of this life."

The Holy Father had received a large number of priests and other people before us. I noticed that he looked sadder than usual; but alas! he has much to sadden him, and his solicitude and anxiety, as Supreme Pontiff, must of necessity sometimes weigh heavily on him.

April 24th, Low Sunday.—To-day we visited, for the last time, Santa Maria degli Angeli, and saw there again the works of Christian art in the quadrangle, but, as these have been before described, I will only add a few words, describing the church and the Baths of Diocletian, the *pinacotheca* of which was converted by Michael Angelo into this splendid church. This church has the largest roof in existence. Its size, its mosaic pavements, its frescoes, and its columns of precious marble make this hall the wonder of the Baths of Diocletian, and even of the Eternal City. In beholding this the mind will naturally recur to the circumstances under which it was built. Forty thousand Christians, condemned to the mines, many of whom shed their blood for the faith, raised these walls, which the providence of God has preserved to have His praises daily chanted in them; and these walls, raised by Diocletian, are consecrated to the honour of the Queen of Angels. Whilst other baths are but a heap of ruins, those of Diocletian, built by the hands of martyrs, remain as a monument of the impotence of the martyrs' persecutors, and as witness of the triumph of Christianity. The monastery of the Carthusians, to whom the church belongs, is formed out of the Baths. The church possesses four beautiful paintings, *chefs d'œuvre* of the best epoch.* In the choir is the famous fresco of St. Sebastian, by Domenichino. There is also a splendid work of art, which every one who has ever visited it cannot fail to have noticed—it is the statue of St. Bruno, which is such a lifelike representation that Clement XIV. said of it that " it would speak, were not silence enjoined by the rules of its order."

That the Baths of Diocletian were of magnificent proportions must be evident to every one who has visited the site, the remains mentioned above, the circular church of St. Bernard, the prison of the Termini, and the ruins beyond it, all of which formed part of these baths, although these different portions are situated a considerable distance from each other. These Baths consisted of a quadrangle, 1,069 feet

* " The Fall of Simon the Magician," by Pompeo Battoni; " St. Basil Refusing Communion to the Emperor Valens," by Subleyras; and "The Blessed Nicholas Albergati," by Hercules Groziani.

long. On each of the four sides, at the angles, there were circular rooms, which served for the *calidarium*, or the reservoirs of warm water. One of these yet remains, and forms part of the circular church of St. Bernard.

These baths exceeded in magnificence all that the imagination can picture. Some of the choicest specimens of sculpture that have been discovered in Rome were found in the ruins of the different baths, so that it would appear they were ornamented with beautiful statues, arranged in suitable places. The baths of Diocletian had more than three thousand bath-rooms, so that this number of persons could bathe at the same time without seeing each other. Each bath was most magnificent. Mosaics, formed of basalt and Numidian marble, surrounded with borders of stones of different colours, produced an effect like painting. The roof was formed of glass; the places in which the water flowed were surrounded by marbles from Thasus.

Streams of water flowed from silver pipes into the baths, made of silver and precious stones.* The first room entered was the *apodyterium*, where persons took off their clothes. After that was the *frigidarium*, where all took the cold bath in common. Pilasters, with niches and statues, decorated this place. Around it was a double row of steps, called the *schola*, where those sat who came to look at persons bathing, or were waiting for their turn. The *tepidarium* followed immediately after the cold bath; there were in it two large basins for swimming in. After this followed the *sudarium*, where the air was heated. An extensive furnace, placed on the outside, heated the water and the entire *sudarium* by means of pipes placed in the walls. The *unctorium*, where the bathers were anointed with the choicest perfumes, completed the entire number of rooms. The baths were the general *rendezvous* of all classes of the citizens. The degenerate sons of the Scipios and the Gracchi might be seen wending their way there, followed by a crowd of slaves, who had each their duties assigned to them.

* See " Rome, its Churches," &c., by Rev. W. H. Neligan, LL.D., M.A.

April 25.—Visited the seven Basilicas of San Pietro, San Paolo, San Sebastiano, San Giovanni Laterano, Santa Croce, San Lorenzo fuor le mura, and Santa Maria Maggiore. In the evening went with Duke to San Carlo al Corso, and to Sant' Agostino, where was kept the Feast of Our Blessed Lady of Good Counsel. We went afterwards to visit Father Ffrench, and to wish him "Good bye;" then we met our other friends, dined with them, and all said adieu and "*au revoir*" to Duke, who was about to leave next day, with his company, for Montefiascone.

26th.—We visited in the morning S. Andrea al Quirinale, and in the evening, for the last time, Santa Croce and its most precious relics, Santa Maria Nuova, St. John Lateran, La Madonna del Soccorso Perpetuo, and St. Maria Maggiore. Santa Croce contains one feature which I have before only slightly noticed. In one of the chapels, behind the high altar, was deposited by St. Helen, the mother of Constantine the Great, a considerable quantity of earth, brought from Mount Calvary; this she brought from Jerusalem, together with the True Cross of our Lord, which she had discovered, after an immense quantity of soil and rubbish the accumulation of nearly three centuries, had been removed under her directions. This Basilica, called Santa Croce in Gerusalemme, was specially founded by the Emperor Constantine to contain this precious instrument of our redemption. The other relics of Our Lord's Passion have been mentioned in a former visit here. The pictures inside the church represent the history of the Invention, or finding of the Cross by St. Helen. With the exception of the Holy Land and Jerusalem itself, no other spot in the world can claim so much interest, connected with the Passion, as this Basilica. Where else can we so easily picture to ourselves Mount Calvary, Our Blessed Lord crowned with thorns, and nailed to the Cross between two thieves, as here on Mount Calvary, represented by its very earth, surrounded by part of the True Cross, its title, "*Jesus of Nazareth, King of the Jews*," one of the very nails which fixed Him to the Cross, and by part of the crown of thorns which pierced His sacred Head?

The cross of the good thief will remind us of the other circumstances of the Crucifixion, and the relic of St. Thomas of those following the Resurrection.

27th.—We visited for the last time to-day many places endeared to us during our life in Rome, of these I need only mention here the altar of St. Aloysius in Sant' Ignazio, and the church of the Gesù. I called on Captain Thomalé and Captain Talmann, and my Sous-Lieutenant, M. Villélc, on the Right Rev. Dr. Brown, Bishop of Shrewsbury, for the purpose of bidding them adieu; they were all very kind. At the English college we said "Good-bye" to our particular friends, as well as to all our other kind acquaintances in the college.

We saw Mgr. Stonor at the Library, where we thanked him for the many services he had kindly rendered us. The Rev. Mr. Roe very kindly came there, provided with several photographs for both R—— and myself; these were his farewell gifts to us, and we were not insensible to these tokens of friendship, nor to those which Father Robinson gave us, nor to the cordiality of his farewell. This evening we dined with our Zouave friends, and afterwards assembled together to the number of eight, amongst whom were M. Desnoyers, a Canadian, and Mr. Bolingbroke, who were in the first depôt with me at Monte Rotondo. It was a great pleasure to us thus to meet together for the last time before we quitted Rome, and we much enjoyed this last social evening in the Eternal City, spent in the company of those comrades whose society we had so much relished. We did not forget to pay a farewell visit to our other friends in the city. This day we received our *Congés* for "*tempo finito*," or certificates of service completed in the Corps of the Pontifical Zouaves. To-morrow we start to return to our homes and friends in England.

Before, however, we leave the subject of the Eternal City, it will perhaps interest some of our readers to hear something of the unrivalled monuments of antiquity it contains. I will therefore devote the three succeeding chapters principally to this subject.

CHAPTER XXII.

THE COLISEUM—CHURCHES ON THE CŒLIAN, ETC.—THE CAPITOL—ARA CŒLI—ROMAN FORUM—ARCH OF TITUS—ST. SEBASTIAN.

> "A ruin, yet what ruin! from its mass
> Walls, palaces, half-cities, have been reared."
>   *   *   *   *   *
> "'While stands the Coliseum, Rome shall stand;
> When falls the Coliseum, Rome shall fall;
> And when Rome falls—the World.' From our own land
> Thus spake the pilgrims o'er this mighty wall
> In Saxon times, which we are wont to call
> Ancient; and these three mortal things are still
> On their foundations, and unalter'd all;
> Rome and her Ruin past redemption's skill,
> The World, the same wide den—of thieves, or what ye will."
>   BYRON.

THIS, the finest ruin of ancient Rome, if not of the whole world, one can hardly contemplate without experiencing deep feelings of wonder and admiration. The conception, design, and execution of it was altogether extraordinary. It is said to have occupied only five years in its erection, which, considering that it was originally larger than any building now existing, was marvellously rapid. Twelve thousand Jews, as well as an immense number of Christians, were employed in its construction, and the rapidity with which the work was completed is said to have astonished even the builders themselves.*

* Its form is that of an ellipse, and its longer axis measures 620 feet, the shorter one 513, so that it covered nearly six acres. The length of the arena is 287 feet, its breadth 180 feet. The arena was in the centre, and from it, to the fourth storey, the seats were raised on an inclined

The exterior wall *appears* to be about 200 feet high.*
The Coliseum was erected for the amusement of the people
by the Imperial games; among these were a great number
of gladiatorial contests. It was here also that an immense
number of martyrs suffered death for the Christian Faith, by
being torn to pieces in the arena by wild beasts. This fact
will create an additional attraction to every Christian; he
will here admire the Providence which so disposed events,
that in the Coliseum—erected for the celebration of profane
Pagan games—was exhibited to people, collected together
from every country, the sublime spectacle of thousands of
heroic disciples of Christ sacrificing their lives in the most
ignominious manner, rather than renounce their faith. This
could not but move the hearts of many among the immense
multitudes there assembled, and lead them to the consideration of the religion professed by these numbers of joyful
martyrs. When we consider the number of persecutions
the Church underwent between the reign of the Emperor
Titus, A.D. 79, and that of the Emperor Constantine the
Great, A.D. 306, we may form some idea of the number of
martyrs who here sealed their faith with their blood;
amongst them may be mentioned St. Ignatius, Bishop of
Antioch, St. Eleutherius, St. Alexander, St. Martina, and
St. Prisca.†

---

plane. The exterior is composed of travertine; it was four stories high,
and was adorned with columns, the lower being of the Doric order, in
the second tier the columns being of the Ionic, in the third of the Corinthian, and in the fourth of the composite order; there are also arcades,
these were the entrances to the rows of seats, which ascended from the
arena one above the other. There were arrangements by which the
Coliseum could be covered by the "*velaria*," or sail cloths, to protect the
spectators from the sun and rain. The third row of seats was surrounded
by eighty marble columns. The Coliseum was capable of containing
107,000 spectators. These figures and some other particulars are taken
from "Rome, its Churches, &c." By Rev. W. H. Neligan, LL.D., M.A.

* The work just quoted states it to be 157 feet.
† It should have been mentioned before, that the building of the Coli-
seum was commenced by the Emperor Vespasian, and finished by his son
Titus, who dedicated it to his father; hence it is called the Flavian
Amphitheatre, from Flavius Vespasian.

Part of the exterior wall of the structure was carried away in the middle ages, and served in the building of several palaces in Rome; however, the vast mass remains, and is still an imposing ruin, the effect of which from the interior is best seen by moonlight.

> "It will not bear the brightness of the day;
> But when the rising moon begins to climb
> Its topmost arch, and gently pauses there;
> When the stars twinkle through the loops of time,
> And the low night-breeze waves along the air,
> The garland forest, which the grey walls wear,
> Like laurels on the bald first Cæsar's head;
> When the light shines serene, but doth not glare,
> Then in this magic circle raise the dead:
> Heroes have trod this spot—'tis on their dust ye tread."
> CHILDE HAROLD.

Near the Coliseum is the ruin of the *Meta Sudans, i.e.* dripping pillar; this was a splendid fountain used by those who frequented the amphitheatre.

Several Popes have done much to preserve the ruins of the Coliseum from further decay, by the addition of immense buttresses, &c. The one erected by the present pope is a fine piece of brickwork.

The triumphal arch of Constantine is near the Coliseum, and exhibits some of the finest sculptured bas-reliefs of the Imperial period; hence the opinion that some of them are of older date than the time of Constantine, and originally adorned a more ancient triumphal arch of Trajan.

On the Cœlian hill, not far from the arch of Constantine, is the church of SS. John and Paul, built on the spot where these holy martyrs suffered in the precincts of their own house, as the inscription in the church testifies. Their bodies repose in the porphyry urn under the high altar. This church now belongs to the Passionists, and underneath the altar of the chapel of the Blessed Sacrament one sees, perfect and entire, the body of their founder, St. Paul of the Cross, who died in the last century. The *campanile* adjoining is built on a base of great antiquity, composed of huge blocks of travertine. This is the masonry of the most ancient substructions now to be found in Rome, and belonged to the time of the kings. It is supposed to be the remains of the *Curia Hostilia* or Senate House, built by Tullus Hostilius, third king of Rome. Here are also remains of the *vivarium*, or dens for the wild beasts used in the games of the Coliseum.

The Church of St. Gregory the Great is also on the Cœlian, built on the site of the house of the Saint. It is a conspicuous object from the south side of Rome. The approach to and façade of the church are very fine.

In the convent adjoining lived St. Augustine and St. Lawrence, archbishops of Canterbury, and St. Mellitus, bishop of London. This spot may be justly called the cradle of England's civilisation, for here were nurtured the men— St. Augustine, St. Laurence, St. Mellitus, and, before them, St. Gregory himself—who were most instrumental in her conversion from Paganism to Christianity, and to Christianity alone does England owe her present civilisation.

On the left of the ascent to the church are three chapels, built by St. Gregory, and dedicated under the invocation of St. Silvia, mother of St. Gregory, of St. Andrew, and of St. Barbara. In the chapel of St. Barbara is the table on which St. Gregory fed twelve poor men every day, and where our Lord, as the thirteenth, sat amongst them. There is a fresco painting in the chapel representing this event.

On the Cœlian, which is one of seven hills of ancient Rome, are many other objects of interest, such as the church of the Quattro Coronati, Santa Maria della Navicella, San Stefano Rotondo, already described last year, the Arch of Dolabella,* and the remains of the house of Scaurus, and of the Golden House of Nero.

* "The Arch of Dolabella and Silanus is supposed to have formed one of the entrances to the Campus Martialis, where the public games in honour of Mars were celebrated when the Campus Martius was inundated by the Tiber. It is a single arch of travertine, with an inscription, from which we gather that it was erected A.D. 10.

"A short way beyond this, towards St. Stefano Rotondo, is a fine

Sette Sale.*—These words, which mean "seven halls," are applied to some ruins on the Esquiline, very near to the Coliseum, from which side they are entered.

First we enter the substructions, or lower portions. The different chambers are of great height, and appear, from the remnants of mural painting, to have been richly decorated. On ascending above these we find ourselves on the present level of the top of that part of the Esquiline, and it was on this floor probably that the "seven halls" and the best part of the palace was placed. Judging from the portion of the ruins now standing—part of which is now used as a powder magazine, the other portions being in the vineyards adjoining—they must have been of magnificent dimensions; but I have not been able to find any account of the Emperor to whom they are to be assigned. The ruins may have formed part of the immense golden house of Nero, or of the baths of Titus, part of which were converted into the subterranean church of San Martino ai Monti.

The *Cloaca maxima* or immense sewer, constructed in the reign of Tarquinius Priscus is a remarkable memorial of early Roman architecture. It is formed of immense blocks of stone, six feet long and three feet wide, joined together without mortar or cement. The width of the sewer is twelve feet, its depth the same. Formerly it was easy to row through it in a boat, but now this is more difficult on account of the rise of the bed of the Tiber. This is indeed one of the wonderful works of the ancients, and now, after 2,400 years, is as perfect as ever.

The Capitol was so called because this hill was considered the chief place, and here was situated the citadel and the chief temple of ancient Rome, viz., that of Jupiter Capitolinus.

---

mediæval arch, surmounted by a canopy with a mosaic, a beautiful specimen of the architecture of the thirteenth century, having been erected by two of the Cosimatis."—Murray's Handbook.

* Murray says the Sette Sale is the ruined building near the Via San Clemente, and that it was the reservoir of the Thermæ of Titus.

On ascending from the Piazza d'Ara Cœli, the beautiful flight of cemented steps, we have a full view of the buildings of the Capitol of the present day. On the summit, to the left, is the fine old Church of Ara Cœli, leading up to which is a very steep ascent. Immediately below this is the small but pretty garden of the Capitol. At the bottom the balustrade is surmounted on either side by a lion of black granite, and at the top by the statues of Castor and Pollux, of colossal size, in white marble. On arriving at the top we find ourselves in a small piazza, or square, in the centre of which is a superb equestrian statue in bronze of the Emperor Marcus Aurelius. Opposite to us is the palace of the Senator, on the site of the *tabularium* or place of records, surmounted by an elegant tower, from which a good view of the site of the ancient as well as of the modern city can be obtained. On the left are the halls of sculpture, and above, in the background, the monastery and barracks of Ara Cœli. On the right is the .Promoteca—containing a collection of modern statues—and the picture gallery. In the halls of sculpture are some of the most beautiful specimens of that art which have come down from antiquity. Amongst these the "Dying Gladiator" is the most famous, and it suggested the following beautiful lines in "Childe Harold."

"I see before me the gladiator lie:
He leans upon his hand—his manly brow
Consents to death, but conquers agony
And his drooped head sinks gradually low—
And through his side the last drops' ebbing slow
From the red gash fall heavy, one by one,
Like the first of a thunder-shower. And now
The arena swims around him—he is gone,
Ere ceased the inhuman shout which hailed the wretch who won."

In the Promoteca is the hall opened by Pius VII. in 1820, containing some very beautiful specimens of modern sculpture by Canova, and other artists. In the *atrium*, or court, are the remains of some colossal ancient statues. The picture gallery contains some very fine paintings. In the superb suite of rooms adjoining are very many interesting objects, including the bronze " Wolf of the Capitol."

The Capitol was the scene, in the time of the Roman republic, B.C. 390, of an act of patriotism which saved the Roman power from utter destruction.

The Gauls, under Brennus, had defeated the Romans in a pitched battle near the river Allia, had laid waste the city, and put to death the eighty senators whom they found in it, while the remnant of the Roman army retired to the citadel, situated on the top of the steep Capitoline Mount. In the "Universal History" we find the following account of the event, the Cominius here mentioned being sent from Furius Camillus to the military tribune in the citadel.

"The way Cominus made this dangerous expedition was by getting down the Tiber by night. He then landed at the foot of the Tarpeian rock, clambering up a most difficult path till he gained the wall that surrounded the Capitol. But though he escaped, the Gauls perceived that some one had passed that way, and Brennus resolved to attempt a surprise by the path he now discovered. The Romans were so secure as to that quarter as to deem a guard unnecessary. From this neglect the two foremost Gauls who were sent on this duty reached the foot of the wall before the least alarm had been given. But a flock of geese, sacred to Juno, who were kept in that place, then began to cackle, and Manlius, a gallant Roman, happening to be awake, ran to see the occasion of it. By this time the two first Gauls had gained the top of the rampart. Manlius, however, with the first stroke of his sword, disabled one, and immediately tumbled the other down the precipice. The alarm then became general, and the forces of Brennus having no longer any chance of success, abandoned this enterprise."

Thus was Rome saved for the time by means of the geese, and the unflinching courage of one of her bravest sons. The danger had not yet altogether passed away, for the Gauls were still in the possession of the city, and it required all the skill and energy of that distinguished

Roman, Furius Camillus, to save the citadel from a disgraceful capitulation, and his country from dishonour.

"He came to relieve the Capitol at a very critical moment, and perceiving the present disgraceful state of things, cried out that by steel alone, and not by gold, was Rome to be recovered from the hands of its enemies. He then charged with great vigour the astonished Gauls, obliged them to abandon their prey, and shortly after, in a decisive battle, fought at a short distance from Rome, amply revenged the disaster that his countrymen had suffered on the banks of the Allia."*

For this and many other acts of distinguished patriotism during a long life, Camillus earned the title of father of his country, and second founder of Rome, and his fame and virtues have caused him to be considered one of the greatest men the Roman Republic produced.

The Tarpeian Rock forms the south-western side of the Capitol. It was here, in ancient time, that traitors were precipitated into the valley below, causing them instant death; at present the accumulations of ages have filled up the precipice, and it would be difficult to determine the exact site of the Rock.

The church of Ara Cœli, *i.e.*, *Altar of Heaven*, is, according to tradition, "built on the spot where the Blessed Mother of God, holding her Son in her arms, showed herself to the Emperor Augustus in the centre of a circle of gold."†
"According to some historians the Emperor consulted the Sybil of Tivoli, to know if he should allow himself to be honoured as a god; and that, after fasting three days, Augustus saw the heavens opening, and a virgin of great beauty, sitting on an altar, and holding in her hands an infant, and saying, 'This is the altar of the Son of God.' In consequence of this Augustus forbad himself to be called god, and caused an altar to be erected on the Capitol to the 'first-born of God.'"‡

---

* "Fredet's Ancient History."
† *Vide* inscription on the baldachino inside the church.
‡ "Rome and its Churches."

The church contains twenty-two pillars of Egyptian granite of different orders, supposed to be taken from the ancient temple of Jupiter, some fine paintings, and interesting inscriptions; in one of the chapels is the famous *Bambino*, which is held in high veneration in Rome.

The Roman Forum was situated immediately to the southeast of the Capitol, and at a considerable depth below it; and the view of its ruins cannot but raise the deepest feelings in the breast of the traveller who sees them for the first time, and beholds the wreck of the beautiful temples before him. This part of the Forum consisted of a series of temples, on different levels, of the Arch of Septimius Severus, and of the *Via Sacra*, or *Clivus Capitolinus*, descending by a circuit, and passing through this arch; farther on is the column of Phocas, and three pillars of the Corinthian order, supposed to have formed part of the *Curia Julia*. Most of these ruins are of beautiful marble, and of exquisite workmanship.

Between the column of Phocas and the circular base, which bears a small pedestal—this may have been the *milliarium aureum*, or golden pillar from which all distances were measured—was the *rostrum*, or tribune, from which the orators addressed the people in the Forum.

As we look on this Forum, how many recollections of a great people present themselves to the mind; Cicero, and Cæsar, and other great orators come up before us, addressing the people with words of burning eloquence, and the multitude listening in breathless suspense; we picture to ourselves the beautiful temples, once more in pristine splendour; then, recalling the mind to the realities of the present, the image vanishes, and ruin and desolation appear again. This great but Pagan people has passed away, and its descendants have merged into the followers of a greater Conqueror than Cæsar. Such are our thoughts on beholding the Forum, and the site of that *rostrum* of its orators. First we are struck with admiration; then a feeling of sadness comes over us; and at last we are content to depart consoled from the scene, to visit some other wonder of the ancient, or to wend our way to some venerated shrine of the modern Rome.

On descending the Capitol, towards the present church of San Giuseppe de Falegnami, we behold, on looking back, the massive substructions of the ancient *Tabularium*, below the present Palace of the Senator. Continuing, we enter this church, built above the Mamertine Prison, where St. Peter and St. Paul were imprisoned up till the time of their execution. We then descend into the prison, and drink water from the fountain which St. Peter caused to come forth from the floor, that he might baptize their gaolers, Processus and Martinianus, with the twenty-seven soldiers, who were converted by him in prison, and all of whom suffered in their turn martyrdom for the Christian Faith. The Mamertine Prison is hewn out of the solid rock, its walls being built of volcanic tufa in the Etruscan style, and it was excavated and constructed by Ancus Martius and Servius Tullius, Kings of Rome. It consists of two floors, one below the other, and formerly the only entrance to both was through a small circular aperture in the roof of the upper prison— the entrance again from this to the lower one being effected in like manner through another small opening in the floor of the upper prison. Through these holes the prisoners were let down into the bowels of the earth, and through them only could any light or air reach the suffering inmates in their gloomy abodes. It was here, in this loathsome den, far removed from the influence of the beautiful sun, which our Beneficent Creator has made to gladden the hearts of His creatures, that the glorious Apostles of Rome, St. Peter and St. Paul, exhibited an example of constancy and patience in suffering, rewarded by the conversion to the true faith of their fellow-prisoners.

Very near is the church of Santa Martina. This holy virgin was the daughter of a consul, and she received the crown of martyrdom in the Flavian Amphitheatre ; her body reposes in the subterranean church. The church belongs to the Academy of Painters.

The present *Campo Vaccino* covers the site of part of the

Forum, and here are the churches of St. Adrian, San Lorenzo in Miranda, and SS. Cosmas and Damian. The second, named *in Miranda* from the wonderful ruins by which it is surrounded, is formed out of the temple erected by the Roman Senate to Antoninus and Faustina, A.D. 168. The portico and side walls are still standing. The portico is formed of ten large columns, each fifteen feet in circumference, and forty-six feet in height. The entablature consists of immense blocks of Parian marble, finely worked, and bears the following inscription—" Divo Antonino et Divæ Faustinæ, Ex. S. C."* SS. Cosmo e Damiano occupies the site of the temple of Remus, part of which now forms its vestibule, or portico; and the ancient bronze door of the temple now closes the entrance of the church. Under the high altar are the bodies of SS. Cosmas and Damian ; in the apse is an ancient mosaic. This church was formed by Pope Felix III., in 527, from the ruins of the temple before mentioned.

The *Forum Romanum*, adorned with beautiful temples, exhibiting elaborate skill in their execution, as well as with the Basilica and *Curia Julia*, pillars, statues, and the School of Zanthus, was the great centre of the ancient Romans, both in Republican and Imperial times. Here the people congregated, the Senate deliberated, the orators addressed the multitude; here the Emperors commanded, and victorious consuls and generals have been often borne aloft in triumph, while unhappy conquered foes have been forced to follow in sadness, lamenting their hard fate.

The three large ruined arches, near the church of S. Maria Nuova, at the same side of the Campo Vaccino as the last-mentioned churches, are generally supposed to have formed part of the ancient temple of Peace. There is no doubt but that its site was here, but an opinion exists that the present ruins of colossal size belonged to the Basilica of Constantine ; above the entablature are the remains of another series of arcades, apparently corresponding to the lower ones, and the whole structure appears to have been of magnificent proportions. Farther on, towards the Coliseum, are the ruins

---

* " To the divine Antoninus and Faustina, by decree of the Senate."

of the temples of Venus and Rome, which cannot fail to have been observed by every visitor to the Eternal City, as they appear to have formed a double temple, joined in the centre, and entered from opposite directions. The church before named, also called Santa Francesca Romana, was built on part of the site of these temples. The *campanile* attached to it belongs probably to the more ancient church built here by Pope Paul I. in the middle of the eighth century.

The Arch of Titus is situated between the Campo Vaccino and the Coliseum, and was erected over the Via Sacra to his honour by the Senate and Roman people; it is one of the best preserved monuments of ancient Rome. It is of white marble; it consists of only one arcade. It was adorned by four fluted pillars of the composite order. In the interior of the arch are two basso-relievos, which, though much injured by time, are the finest known. On the left side Titus is seated in a triumphal car, drawn by six horses abreast. The rein is guided by a female figure representing Rome. The corresponding one on the right side is a continuation of the triumph; it represents several soldiers, the Jewish captives, the golden table, the silver trumpet, and the seven-branched candlestick, with other spoils, carried on the shoulders of soldiers wearing crowns. It is remarkable that all the figures except the Emperor have the Grecian nose and face. He alone has the short neck and features of the ancient Romans. There are four very fine figures on the archivaults.*

You meet a Jew in the Campo Vaccino; he never passes under this arch; he will pass along the side of it. Vain protestation! for the memorial of his servitude and of his fall stands near him.†

---

* The side towards the capitol bears the following inscription: "S. P. Q. R. Imp. Tito Caes. Divi Vespasiani filio Vespasiano Aug. Pont. Max. Tr. Pot. X., Imp. XVII., Cos. VIII., P.P., principi suo qui, preceptis patriæ consiliisque et auspiciis gentem Judæorum domuit, et urbem Hierosolimam omnibus ante se ducibus, regibus, gentibus aut frustra petitam aut intentam delevit."

† "Rome, its Churches," &c.

Beyond this arch, on both sides of the road leading to the Coliseum, are the remains of departed grandeur; on the left we see broken marble pillars of enormous size; on the right, immense masses of crumbling brickwork, dust, and soil, accumulated from the fallen buildings of the ruined palace of the Cæsars. Here we stand to look at the memorials of the former greatness of the Imperial Palatine, and one cannot contemplate them without experiencing some feelings of sadness.

We must not, however, forget to visit the spot hallowed by the martyrdom of a great Christian hero, who lived at the time when the ruins we have now spoken of existed in all their grandeur, viz., the small church of St. Sebastian, on the Palatine hill, where this Christian soldier fell, pierced with arrows, for refusing to conform to the idolatry of the Empire.

It will be known to all readers of the "Lives of the Saints," that this Saint was a captain of the Prætorian Guard, under the Emperors Carinus, Diocletian, and Maximian, and that he spent his life in Rome in furthering the progress of the Christian religion, and used his influence in protecting the Christians. In the year A.D. 288, he was denounced as a disciple of Christ before the Emperor Diocletian, who delivered him over to Mauritanian archers to be shot to death. "His body was covered with arrows, and he was left for dead. Irene, the widow of St. Castulus, going to bury him, found him still alive, and took him to her lodgings, where, by care, he recovered from his wounds, but refused to fly, and even placed himself one day by a staircase, where the Emperor was to pass, whom he first accosted, reproaching him for his unjust cruelties against the Christians. This freedom of speech, and from a person, too, whom he supposed to have been dead, greatly astonished the Emperor; but recovering from his surprise, he gave orders for his being seized and beat to death with cudgels, and his body thrown into the common sewer. A pious lady called Lucina, admonished by the Martyr in a vision, got it privately removed, and buried it in the catacombs at the entrance to the cemetery of Calixtus."* The church on the Via Appia, which has been mentioned before, was built over the tomb of St. Sebastian by Pope Damasus in the fourth century.

* "Butler's Lives of the Saints," Vol. I.

CHAPTER XXIII.

THE PANTHEON—COLUMNS—OBELISKS—AQUEDUCTS.

> "Simple, erect, severe, austere, sublime—
> Shrine of all saints, and temple of all gods,
> From Jove to Jesus—spared and blest by time;
> Looking tranquillity, while falls or nods
> Arch, empire, each thing round thee, and man plods
> His way through thorns to ashes—glorious dome!
> Shalt thou not last? Time's scythe and tyrants' rods
> Shiver upon thee—sanctuary and home
> Of art and piety—Pantheon!—pride of Rome!"
> "Relic of nobler days and noblest arts!
> Despoiled, yet perfect, with thy circle spreads
> A holiness appealing to all hearts—"
>
> CHILDE HAROLD.

THE Pantheon, as its name implies, was originally built as a temple for *all the gods* of Pagan Rome; its form is circular, hence it is also known by the name of the Rotunda. It is also called "S. Maria ad Martyres," from its conversion into a Christian church, and its dedication by Pope Gregory IV. under the invocation of the Blessed Virgin, and all the martyrs and saints, in the beginning of the ninth century, as well as from the relics of a great number of martyrs preserved in it. The portico is of magnificent proportions, the shafts of the sixteen pillars being each one block of oriental granite, nearly five feet in diameter at the base, and forty feet high. These pillars are of the Corinthian order, and support an entablature of the finest proportions. On the frieze of this entablature is the following inscription: "M.

Agrippa L. F. Cos. Tertium Fecit."* This M. Agrippa was son-in-law to Octavius, and he built the Pantheon twenty-seven years before the Christian era.

The façade of the portico has withstood the ravages of time, and is now as perfect as ever, and the view of it from the Piazza is very fine; it was probably this exterior façade that the poet had in mind when he wrote the commencement of the lines quoted above, which are so well calculated to convey a just idea of this, the most perfect work that has come down to us from ancient times. The interior is one hundred and forty-three feet in diameter, the walls are of immense thickness, the height to the top of the dome is equal to the diameter; the building is only lighted from a circular opening in the top, twenty-eight feet in diameter. I have myself measured the dimensions of the diameters of the Pantheon and of the cupola of St. Peter's, and found the latter to be slightly less, hence the promise of Michael Angelo was all but accomplished, when he said he would build in the air what Agrippa had placed on the ground. The dome occupies one half the height of the building, and in it were placed the niches for the statues of the gods, as well as in the lower part; these latter were easily converted into receptacles for the Christian altars. The great painter, Raffaele, is buried here. The baths of Agrippa were formerly near the Pantheon.

The Commandant, or Military Governor of Rome, resides in the Palace of the Piazza Colonna, also called Piazza di Roma; in the same palace are the rooms of the *casino*, or Military Club of the officers of the Pontifical Army.

The Column of Antoninus Pius, one hundred and sixty feet high, which is in the centre of the piazza, is now surmounted by a statue of the Apostle St. Paul; the column is ornamented with basso-relievos representing the victories of Marcus Aurelius, and the miracle of the *thundering legion.* "About A.D. 176, this Emperor was in the centre of Germany with his army, where, being deceived by the Quades, he had been led into a deep defile, surrounded by high mountains,

* "Erected by Marcus Agrippa when consul for the third time."

on which the enemy suddenly appeared. There was no means of escape. In addition to this the army had been suffering for want of water for more than five days. The leader of the Prætorian Guards came to tell the Emperor that the Melitine legion, nearly all composed of Christians, formed part of the army, and that they could obtain anything they desired through their prayers. The Emperor expressed his wish that they should offer up their prayers. Scarcely had these old soldiers fallen on their knees, and entreated the true God to send them rain, than the heavens soon darkened with clouds, and loud claps of thunder were heard, accompanied with lightning and a fearful hail, which fell on the enemy, while it only rained on the army. The account of Dio, a heathen writer, is interesting :—'There could be seen, at the same time, both fire and water descending from heaven. The army were refreshed by the one, and the enemy were burnt with the other, for the fire did not touch the Romans, and the water burned the barbarians like burning oil. In their despair they threw themselves amongst the Romans, where the water refreshed them. The Emperor took pity on them.' . . . . In memory of this fact the legion was called the *thundering legion*, and the Emperor stopped the persecutions against the Christians by an edict he then published." *

The Forum of Trajan, also called the *Forum Ulpium*, was formerly of great extent and magnificence, as one may judge from the ruins of it now remaining.

The Column of Trajan, now crowned with a statue of St. Peter, of gilt bronze, is about one hundred and forty feet high, including the statue; it is ornamented with basso-relievos representing the expeditions of Trajan. These—the work of an artist named Apollodorus—have been considered as masterpieces of art, and have served as models for many eminent artists. These basso-relievos commence from the bottom of the shaft, and are continued round it, winding and ascending as a spiral cordon until the top is reached. The shaft contains 2,500 figures, many two feet high. "The shaft, a hundred Roman feet in height, is composed of nine-

* "Rome, its Churches," etc.

teen solid blocks, some five feet in height, over twelve feet in diameter, and that after reduction by cutting away to the surface of the sculpture. The block out of which the upper cornice of the plinth is cut is twenty-two feet square. Each of these enormous masses contains a certain proportion of the stairs, and of the column in which it centres. These are excavated out of the blocks. The blocks, or drums, are connected by T-shaped iron dowels. The foundations must be admirably constructed, as the enormous weight of material, so close in grain, presses on a limited area of ground. It remains, however, perfectly perpendicular to this day."*

The height of the column, as we gather from the inscription on it, was designed to represent the height of the hill which was here removed by the Roman engineers, in order to construct the Forum, or Ulpian Basilica, the court of which was adorned with this column.

The obelisks of Egyptian granite which adorn several "*piazze*" in the city are wonderful as exhibiting the enduring nature of this stone, the skill of the ancient Egyptians in carving hieroglyphics, and the extent of the dominions of ancient Rome, whose generals brought these trophies from that far distant land after its conquest. The one in the Piazza of St. John Lateran is said, by those learned in hieroglyphics, to be as old as the time of the Jewish captivity, which ended B.C. 1491; thus the obelisk would be 3,360 years old.

The obelisk in the Piazza San Pietro is a fine column of a single block, but there is no hieroglyphic to determine its exact date. It is placed on four small bronze lions, and above it is a portion of the True Cross; in the panels of the base are the inscriptions—"Ecce crux Domini, fugite partes adversæ;" "Vicit leo de tribu Juda;" "Christus vincit, Christus regnat, Christus imperat." † Thus the eternal victory of Christianity over Pagan superstition is proclaimed.

* "Month," Vol. 6.
† "Behold the cross of the Lord, let all enemies fly;" "The lion of the tribe of Juda has conquered;" "Christ conquers, Christ reigns, Christ rules."

> The Cross its victory proclaims,
> O'er proudest laurels won of yore;
> Now Christ alone supremely reigns
> Where superstition swayed before.

This column was placed in its present position by the great Pope Sixtus V., and, as its weight was enormous, it was the occasion for the exercise of a considerable feat of engineering skill. High Mass was celebrated in St. Peter's, the Pope bestowed his benediction on the workmen, and the shaft was being raised from a horizontal position by means of ropes, in the presence of a great multitude—who had been commanded to observe perfect silence—when it was seen that the strain on the ropes was too great, and there was danger of an accident. At this juncture a Genoese sailor called for water to sprinkle the ropes, which, being applied, contracted them to their original tension, and, after some other efforts, the shaft was fixed in its place without further difficulty. The Pope demanded what reward the sailor desired for his courage and coolness; to which the latter said, that he would only ask for the privilege of supplying the Holy Father and St. Peter's with palms for the ceremony of Palm Sunday, and it is said that the privilege is still enjoyed by his descendants at the present day. The fountains on either side of the obelisk are perhaps the most beautiful in the whole world, the jets being of great height and exquisite delicacy, and producing a crystal shower in which are reflected the colours of the rainbow.

Marmorata.—The ancient port of the Tiber—recently discovered, and now known by the above name from the marbles there brought to light again—is an interesting object. It is situated below the present city, and very valuable marbles have been re-discovered, after lying buried in the mud on the banks of the river for many centuries. How such a store could ever have been buried remains an unexplained mystery; but I suppose the fact must be put down to the account of the Goths, Huns, or Vandals, or of the other barbarians who devastated the city in former times.

The *Sette Vigili*, or barracks of the *seventh cohort*, near the Lungaretta of the Trastevere, has also been recently discovered; it is situated below the present level, as are so many of the ancient remains. On descending we enter a small *atrium*, in the centre of which was a fountain. We walk through the other chambers, which are small but tastefully decorated, and we then examine the scratchings in the mortar, on the wall of the *atrium*, and we find they were done by certain members of the seventh cohort of the Roman army. The excavations here were not completed at the time of our visit, and it was thought that other interesting remains would be discovered under the houses adjoining.

Aqueducts.—No ancient or modern city was ever better supplied with water than Rome was, and is at present; pure water brought from the distant mountains and lakes. In the Campagna the ruined aqueducts form quite a feature in its scenery. Appius Claudius, the Censor, was the first who brought water to Rome by means of an aqueduct; this was in the year B.C. 311. The mention only of the various ancient aqueducts, will give some idea of the quantity of water they brought.

The *Aqua Appia*, mentioned above, brought from the Via Prænestina. The *Anio Vetus*, brought from Augusta, twenty miles beyond Tivoli, by C. Dentatus and L. Papirius, in the year B.C. 272. The *Aqua Tepula*, from the Via Latina, B.C. 125. The *Aqua Julia*, by Agrippa, the son-in-law of Augustus. The *Aqua Marcia*, from the Sabine Mountains. The *Aqua Virgo*—so called from its being discovered by a young girl—was brought to the city by Agrippa. The aqueduct which he constructed had been rendered useless by war and devastation, when it was restored by the munificence of different Popes, and in particular by Gregory XIII., who distributed the water through the city. It is this water which supplies the Fountain of Trevi, and the district of the city near it. The *Aqua Alsietina*, brought to Rome by Augustus. The *Anio Novus* was conveyed to the city by the Claudian

Aqueduct, the ruins of which, in the Campagna, are very remarkable. It is still used to convey water to the city, although the old conduit—which was for a long way at a great height from the ground—is not now available. This aqueduct—*Aqua Claudia*—was commenced by Caligula, and finished by Claudius, and conveyed the water from Subiaco, forty miles from Rome. The *Aqua Sabatina*, brought from Lake Sabatino, now Bracciano, by the Emperor Trajan, but the aqueduct having become useless, Pope Paul V. repaired it, and constructed a splendid fountain—la Fontana Paolina—on the Janiculum, to receive and distribute its waters. I need not enumerate all the other fountains of the city, but will mention some of the most remarkable. The matchless fountains of the Piazza San Pietro have been previously spoken of; then there are the fountains of Trevi, of Moses, of the Piazza del Popolo, Piazza Colonna, and of the Piazza Navona. Every palace, or considerable building, has one or more fountains.

CHAPTER XXIV.

THE KIRCHERIAN MUSEUM—CHURCHES OF S. MARIA IN TRASTEVERE, SAN PIETRO IN MONTORIO, AND THE GESU —CAMPO SANTO AND TOMB OF JULIAN WATTS-RUSSELL.

ON one of our visits to the Roman College we saw the Observatory there, which is very interesting to lovers of astronomy. The telescopes are of great magnifying power. We much admired the mechanism of Padre Secchi's beautiful machine. The Observatory was under the entire control of this Father, whose authority as an astronomer is one of the highest in Europe.

The Kircherian Museum contains very many objects of interest to the antiquarian; amongst them are a large number of Etruscan remains, such as coins, medals, rude figures in bronze; there is also a caricature of an early Christian, which calls for the attention of every one who visits this museum, as showing what was the practice of the early Church respecting the crucifix and other holy images. The caricature consists of the figure of a man with an ass's head, nailed to a cross; underneath is the kneeling Christian engaged in prayer. There is an inscription scratched in the mortar in Greek characters—" Alexamenos adoring his God." There can be no doubt but that this was really done by a Pagan, in derision of the Christian religion. It was taken from one of the rooms of the Palace of the Cæsars, and was found cut in the mortar, which has been removed to the Museum. It may be supposed to have been scratched by a Pagan domestic of the palace, in order to deride his Christian fellow-servant.

The church of Santa Maria, in Trastevere, is built on the site of the *Taberna Mercatoria*, whence sprung up, at the birth of Christ, a miraculous fountain of oil, of so great power, that it flowed hence to the Tiber. The identical spot is shown in the church, and over it is inscribed "Fons olei," and on the right, "Hinc oleum fluxit, cum Christus Virgine luxit."* This fact, well authenticated by the Pagan historians of the time, is mentioned by later writers.†

In 224, Pope St. Calixtus erected a small church here, which was the first in Rome dedicated under the invocation of Our Blessed Lady. The present is a fine old church, surmounted by a "campanile" of the time of Innocent II., who reigned about the middle of the twelfth century. The portico, sustained by four granite pillars, was added under Clement XI., and the beautiful mosaics adorning it have just been restored (April, 1870). The church is at present undergoing restoration, and when it is completed, it will be very beautiful. The picture of the Madonna, in one of the chapels, is an admirable one, but it is not always exposed to public view.

San Pietro in Montorio is built near where St. Peter was crucified. A circular chapel, built over the identical spot, was erected by Ferdinand IV., King of Spain, and is situated in the cloister of the convent adjoining. In the church are the tombs of two Irish chieftains, the brave O'Neil and O'Donnell. The newly constructed carriage-way is due, I have heard, to the exertions of Cardinal Cullen.

On the raised plateau in front of the church, a fine view of Rome can be obtained, and very many times have I enjoyed it, and counted up with a comrade the different edifices of the ancient and the modern city. Extending our view, we rejoiced in the sight of the grand scenery beyond and around Rome, including the Campagna, the Alban Hills, the Sabines, and the distant Apennines, as well as Monte Soracte, Monte Rotondo, and the Tolfa.

---

* "Hence flowed the fountain of oil, when Christ was born of a virgin."

† The fact of the issue of the *fountain of oil* at the birth of Christ, is related by Osorius, lib. 6, cap. 19; by Eusebius, in his Chronicle; by Paul the Deacon, and on their authority by Baronius. These citations are taken from Cornelius a Lapide.

The Corsini picture gallery is considered to contain one of the finest collections in Rome. For my own part, I must say, I wish I had been able to spend more time in admiring and examining the masterpieces there to be seen. If I recollect rightly, the original Madonna of Carlo Dolce, which is a great favourite of mine, is in this collection; but, as we paid it only one rapid visit, memory fails me in particulars —I only recollect that I was very pleased with the whole.

The church of the Gesù, having been a great favourite of the Zouaves, demands a few words from me.

The high altar is of marble, which is so arranged and joined as to form a design. The tabernacle is a very fine one, and above is a beautiful painting, representing the Circumcision of Our Lord, and His receiving the Holy Name of Jesus. On each side of the altar are two columns of *giallo antico* marble. On the left is the altar of St. Ignatius, under which reposes the body of the Saint, while above it is a statue representing him. Formerly the statue was of silver, but the present one is of metal, the chasuble worn by the Saint being silver. The four columns are ornamented with lapis-lazuli and gilt bronze. In the middle of the pediment is a group of white marble, representing the Holy Trinity. The globe of lapis-lazuli, which the Eternal Father holds in His hand, is considered the finest and largest piece known. The inside of the tabernacle is also ornamented with precious stones, the outside being quite plain. To see this altar in all its glory, it should be visited on the festival of the Saint, when the altar is radiant with lights and candelabras.

On the same side is the chapel of the Blessed Virgin, which is quite a gem. On either side of the chapel are rich stores of relics, but these are not usually exposed, but are concealed by panels, on which are painted with exquisite taste different scenes in the life of Our Blessed Lady. The altar and balustrade are formed of rich marbles of beautiful colours, and above is the painting of "La Madonna della Strada," before which St. Ignatius often prayed. Opposite the altar of St. Ignatius is that of St. Francis Xavier, whose incorrupt arm is there kept in a rich shrine of gold—that arm which was raised to bless, to baptize, and was instrumental in the conversion to the Christian Faith of so many hundreds of thousands of souls in India, China, and Japan. The altar is very beautifully gilt, and above it is a picture representing some incident in the life of the Saint. This church, when illuminated, presents a magnificent appearance, and all its arrangements are as perfect as possible. Great numbers of persons here approach to Holy Communion every Sunday, and even every day of the week.

The Fathers of the Society of Jesus, so much calumniated and persecuted, may be considered as the *advanced guard* of the Church, both because they are always singled out by her enemies for the first attack,* and on account of the great services they have rendered and are rendering at the present moment to the cause of religion, science, and learning. In Rome at present (April, 1870) the first preachers, the most crowded churches and schools belong to their Order. And who can ever forget their services as missionaries in every country, the hundreds of thousands of American Indians they converted at the peril of their lives, and their models of primitive Christian life, the reductions of Paraguay and Uruguay, interrupted, alas! only by the cupidity and infidelity of so-called Christians. To the Zouaves they have ever shown themselves most obliging, affable, and self-sacrificing.

The *Campo Santo*, or principal cemetery of Rome, is situated near the Basilica of San Lorenzo, outside the walls; at one point are seen the remains of an ancient Catacomb. The general plan of the cemetery is different to any I have before seen, but the raised portion near the Basilica is arranged with the greatest taste, and here may be seen very many beautiful monuments of rich marble. The Zouave will be interested to examine the tomb of Julian Watts-Russell—on his right as he ascends to this portion—on

---

* The Communists directed their mad fury especially against them, as shown by the number of Jesuits shot or imprisoned during the last siege of Paris.

which there is the following beautiful inscription, composed by Father Cardella :—

> "HEIC AD MARTYRUM CRYPTAS
> DORMIT IN PACE
> JULIANUS WATTS-RUSSELL MICHAELIS F.
> ANGLUS CLARO GENERE
> PRO PETRI SEDE STRENUE DIMICANS
> IN ACIE AD NOMENTUM OCCUBUIT
> III. NON. NOVEMB., AN. MDCCCLXVII.
> AN. N. XVII. MENS. X.
> ADOLESCENS CHRISTI MILES
> VIVE IN DEO."*

The tomb of this heroic champion of Holy Church is near to that of another of our countrymen, also a soldier—General Tylee—who died a holy death, as Father Cardella tells us, in the Eternal City in 1865. Giulio, as he was familiarly called, died on the field of victory; after a few years spent in innocence he gladly sacrificed his young life in the cause of justice and religion. He was the youngest victim of the battle-field, and he fell the nearest to Mentana; his comrades may well envy his happy fate, and be ready to offer up their lives in the same cause. He was first buried at Monte Rotondo, but his body was afterwards removed here; his memory is held in great veneration by those who knew him in the Zouaves, and before his entry into the corps.†

---

* "Here, near the Crypt of the Martyrs,
  Sleeps in peace
Julian Watts-Russell, the son of Michael,
 An Englishman of illustrious family,
Who fell, bravely fighting for the See of Peter,
  In the battle of Mentana,
  The 3rd of November, 1867,
  Aged 17 years and 10 months.
  O! youthful soldier of Christ!
  Live in God."

† His biography has been written by Father Cardella in Italian, and translated into English by the Rev. W. Tylee, B.A. (J. Philp, Orchard Street). I would strongly advise all those who are interested in the Zouaves to read it, especially as it is short and inexpensive.

TOMB OF JULIAN WATTS-RUSSELL.

.... Beneath this tomb
In peace, a youthful martyr lies;
To justice, right, religion, faith,
A pure and noble sacrifice.

Britannia's son, of gentle race,
Her children claim thee as a prize
Of victory, and love, and grace:
To win the brightest crown he dies—
Unconquer'd soul! aloft arise!

When we last visited the Campo Santo, the fine monument to those who fell at Mentana was in course of erection; on the panels of the base, which is of considerable size, are to be inscribed the names of all those who fell in the campaign. Above the base there is a pedestal, on which is to be placed a colossal statue of St. Peter, in the act of presenting to a crusader the standard of Holy Church and the sword, with those words heard of old in the vision of Judas Maccabeus:—" Accipe sanctum gladium munus a Deo, in quo dejicies adversarios populi mei Israel."* This beautiful design is said to have been suggested by the Holy Father himself, and it is a proof of the high estimation in which he holds those who have shed their blood in defence of the just rights of the Apostolic See, as well as those who have fought in the same high cause.

Near the ancient Catacomb are some small chapels, erected to the memory of Lieutenant Arthur Guillemin, the brothers Dufournel, Captain de Vaux, and Lieutenant the Marquis de Quatrebarbes, all distinguished officers, who fell in the same engagement, bravely fighting in defence of the liberties of the Church.

The Basilica of San Lorenzo is of considerable antiquity, and dates from the reign of Constantine the Great, when it was erected over the tomb of the martyr St. Laurence, in the *Campus Veranus*. It is one of the fine patriarchal Basilicas of the city. The interior is adorned with numerous

---

* "Take this holy sword, a gift from God, wherewith thou shalt overthrow the adversaries of my people Israel." (2 Macc. xv. 16.)

pillars, which appear to be diminished in height by the present floor of the church, which in a manner cuts them in two. They are of different orders, and were probably removed here from some more ancient building. The bases of these columns are placed at the level of the subterranean church. Besides the body of the famous deacon and martyr St. Laurence, there are the relics of several other well-known martyrs underneath the high altar. In the tribune, or choir, is a stone seat, or throne, for the Pope. At the period of our visit the walls of the church were being painted in fresco by an artist of great merit; the exterior façade is also beautifully painted. These restorations, like so many other fine works completed under Pius IX., exhibit his love for the fine arts, and the encouragement he has accorded to men of genius and talent. In the vestibule are some curious ancient paintings. In front of the Basilica is a column, surmounted by a fine statue of St. Laurence, holding the gridiron, the instrument of his martyrdom, in his hand. San Lorenzo in "Paneperna" is built on the identical spot where the martyr suffered.

CHAPTER XXV.

REMARKS ON THE ANCIENT HISTORY OF PLACES VISITED NEAR ROME.

SOME notes on the ancient history of the interesting localities in the neighbourhood of Rome may not be unacceptable to the general reader.

It will be proper to commence with the vicinity of Albano, as the ancient city of Alba Longa, founded by Ascanius, the son of Æneas, the Trojan, was one of the earliest of the Latin cities. The Alban hills are situated to the south-east of Rome, and of them the present Monte Cavo is the highest point.

"Monte Cavo.—This central height of the Alban hills was the *Albanus Mons* of the ancients, and was once crowned with the temple of Jupiter Latiaris, in which the Latins held their congress. This summit commands a magnificent view of the Campagna. Hence Virgil represents Juno as watching from it the fight between the Trojans and the Latins :—

"' At Juno ex summo, qui nunc Albanus habetur,
Prospiciens tumulo, campum spectabat.'*— Æn. xii. 134."†

The modern town of Albano does not occupy the site of Alba Longa, which stood between the lake and the Alban Mount, and was the capital of the Latin cities; it was destroyed by Tullus Hostilius. Its position is now marked by the convent of Palazzolo, overlooking the lake. From various authors we learn that the celebrated Æneas escaped, with a considerable band of followers, from the destruction of

* But Juno from the summit of Mount Alba, looking down, beheld the field of battle.

† Bevan's "Ancient Geography," by Dr. Smith.

Troy, and after a long voyage and many adventures landed near the mouth of the Tiber—then known as the Albula—in the year B.C. 1182. Latinus, the son of Hercules, then reigned over a small territory in this part of Italy, and was at war with the Rutuli. At first he was inclined to treat Æneas and his followers—numbering about six hundred men—as enemies, and marched against him; but on approaching his camp, and seeing the masterly manner in which Æneas arrayed his small army, he thought it better to open negotiations with the Trojan warrior, whom he found only too ready to treat with him in an amicable spirit, and to become his faithful ally against the Rutuli. Latinus afterwards bestowed upon Æneas the hand of his daughter Lavinia, and the Trojan prince gave the name of Lavinium to the settlement or city which he founded.* The kingdom of Latium, which afterwards was of considerable extent, received its name from Latinus, and its inhabitants were then first called Latins,† for before the time of Latinus they had been known by the name *Aborigines*.‡

In a battle which afterwards ensued between the Rutuli —assisted by Turnus, the nephew of Latinus—and the king Latinus, the latter was killed, and Æneas succeeded to his dominions, and reigned four years. Ascanius succeeded his father Æneas, and founded Alba Longa, which he made the capital of the kingdom. It was from this line of kings that Romulus and Remus, the founders of Rome, descended, they being the grandsons of Numitor, the fifteenth king in succession from Æneas.

Tiberius, one of the successors of Æneas, having, in an engagement on the banks of the Albula, been forced into the river, carried away by the great strength of its current, and drowned, its name was changed to that of Tiber, which it has ever since retained.§

* Livy, lib. i., cap. 1.

† "Roman History," by N. Hooke, who follows Dionysius of Halicarnassus.

‡ Livy, lib. i., cap. 1.

§ *Tiberis flumen*, *i.e.*, the Tiber, takes its rise in the Apennines, flows south and then west. About two miles above Rome it joins the Anio—

LAGO DI ALBANO.—The ancient *Albanus Lacus*, six miles in circumference, and undoubtedly the crater of an extinct volcano. There being no natural outlet for the waters, an artificial emissary cut through the rock—still existing—was pierced B.C. 397, and conducts the waters to the Tiber by the Rivo Albano.*

LAGO DI NEMI, anciently the L. Nemorensis, and famed in antiquity for the sanctuary of Diana, *Nemus Dianæ*. The modern village owes its name to the lake.

The ancient Albans retained their independence until the reign of Tullus Hostilius, who ascended the throne as third king of Rome, B.C. 671.

"During his reign an open rupture took place between the Romans and the Albans. The armies of both nations soon took the field, and advancing against each other, met at a distance of five miles from Rome. Here, in order to avoid an unnecessary effusion of blood, it was agreed that instead of a general battle there should be a combat between three champions from each party, with the condition that the issue of this contest should decide the fate of the two armies.

"There were at this time in each army three brothers of great strength and valour, the Horatii and the Curiatii. According to the more common opinion held by ancient authors, and adopted by Livy, the Horatii belonged to the Roman, the Curiatii to the Alban side. On these devolved the honour of the important conflict. They advanced from their respective camps with equal resolution, and carrying within themselves, as the historian expresses it, the courage of two great armies.† As soon as the clashing of their

---

now Teverone—which also rises in the Apennines, near Treba, and at Tivoli forms a remarkable waterfall. The waters of the Anio are very pure, while those of the Tiber are thick and muddy, and liable to sudden risings. Horace says, "Vidimus *flavum Tiberim*," and Macaulay says, "yellow Tiber."—Bevan's "Ancient Geography."

* Bevan's "Ancient Geography."

† "Infestis armis, terni juvenes magnorum exercituum animos gerentes, concurrunt."—Livy, lib. i., cap. 25.

swords was heard, all the beholders were struck with awe, and awaited the result with breathless anxiety.

"Soon after this terrible onset the three Curiatii were wounded, but two of the Horatii fell dead. The Albans at this spectacle shouted for joy, whilst the Romans were dismayed, and trembled for the surviving brother, now surrounded by his opponents. Fortunately for him he was not wounded, and although unequal to the task of fighting the three together, was more than a match for them singly. To separate them he retreated, and as the Curiatii, unable to keep up with him, were soon at some distance from one another, he rushed upon the nearest and slew him on the spot, and successively dispatched the other two. Thus almost the same moment which had witnessed the despair of the Romans, saw them in the enjoyment of a complete victory, won by the prudence and intrepidity of their warrior."*

Victory having been thus declared for the Romans, the Albans professed their submission; but as they afterwards were guilty of perfidy, Tullus Hostilius put their general to death, razed the city of Alba, and transferred the inhabitants to Rome, where they became blended with the mass of the Roman population.

TUSCULUM, near Frascati, on a spur of the Alban hills, with its citadel on a lofty peak east of the town. Founded by Telegonus, son of Ulysses and Circe. People of Tusculum originally steadfast allies of Rome, except during the Latin war. Afterwards many Romans of fame had villas here. Cato, Mæcenas, and Cicero, whose Tusculan Disputations were here composed at his villa, now the villa Rufinella. There are remains of walls, piscina, and two theatres yet to be seen. The town was destroyed in the middle ages, and its inhabitants rebuilt their dwellings lower down the hill, and founded the modern town of Frascati.†

The *Volsci* spread over the greater part of the southern district of Latium, from the sea-coast to the borders of Sam-

---

* Fredet's "Ancient History."
† Bevan's "Ancient Geography." By Dr. Smith.

nium, now Abruzzo; they thus held the Pontine Marshes, the Volscian Hills—now Monte Lupino, Monte Cacume, &c., —and the valley of the Liris, now the river Garigliano. As we were quartered with our company at Ceccano, and this town is situated in the territory of the ancient Volsci, we were able to cross the mountains—the Volscians—and enjoy the beautiful scenery of hill and dell in their vicinity. This has been mentioned in the trip from Ceccano to Piperno in the first year of my Zouave life. Anxur—now Terracina —was the capital of the Volsci.

VIA APPIA, the great southern road of Italy, issued from Rome by the *Porta Capena*, along with the *Via Latina*, and took a direct line for Terracina, thence to Formiæ, and by sea-coast to Sinuessa, and thence inland to Capua, Beneventum, and Brundusium—now Brindisi—constructed as far as Capua in B.C. 312, by the Censor, Appius Claudius.*

VIA CASSIA ran from Rome through the heart of Etruria, by Sutrium and Clusium, to Arretium, and thence by Florentia, across the Apennines.

ETRURIA, ancient boundaries, N. the Apennines; E. and South-east the Tiber; W. the Tyrrhenian Sea; it included the Maremma. In the south-east district were extinct volcanoes, which have now become lakes; some portions are fertile; harbours along the coast deficient. The mountains included Argentarius, now Argentaro, a promontory on the coast; Soracte, now Monte S. Oreste; and Ciminus Mons, now Monte Cimino, forming the northern boundary of the great plain of the Campagna.†

This ancient state was divided into twelve cantons, or Lucumonies, which were subject to twelve heads, who governed with a sort of sovereign authority. "The names of the twelve capital cities of the Lucumonies were, according to Cluverius and Holstius: Clusium, Perusia, Cortona,

* The numerous lamps around the shrine of St. Peter are kept burning with oil of olives, grown on a piece of land, which is said to have been given by A. Claudius for the purpose of keeping his road in repair, but since given to the Basilica of St. Peter, for the purpose of keeping the lights burning around the tomb of the Apostle.

† Bevan's "Ancient Geography." By Dr. Smith.

Arretium, Volaterra, Vetulonium, Rusellæ, Tarquinii, Volsinii, Caere, Falerii, and Veii. Etruria was long the mother of all the learning and politeness of the Romans; they sent their children thither to cultivate their minds, till the conquest of Greece furnished them with a better school."*

These twelve cantons sometimes united together for the common defence of the mother country; they were first reduced to obedience to the Roman power by Lucius Tarquin, fifth king of Rome, he being himself an Etruscan by birth, but a Greek by descent. They were, however, as yet by no means a conquered people, for we find them often engaged in war with the Romans during the next three hundred years, until they were finally subjugated about B.C. 280.

The localities and sites of the ancient Etruscan cities, visited by myself and comrades of the Zouaves, comprise those which were nearest to Rome, *i.e.* in the Pontifical States. I will commence with CORNETO; near it, further inland, on the river Marta, stood *Tarquinii*, the oldest Etruscan city, now called *Turchina*. There are many existing remains.

Tarquinii was the birthplace of Lucumo Damaratus, who afterwards took the name of Lucius Tarquin from his native city, settled in Rome, and became its fifth king, B.C. 614.

BOLSENA, formerly *Volsinii*, on the shore of Lacus Volsinii. The Etruscan town was on the hill, the Roman on the plain, near the lake. The old town destroyed by Romans, B.C. 280. Volsinii was the birthplace of Sejanus, the favourite of Tiberius.†

FALERII, now *Civita Castellana*. The Roman town of the former name stood nearer to Monte Soracte.

VEII stood twelve miles from Rome, at Isola Farnese. In the year B.C. 396 Veii had been besieged unsuccessfully during nine years by the Romans. "Ultimate success might have proved hopeless, had not Furius Camillus been appointed to the supreme office of dictator. This illustrious

---

* See Foot-note in "Roman History." By N. Hooke, Esq. Page 52. Edition of 1825.

† Bevan's "Ancient Geography." By Dr. Smith.

Roman was distinguished alike for his valour, his skill, and the experience which he had acquired in inferior employments. As soon as he assumed the command of the troops, he revived courage and discipline amongst them, increased the fortifications of their camp, defeated the allies of the Veientes, and pressed the siege of Veii more than ever. Still, as he perceived the great difficulty of taking so strong a city by storm, he caused a mine to be dug by his troops, extending from the Roman camp to the enemy's citadel. When it was completed, he ordered a general assault on the place. Whilst the Veientes, not aware of their real danger, ran to the different parts of the wall in order to repel the assailants, a body of choice soldiers entered, by order of Camillus, the subterranean passage, penetrated into the citadel, and thence spread through the city. Some attacked the garrison from behind, some began to fire the houses, whilst others hastened to open the gates of the town to their fellow soldiers. In a few moments this mighty capital was entirely in the hands of the Romans. The quantity of spoils which they found in it was beyond description, and the dictator, loaded with glory, enjoyed triumphal honours suitable to the importance of his conquest."*

Falerii was besieged two years later by the same Camillus. " Here he effected by his justice and generosity what he had effected at Veii by his prudence and valour. One day a schoolmaster, who had under his charge the children of all the chief families of Falerii, led them, under pretence of exercise, to a certain distance from the city, and betrayed them into the hands of the Roman general. Camillus, fired with indignation at this base conduct, exclaimed :—' Have we, then, taken up arms against children, whom we spare even in the storming of cities, and not rather against men, who have provoked our resentment, and who, moreover, can defend themselves ? God forbid that I should avail myself of this base offer of a traitor, to conquer the Falisci !' Having said this, he dismissed the perfidious master, and obliged him to return to the town, with his hands tied

* Dr. Fredet—" Ancient History."

behind him, and under the incessant lashes of his young pupils. This act of humanity and justice so moved the Falisci, that they no longer hesitated to surrender to so generous an enemy."*

AGYLLA, or CAERE, now *Cervetri*, was founded by the Pelasgi, but conquered by the Etruscans; it is mentioned by Herodotus; in B.C. 353 it received the right of Roman citizenship. This site must attract the very highest interest of all students and lovers of antiquity.

CENTUM CELLÆ, now *Civita Vecchia*, owes its magnificent port to Trajan.

SUTRIUM, now *Sutri*, was the scene of a Roman victory over the Etruscans, B.C. 311, gained by the consul, Q. Fabius. "Fabius marched against the Etruscans, and defeated them near Sutrium. The runaways took refuge in the Ciminian forest, a forest, says Livy, more impassable and dreadful than those of Germany, and through which not even a single merchant had ever yet made his way. Fabius was almost the only man in the army who had the boldness to think of entering into it. They were afraid of finding Caudine Forks in Etruria. The general had with him at this time a near relation, named Cœso Fabius, who had been educated at Cære, in Etruria, and spoke the language of the country perfectly well. Cœso undertook to examine the forest, and the places about it. He was accompanied in this enterprise by only one servant, who, having been brought up with him, was also well acquainted with the Tuscan language. They were clad in the habit of shepherds, bearing each a cleaving bill and two javelins, after the manner of the peasants. But neither their dress, their arms, nor their familiar use of the language was so good a security to them against a discovery, as the general notion that no stranger would dare to enter that forest. In this disguise they are said to have travelled as far as Camerinum, in Umbria (two days' journey)."† We learn further, that upon Cœso returning and delivering his report, Fabius

* Dr. Fredet—" Ancient History."
† "Roman History." By N. Hooke.

immediately prepared to enter the forest with his army, and after amusing the Etruscans by a skirmish outside the woods, retired to his camp, and then marched off early next morning, and joined before nightfall the main body of his army, which was already penetrating the dense and hitherto impassable forest. The next morning he reached the top of Mons Ciminus, which was on the farther side of the forest, and gave the name to it. On this mountain he beheld the fertile plains of Etruria, to the conquest of which he had now prepared the way, by passing the impenetrable woods, which had hitherto been its security on this side. Fabius now returned to Sutrium, and the Etruscans immediately prepared to attack him.

Fabius, to deceive the enemy, still pretended fear, and kept close within his intrenchments; but he bade his men refresh themselves, and be ready for action at the first signal. To raise their courage he made a short harangue to them, extolling to a high degree the exploits of the Roman arms in Samnium, and assuring them that the Etruscans were not soldiers comparable to the Samnites for strength or courage. About the fourth watch of the night he drew up his army in order of battle, within the intrenchments of the camp, caused the rampart to be levelled, and the ditch to be filled, and then marched out, and surprised the enemy while half asleep, and lying scattered over the plain. Of the Etruscans 60,000 men were slain, or taken prisoners. Their camp was seized and plundered. Three of the most considerable lucumonies after this overthrow sent deputies to Rome to sue for peace; they obtained a truce for thirty years.*

This same Fabius afterwards obtained another signal victory over this people at Lake *Vadimonius*—which has now disappeared;—it was near Viterbo, the north-east of the Via Cassia. It was in the year B.C. 309 that this battle—contested obstinately by the Etruscans, who had chosen each other for the service,† or bound themselves to conquer or to die—was gained by the Romans, and the whole army of the Etruscans put to flight.

* "Roman History." By N. Hooke, Esq.
† Livy, lib. ix., cap. 39.

It should have been mentioned before that Sutrium was the scene of one of the exploits of the celebrated F. Camillus. This town was in alliance with Rome about 388 B.C., when it was attacked by the Etruscans. Camillus, by order of the Senate, marched to its relief, but before his arrival the city had capitulated to the enemy, and the inhabitants had obtained only their lives and the clothes on their backs. In this destitute condition they were going to seek new habitations, when Camillus met them, bade the women dry up their tears, and promised to transfer their sorrows to the enemy. This promise he performed, for the Etruscans, secure after their victory, and wholly employed in plundering, had left the gates of Sutrium open, and without guards. He came upon them by surprise, slew many, and made an incredible number of prisoners. The Sutrini before night found themselves again in possession of their city, which had been thus taken twice in one day.*

NEPETI, now *Nepi*, became an ally of Rome, B.C. 386. This city, together with Sutrium, on the frontier of Etruria, formed two bulwarks of Rome, and the keys of the former country. Nepeti, having surrendered voluntarily to the Etruscans, was taken by assault by Camillus.†

TUSCANIA, on the river Marta, now *Tuscanella*, was formerly a city of Etruria. On a good map in my possession an ancient Etruscan cemetery is marked out as being in the neighbourhood of Tuscanella, in the direction of Viterbo, and near some of the numerous rivulets which rise in the vicinity, and afterwards run into the Marta.

In one of our trips here mentioned, *i.e.* from this place to Montefiascone, we must have passed near to this cemetery, but as we were ignorant of its existence, we had not the good fortune to visit it.

* "Roman History," by N. Hooke, Esq., page 293.
† *Idem.*

CHAPTER XXVI.

RETURN TO ENGLAND—VOYAGE—MARSEILLES—PARIS—
BOULOGNE—LONDON, ETC.

April 28th, 1870.—AT half-past ten a.m. I left the Eternal City, accompanied by Messrs. R——, Johnson, Raymond, Thomas, and about fifty other Zouaves going home, either on *congé*, or on permission for a limited period.

Mr. Johnson and I regretted very much leaving the holy city of Rome, endeared to us by so many associations, the many kind friends we had left behind, and the beautiful clear skies and fine country of Italy. For myself, I have never yet experienced so many feelings of regret in quitting any other place, not excepting my own home; nevertheless, I console myself with the hope of seeing it again, for as I looked on the scenes I have loved so much, and on St. Peter's, St. John Lateran, Santa Maria Maggiore, I could not bring myself to believe that it was for the *last* time; but the presentiment came that I should behold them again. I may be deceived, for the human mind is often betrayed into illusions; this was, then, my idea of bidding them adieu, and it has often returned.

After waiting a long time at Civita Vecchia, we embarked at last on board the "*Pausilippe*," of the *Messageries Imperiales* line. The weather was such as we are accustomed to in England, the sky overcast, the clouds giving a leaden, muddy appearance to the atmosphere, the wind cold and threatening, everything betokening a stormy passage. On reaching the open sea we found it very agitated, and a very fresh breeze blowing; several on board were taken with sea-sickness. As we proceeded on our voyage the weather became worse. During the night the wind increased to a gale, which continued till the next morning. About seven a.m. one of the paddle-wheels became damaged, and steam had to be shut off to repair it. After a delay of about an hour this was repaired, and we started again; the wind had now calmed somewhat, and there was no further cause for apprehension. We, who were not ill, enjoyed the second day's voyage, but we had passed through a rough night, and R—— and I had remained on deck, although it was raining hard, but I was wrapped up in two blankets. R—— went down below at five in the morning, as he was quite wet through. Raymond and Thomas, more fortunate than we, had managed to secure two berths in the cabin, and they were able to get some sleep when the wind moderated in the morning.

The second day we made better progress on our voyage, although the wind blew quite fresh, and the sky was generally overcast. In the afternoon we enjoyed the passage across the blue Mediterranean, and the view of the coast of France we were approaching. The Maritime Alps, and the port of Toulon, the rocky height of Notre Dame de la Garde, and the port of Marseilles are all striking features which help to produce the beautiful scenery of these coasts; if these, too, be combined with the sea, calm and tinted with its deepest azure hues, a scene of loveliness is produced, which I suppose cannot be surpassed on any other sea-coast in the world. I have looked on many pictures representing the Mediterranean, and wondered whether they were not exaggerated; in my opinion they were not, for I must own that the reality well bears out the representation, and there can be no doubt that this sea far surpasses in beauty the Atlantic, as seen at least from the British Isles.

We arrived safely in port at four a.m., April 30th, having been thirty-eight hours at sea. I should have noticed before the fact that our dashing Lieut.-Colonel de Charette—since famous for his exploits during the Franco-German War, for which he has been raised to the rank of General—accompanied us on our voyage. I believe he was returning to France on leave of absence for a short period.

At daybreak we went on shore. R—— accompanied me to the Sanctuary of Notre Dame de la Garde, where we did not forget to return thanks to God and Our Blessed Lady for our safe voyage so far.

On the rock on which this Sanctuary is situated we admired the position of Marseilles, placed as it is between the mountains and the sea—the lovely blue Mediterranean, with its rocky isles emerging boldly from its depths, one at least of which, were it gifted with speech, could tell its stirring tale of other days now numbered with the past. This scene is varied by vessels, large and small, and by the fine ports of the city, crowded by the masts of ships of every kind.

This Sanctuary of Our Blessed Lady is one of the most famous in France. The church is a fine one, of a peculiar style, resembling the Moorish. The whole of it is not yet completed; the Emperor and Empress are amongst the contributors to its erection. The high altar and sanctuary are adorned with very good taste, and a great number of lights and *ex-voto* offerings show forth the devotion of its numerous pilgrims. On the *fête* of the church the numbers who take part in the pilgrimage and procession are very great, amounting sometimes, if I remember rightly, to 150,000.

The cemetery of Marseilles is laid out with great taste, and it was a great pleasure to me to be able to visit it, and to observe the great respect paid to the memory of the departed here and elsewhere in France.

The foundation of the city and port of Marseilles dates from a very remote period. *Massilia* was once inhabited by a colony of Phœnicians, and is mentioned in the ancient history of Rome.

We left this city in order to continue our journey before mid-day. Now we were *en route* for Paris, and we remarked on our way that the fruit-trees of the south of France were more advanced than in the neighbourhood of Rome, but that the corn was later. The climate of the south of France is very warm, and the air very clear. On passing Marseilles for the first time, on my way to Rome, in the beginning of the month of March, I found many visitors to the gardens of that city sitting out-of-doors and enjoying the warm genial air of early spring, an enjoyment that we in England would hardly venture to indulge in before the month of June.

We remarked, *en passant*, the great skill of the French in the matter of pruning and the cultivation of their fruit-trees, the gardens and fields exhibiting trees without a bit of superfluous wood, but yet of the greatest vigour, health, and regularity. The scenery of the south of France, as seen from the Paris, Lyons, and Mediterranean Railway, following the valley of the Rhone from Arles and Avignon to Lyons, includes in some places a view of the distant Alps, and is in reality very fine, but cannot be compared in grandeur to that of Italy; and we felt it could not compensate to us for the loved scenes we had left behind in Rome and its States. From Lyons to Dijon the railway follows the valley of the Saône, a tributary of the Rhone, and afterwards enters that of the Yonne, which it keeps until the latter falls into the Seine near Fontainebleau. At Avignon is seen the palace which belonged to the Popes till 1790. On our way we amused ourselves together as well as we could, and, as night came on, we tried the experiment of standing up together at the door of the carriage at the different stations, so as to let the passengers on the platform believe, if they liked, that our compartment was full; by this means we managed to get some sleep between the stoppages—about every two hours. We were often not more than four together in one compartment.

The next day I questioned some inhabitants of the provinces as to their feelings regarding the elections, which were coming off in about a week; not one of them had the least sympathy for the "*Irreconcilables*," or "*Reds*," who were then trying to make so much noise in Paris. We arrived in Paris about five p.m., having travelled thirty hours without any considerable intermission.

During our stay of two days in Paris we had an opportunity of admiring the fine Boulevards of the city. These consist of wide streets, ornamented with a row of trees on each side; the centre is a perfectly macadamized road, kept in beautiful order by dint of constant rolling and grinding the broken stones, watering to lay the dust, and scraping to remove the mud. This centre is wide enough to allow an enormous traffic to be carried on over it without any confusion or hindrance, such as arises sometimes in other cities from the narrowness of the ancient streets. It is bounded on either side by trees in the greatest health and vigour; and then we must not forget the wide pavements, which afford the same facilities to foot-passengers as the central road does to the vehicles. The omnibus traffic is so arranged that, by taking a *correspondance* ticket, costing about six sous, one can travel from one part of the city to any other, without inconvenience further than that of perhaps changing "'bus," and waiting a few minutes till one's own district "'bus" arrives; add to this that the different lines are furnished with horses—grey, black, bay—one colour peculiar to one district, another to a second, &c.; thus every possible facility is afforded to locomotion of all kinds. The trees are, I think, also a great improvement to any city, not only as an ornament, but also because they contribute to healthiness by consuming large quantities of carbonic acid gas, and evolving oxygen.

We went to the Louvre, with the intention of visiting its galleries, but it was unfortunately Monday, and we were told that they were always closed to the public on that day.

On walking through the precincts of the Louvre, we could not help being struck by a feeling of familiarity with the statues which are there seen adorning the quadrangles; and it was no wonder, for these were copies of the ancient models we had admired in Rome.

We prepared to leave Paris for Boulogne the next day, but we missed our train, and thus we were obliged to defer our departure till night. This delay turned out an advantage to us, for it gave us the opportunity of seeing Paris from the best possible point of view, *i.e.*, the *Arc de Triomphe*. This triumphal arch, beautifully executed, and designed after the Arch of Constantine in Rome, is a very fine work; it represents all the victories of the First Napoleon, and is ornamented with numerous figures in relievo. Its position being on a slight eminence, to the centre of which converge ten different streets, it forms an interesting object, viewed either from the gardens of the Palace of the Tuileries, La Place de la Concorde, the Champs Elysées—all of which are in a direct line leading up to it—or from the Avenue de l'Impératrice, which is on the opposite side, the entrance to the Bois de Boulogne. During our stay we also visited La Madeleine, which possesses a fine classic exterior, ornamented with a forest of pillars; Notre Dame des Victoires, a very remarkable sanctuary of Our Blessed Lady, adorned with innumerable votive offerings, in thanksgiving for favours received; La Bourse, remarkable for the intense animation there to be seen displayed in the transaction of business.

On our way from Paris we passed Amiens, where there is a splendid old Gothic cathedral; its age and style is of the lancet period, in process of transition to the decorated. The cathedral itself is a perfect building in one style, or period, of Gothic; of the altars I admired that of the parish, the one given by the Empress—these both possess Gothic decorations and canopies—and the altar of the Blessed Sacrament. If I am not mistaken, there was also a fine statue here of a weeping angel.

Boulogne comprises three distinct towns, viz., La Haute Ville, or upper town, within the ramparts, of considerable antiquity; La Basse Ville, or lower town; and St. Pierre, on the cliffs, where dwell the fishermen, who are almost a distinct race from the other inhabitants. Boulogne is famous as a watering-place, and it is the resort and residence of numbers of English visitors. It possesses a fine sandy beach, and its environs are very pretty and interesting; it is also noted for its educational establishments.

I visited Boulogne for the first time in 1865, and the fine cathedral was not then completed. Up till this time I must confess to a certain amount of prejudice against the suitability of the classic style for churches or cathedrals; there was, however, quite sufficient to be seen in Notre Dame de Boulogne to claim my admiration, and to induce me to change somewhat my opinion. Notre Dame is of the classic, or what may be more properly called the Italian style; it is surmounted by a fine lofty dome, about three hundred feet high, and this is always a most conspicuous object on approaching Boulogne, either by sea or land. The paintings are well executed by Paul Delacroix, and form one great attraction of the cathedral; the roof of the nave and transepts is semi-circular, and it is enriched with these paintings, which, whether viewed through the circular openings in the ceiling—which almost give the idea of every painting being enclosed in a separate dome—or viewed in a body from one point, have a beautiful effect. I was much struck with the great reverberation of sound which this cathedral possessed at the period of my first visit; this I imagine to be a good point in so large a building.

In the choir, over the high altar, is a statue of Notre Dame de Boulogne, or, our Lady of Boulogne, in a boat, and around, the choir is enriched with the votive offerings of the fishermen of St. Pierre, who are very devout to our Lady. Under the cathedral is a very large ancient crypt, which possesses fine groined arches, ancient inscriptions, and some very old paintings of the Evangelists and Apostles. One portion is fitted up as a Calvary, and lighted with a reflected crimson light; another as a chapel of Our Lady, with a blue light. This arrangement was most effective and beautiful.

I give the following tradition of Notre Dame de Boulogne, without vouching for its authenticity in every particular. About A.D. 620 a statue of our Lady in a boat without pilot or rowers, arrived at Boulogne. The people flocked to the shore to see the prodigy, and carried the statue with great respect to the cathedral church, where it was held in high veneration until the sacking of the building by Henry VIII., King of England, when the statue was cast into the fire, but refused to burn. It was, however, destroyed at that period of sacrilegious desecration, the Revolution of 1793.

I visited at the same time the church of St. Francis of Sales, and the chapel of Notre Dame du Saint Sang, both of which are the works of Messrs. H. and C. Hansom. The former is a pretty building in the Romanesque style, and the latter is a small but beautiful Gothic structure. The traditions of the chapel are of great antiquity, and we learn from an inscription on the wall that the foundation of the original structure is assigned to St. Victorique in the year 280, that in it the Gospel was preached to the Boulonnais, and that about the year 1100 the *Relique du Saint Sang de Notre Sauveur Jésus Christ* was brought from Jerusalem to St. Ide by Godefroi de Bouillon.

La Haute Ville contains La Place Godefroi de Bouillon, in which is seen the remains of the palace of the Counts of Boulogne, consisting of a belfry, formerly the keep of the castle.

A pleasant walk brings one to the statue of Napoleon I., which is erected on the spot where this Emperor pitched his tent during the time he encamped his army here previous to his intended invasion of England. From these heights Napoleon I. beheld the white cliffs of that Albion he was destined never to conquer. But the third Napoleon showed more wisdom in recognising that the true interests of France and England counsel them to alliance instead of enmity. This statue is situated between the Tour d'Odre—a relic of antiquity—and a Calvary, due probably to the piety of the fishermen, for it is here, as in so many other places in the north of France, a striking object on approaching the port from the sea.

On this particular visit of ours to Boulogne we enjoyed a very pleasant walk to the column of Napoleon I., situated at some little distance from the town. We also were most kindly received by a gentleman on whom we called. He and his good lady felt the most lively interest in the corps of the Zouaves, as their son was thinking of joining it.

After spending a most agreeable day—we must not forget another visit which we paid to a lady, a relative of one of our intimate Zouave friends, who was very pleased to hear of him—we went down to the London Bridge steamboat, and secured our berths. The sea was very calm, so that we were able to sleep very comfortably till the early morning, when on going on deck we found ourselves amongst the fogs and mists for which the river Thames and shores of England are so much noted. As the day dawned the scene did not much improve. It was indeed a dull, heavy, dreary welcome this to our native country after more than two years' absence in bright, sunny Italy. Who could not but feel some regret in exchanging the bright sunshine and clear air of that favoured clime for the heavy, oppressive atmosphere of the Thames, which weighed on our souls with the effect of lead?

Both days we were in London the weather exhibited the same dull, misty features, and it was only on leaving the metropolis and emerging into the open country by the Great Western railway, that I experienced some sense of relief from the oppressiveness and fog which characterised the atmosphere of London.

Although the climate of England has many objectionable features, yet its homes are generally prepared to give one a hearty welcome, and it was with great pleasure that I entered my home, and was united once more to my family and friends.

Nothing very remarkable happened in relation to our corps after my return till about the time of the sudden breaking out of war between France and Germany. At that time Sergeant Shee, of the Zouaves, had been spending some few days with me, he being then on leave of absence from Rome. I well remember accompanying him to the Swindon Station on a Monday in July, for it was then we both first learnt the news of the declaration of war by France. This news occasioned us some very deep reflections, for we both at once saw the possibility of another raid upon Rome. I felt some regret at being absent at this critical period; but still I was inclined to hope that France would continue her protection to the Holy Father, and would not abandon him at this juncture to his enemies. The event unfortunately proved otherwise. Sergeant Shee returned to his post in the Eternal City immediately there was the slightest appearance of danger.

In this same month a great friend of mine wrote from Montefiascone, telling me that the revolutionaries had crossed the Pontifical frontier, but they were immediately dispersed through the prompt measures taken by the Papal and Italian troops, Captain D'Arcy's company on this occasion acting as a "flying column." The company to which my friend belonged kept their *sacs* made up for ten days, and were employed in patrol duty on the frontier. Carrigan, he says, has distinguished himself in taking a brigand chief. Carrigan and a gendarme were the first to go upstairs into the room to arrest this chief. Two of the least Zouaves one could find (an Englishman named Dew being one) were fired upon by four brigands one dark night, between Bassano and Sutri. The first shot from a Zouave rifle brought one of the brigands to the ground. These two small Zouaves received silver medals for their bravery in taking these brigands, as also did Carrigan. The friend who furnished me with the above particulars has always been most devoted in his attachment to the Holy Father and his sacred cause. His sentiments will be seen by this extract from his letter to me—

"I had thought of coming to England, but being so well off here, having a good chance of being in for the first "*coup de fusil*," and being so near the frontier I told Mr. —— that I had made up my mind to stop; otherwise I had thought of starting to England with him."

He also informed me that the French troops had left Civita Vecchia, so that the Holy Father had now only to depend on the fidelity of his own little army in case of attack.

Both in this letter, and in one he wrote to me on August 29th, he urged me most strongly to return to the Zouaves at the hour of danger, for they were (at Montefiascone) prepared for any emergency, and might be attacked any moment by the Italians, who were massing on the frontier. "Who knows," he says, "now the troops are on the frontier again, but we may be fighting before the week is out?" Such an appeal could not but produce a response in the heart of a friend and comrade.

CHAPTER XXVII.

THE ZOUAVES AT MONTEFIASCONE.—THE MASTERLY RETREAT OF LIEUT.-COLONEL DE CHARETTE.

THE friend before mentioned has kindly furnished me with the following graphic narrative.

On the evening of August 19th intelligence was received by the officers of the Zouaves in Montefiascone that an attack was intended by the Italians that night or early the next morning. Two companies of the fourth battalion were then in garrison at Montefiascone, under Captains D'Arcy and de Messeliere. The commandant and superior officers of the battalion had their quarters in the town. On receiving the aforesaid intelligence all necessary preparations were made, the officers of the companies passing the night in the barracks, while, as usual, scouting parties were sent out to watch the approaches to the town. The men were so accustomed to the thought of being called out at any moment to face the enemy that it caused no excitement, and no alarm being given, the night passed quietly away.

The companies were exercised principally in the skirmishing drill. The words uttered one morning by the commandant—M. de Saisy—were well worthy of note.

The men had just been halted on the undulating downs about a couple of miles from the town. Previous to sending out skirmishers M. de Saisy made them a short address, advising them to pay great attention, saying: "In a few days you may have to do it in earnest over the same ground, and let me recommend you all to prepare yourselves by a good confession, for with clear consciences you can but fight well. The Zouaves have never flinched yet, however great the odds against them, and let us remember *that*, when the occasion comes."

In much more telling language did this brave old defender of the Holy See encourage his men. A Dominican Father, Père Doussot, who spoke English very well, came from Viterbo to assist Père Flamand (a Belgian, and also an active and zealous son of St. Dominic), so that all the Zouaves might have an opportunity of confessing in their own language. Thus till late that night and early the following morning the chaplains were busy at their work.

Captain Adjutant Major Vyart, who had been out all night, came into the barracks, throwing himself down on a bed among the men, who were busy cleaning their accoutrements, went off fast asleep, thus waiting for the Mass at which the general Communion was to take place.

Père Doussot celebrated the Mass, and, while the communicants were kneeling at the altar-steps waiting to receive, he made them a short but touching exhortation, winding up by saying that the Holy Father had sent his blessing in a special way to all the Zouaves in the Viterbo Province.

For several weeks were the Italians expected. A small detachment of Zouaves, under a sergeant and corporal, were quartered in the centre of the town. Guards were mounted at several of the gates every night. The Porta Pia, being commanded by the guard at the San Francisco barracks, was considered sufficiently secure without any addition being made for it. Sergeants, with several men, were despatched every night along the roads leading to the frontier, in order to give the alert in case of any unexpected movement. On the morning of September 11th a rumour came that the Italians had crossed the frontier, but it turned out to have no foundation. A section of the fourth company was sent off, in charge of Lieutenant Algand, but they returned after a fruitless march. The idea among the officers and men appeared to be that resistance was to be made as long as it was possible, and then those who were not killed would try and retreat to Rome. Sealed orders, however, which were only to be opened when the Italians had crossed the frontier, directed M. de Saisy to retire on Viterbo and join Colonel de Charette. Early on the morning of September 11th the men of each company were roused in silence. In a few minutes all were up, and the barracks, which shortly before had been wrapped in the quiet of night, became a scene of bustle and animation. Baggage was packed and carried into the corridors, and from thence transferred to the carts, which were in readiness at the barrack-gates. All was effected in silence and order, and before three, a.m., the carts were loaded and on their way to Civita Vecchia, leaving behind only the straw mattresses.

The men wore their best uniforms, so as to be well provided for the campaign. All then lay down again in their clothes, knapsack and rifle at their heads, ready for the first summons. The military Mass, for it was Sunday, was deferred till nine o'clock, a little before which hour the companies met under arms in the Piazza, and then marched to the cathedral church. After the Mass the Commandant reviewed the companies, and complimented the men on their well-filled ranks after the alert of the night. The Zouaves were then free to employ themselves as they liked, provided they did not go beyond bugle call. They were required to be in the barracks from mid-day till four o'clock, so as to secure some repose, in case of a night march. The retreat sounded an hour earlier than usual, all the men paraded with their knapsacks and arms, and forty rounds of cartridges were served out to each man, making a hundred in all.

The men were then sent to lie down, with orders to be ready for an immediate start. Scarcely half an hour had elapsed when the bugle called to arms; five minutes more, and the companies drew up on the road leading to Viterbo, just outside the gate of the town. Perfect stillness reigned within the walls. The ground sloped downward from the gate, and some distance in front there stretched a grassy plot, shaded by trees; the peaceful moonlight playing on the arched gateway. The quiet of the slumbering town was not in consonance with the thoughts of war and invasion. Meanwhile skirmishers of the 4th company were thrown out in line, in front of the gate, while two squads were sent inside to man the walls. The rest of the company was drawn up in reserve below the gate. The 3rd company gradually withdrew towards Viterbo, after which the squads, being called out from the town, rejoined their company, which followed the 3rd, marching in section ; the skirmishers were then called in, and the small body moved forward on its way to Viterbo. The town was only quitted on the approach of the Italians. A few Dragoons, part of the garrison of Montefiascone, formed our advance and rear-guard. A halt was made a few miles from Viterbo, while scouts were sent on to learn if the town was still held by the Pontifical troops. Finding that all was right, the word was given to advance, and about two o'clock in the morning the two companies entered the gates of Viterbo, and halted in the large Piazza. Everything had been prepared to give the enemy a warm reception ; earthworks had been thrown up outside the gate, which was covered with mattresses. Lieutenant-Colonel de Charette came into the Piazza, looking every inch a soldier, and surveying with marked pleasure the well-filled ranks of the two companies that had just arrived. The 1st of the 4th was immediately called under arms to go out *en reconnaissance*, and to cut the telegraph wires, while the 3rd and 4th took up the quarters which the others had just left. Viterbo presented that morning a curious appearance, the soldiers passing rapidly up and down the streets, with cheerful but earnest countenances ; the grave and bewildered looks of the population showing that unusual events were about to happen. In the Piazza were all the horses of the cavalry ready saddled, the ammunition and artillery horses ready harnessed. Dragoons galloped backwards and forwards with despatches. Speculations were rife as to whether a stand would be made in the town. It turned out, however, that the Colonel's orders were to retire upon Rome on the coming of the Italians. At two o'clock the bugles sounded to arms, as the videttes came galloping into the town; the men fell into the ranks, while the artillery, with the train and baggage, started to quit it by the road leading to Vetralla. The 3rd and 4th formed the advanced guard, while the 1st company was the last to leave. The little troop was quickly out of the gates, accompanied by the good wishes of the inhabitants, who prayed the Madonna and St. Rose to protect it. Up the steep hilly road, inches deep in dust, which thickened the air, we mounted with unrelaxed speed, while the hot Italian sun poured down its burning rays. The advanced guard was then sent into the vineyards on each side of the road, and thrown out in skirmishing order, to cover the retreat of the main body. The bunches of ripe grapes were godsends to clear the choking dust from our parched throats, as water was not to be had. After about three-quarters of an hour the 3rd and 4th were called back to the road, and formed the rear-guard. Thus the march continued till the town of Vetralla was reached, and nothing occurred beyond the rear-guard being thrown out in skirmishing order, to repel the attack of some Italian Lancers.

Some of the Dragoons narrowly missed being taken prisoners at Viterbo by the Lancers. One officer, and his orderly half-a-dozen paces in front of him, were pursued by them. The officer rode coolly away from them, turning round and brandishing his sword, while he invited them to come on. The Zouave guard in the Piazza remained behind, having received orders to leave as soon as the troops were out of the town; but not receiving any further orders, and not knowing when the retreat had been completed, they stayed and were made prisoners.

Lieutenant-Colonel de Charette would gladly have made a stand in Viterbo, but, as he himself said, "I have my orders, and must obey them." He executed the retreat from Viterbo in a most masterly manner, as two *corps d'armée* of the Italians were advancing on each side of the town. He remained till the last moment, in case some of the other companies in their retreat might have tried to join him there. A detachment had been taken unawares by the

Italians at Bagnorea. Captain de Kermouil's company from Valentano had been heard nothing of; it seemed impossible that he could have escaped, but, on account of his perfect knowledge of the country, some hopes were entertained that he had. On the retreat from Viterbo one bridge was blown up to retard the advance of the enemy. Arrived at Vetralla, the advance guard was placed with the artillery at the entrance to the town, while the others marched and encamped in an olive grove. In Vetralla were collected about two hundred gendarmes, who had retreated from their respective stations, and assembled there to join the main body. It was a sad sight to see these brave men, some of them grown grey in the service, thus driven from their homes and families. They might have stopped and taken service under the flag of Piedmont, but men who had previously left their homes in the States seized by Victor Emmanuel after Castelfidardo, would not now desert the Holy Father in his hour of need. It was their boast to serve him from father to son.

The night was spent in the open air among the olive-trees, while several fires, being lighted, threw a partial glow over the Zouave camp. The men lay on the ground, their arms being piled. One hour or more before daylight most were awake and stirring, warming themselves at the camp-fires, and smoking; news seemed to have made its way among them. The most inspiriting report was that Captain de Kermouil, commanding the 2nd company, had effected his retreat from Valentano, and that he was somewhere ahead. The other piece of information, which proved to be true, was that his retreat was cut off by the Italians, who were in possession of the road to Corneto, the only road by which he could retire. The road leads from Vetralla to Corneto, where you take the railway to Civita Vecchia. We drank a draught of hot coffee before sunrise, and then everything was got in readiness for resuming the march. The town stands on an abrupt eminence, with a valley on either side. The Corneto road winds round one side of the town, gradually descending till you are in the valley, where the road bends to the right and ascends the other side of the valley.

We were again under arms, and commenced the march, the 1st and 4th companies occupying the post of honour as the advanced guard. A few Dragoons and the mounted Gendarmes went first, then the Zouaves, after which followed the Artillery, a *mitrailleuse*, the ammunition and baggage waggons, the foot Gendarmes, and the rear brought up by the Zouaves—the 4th battalion forming both advance and rear-guard. As the head of the column gained the summit of the hill on the opposite side of the valley, a prolonged "Viva Pio Nono!" rung back on the town, as some hundred voices sang the Pope's Hymn. Such was the last "viva" for the Holy Father in Vetralla. The day, which had dawned threateningly, gradually improved, though the sky was clouded. Once clear of the valley of Vetralla, the road ran straight, over a slightly undulating country, to the little town of Monte Romano. The telegraph wires were cut as soon as the march began. About half-past ten Colonel de Charette halted his little troop in Monte Romano; the rifles were piled, guards told off and placed. The 1st of the 4th, as advanced post, took up position on the hill overlooking the road and plain towards Corneto; the rest scattered about the place and through the town, and an air of life and bustle was imparted to it that it rarely wore. The men brought wood and water, and all the few preparations for cooking the rations were speedily made. Groups of soldiers were everywhere standing, sitting, and strolling about, while others sought the fountains to wash away the dust and dirt of the march.

While at Monte Romano, authentic confirmation arrived of the news that the Italians had entered Corneto. This is the next town on the road after Monte Romano. By this road we had hoped to reach the railway and proceed to Rome, and now we found that we were intercepted. The day had turned out most gloriously, the sun was shining in all its splendour, and scarce a cloud appeared to hide the clear blue sky. Doubt had given place to certainty, and our suspense was ended, the Italians lay between Rome and the Zouaves; the orders were to retire to Rome, and so Rome must be reached.

Our spirits went up, and everyone felt that, come fighting or not, no triumph was at hand for the enemy. Again, the news that Captain de Kermouil had reached Civita Vecchia, proved most inspiriting. At three in the afternoon preparations were made to resume the march, and by half-past the advance guard had issued forth from the gate and gained the road leading to Corneto. About half a mile from the gate the road was abandoned, and turning to the left, the column pursued its way down a rough hill-side. It was a pretty sight to see them winding down into the valley, a beautiful miniature army, with its picturesque uniform and the flashes of the sunlight glancing off the bright scabbards and rifles at every moment.

A looker-on would almost have imagined that a review or sham-fight was going to take place, rather than that the little army expected to have to cut its way through the enemy before night. Small as the column was, the extended line descending the valley made it look double its number.

The weather was delightful after the greatest heat of the day was over; the scenery too was very charming, though wild and uncultivated. The march led us along a grassy country broken occasionally by clumps of trees. Later on the vanguard reached the bank of a river; descending, they plunged in, and emerging on the opposite side ascended a high, steep hill, crowned by a verdant wood. The scouts always a head, had made a careful *reconnaissance*, and the troop halted at length on the summit, where the wood was partially open. Few persons passing over the same country would believe that artillery with ammunition and baggage-waggons had been brought up those heights. Even the horses seemed to know that it was no ordinary occasion that called on them to tax their iron muscles to the utmost; all however, safely reached the top. The last rays of the sun had left the mountain-top, and darkness had set in before the march was resumed, so it became difficult to mark the features of the ground we passed over. Owing to the skill of the officers the march was kept up pretty briskly, though marked by great caution. Not a word was allowed to be spoken, and all noise was avoided as far as possible; pipes and cigarettes were absolutely forbidden, Nor did this prove an excess of caution, for after about an hour's ascent, as we gained at length the high road which ran along for some miles nearly at a level, down below on the right hand were plainly visible the camp fires of the Italians. They had left Corneto and were on their way to Civita Vecchia.

It might not be amiss to mention here, that the 5th of the 4th battalion of Zouaves, stationed at Civita Castellana, under the command of M. de Resimont, having received orders some time previously to offer all the resistance it reasonably could, in order to keep open the line of retreat for Colonel de Charette, had only surrendered to 15,000 Italians, when the little fort was ready to crumble from the effect of the fierce cannonade. As many of the enemy fell, they could hardly realize the fact that scarcely a Zouave was hit. By the occupation of Civita Castellana, the retreat by that road was rendered impossible.

The camp fires of the enemy before mentioned gradually faded from our view, one mile after another was accomplished, till the road began to descend, and to wind round the hill-sides, then it traversed a valley, after which it ascended again and seemed to wind back in the old direction. By this time the moon had risen, and though it was hard to distinguish much, the effect of the moonlight, breaking through the trees that skirted the roadside, was very beautiful, contrasting with the gloom of the valley just passed, where the moon was not yet high enough to illuminate it; a table-land appeared to stretch away in the distance from the now level road, though woods appeared again on some sides. A halt of half an hour took place, during which it was determined again to abandon the high road, taking only the two pieces of artillery and the *mitrailleuse*, thus leaving the baggage to make its way into Civita Vecchia by the road if they should chance to escape the attention of the enemy. The hardest part of the march now really began, there was no road, and the direction taken led through woods which opened out occasionally, but at other times barely left room for the artillery to force its way through. About an hour and a half was spent in getting the artillery up a frightfully steep and stony ravine, which was only accomplished by the untiring energy of the men, who exerted their united efforts to get them up foot by foot.

This difficulty over, the woods were left behind, and now an apparently interminable plain, thickly strewn with rocks and nearly destitute of soil, stretched itself before us; those were weary hours as each slowly passed by, and still the same rocky plain reached far away before us.

The Colonel was on foot, exchanging now and then a kind word with his men, whom he styled familiarly "*mes enfants*." As mile succeeded mile some began to wonder where we were going; others imagined that Civita Vecchia had been occupied by the Italians, and that the object was to try to gain the railway nearer Rome. At last, however, it was seen that we were approaching the end of the plain, and it was with the most intense satisfaction that we descried the lighthouse of the harbour rising above the level. We were now descending a slope, when the shipping came in sight, and an English frigate gracefully floating outside the harbour was disclosed to our view. Then gradually the town of Civita Vecchia was unfolded before us, and three quarters of an hour later the streets of the town echoed back the tramp of the little troop, which had just completed a forced march of about 35 miles in 22 hours, and 42 miles in all. The baggage wagons had arrived safely.

It would have been something to have effected the retreat even had the artillery and baggage been left behind, but to have slipped about the country surrounded by some 60,000 Italians, without leaving them so much as a bit of baggage, must have proved very annoying to the enemy. It was 4 o'clock in the morning of the 14th of September, before the men entered the barracks, and at once they threw themselves down on the straw, and soon hunger and thirst and weariness were forgotten in slumber. By seven o'clock most of them were stirring again, and by eight the rappel had sounded. At the first dawn of daylight the smoke of some half-dozen vessels of the Italian fleet was seen on the horizon, and later on their unsightly hulks were visible. Before nine they had arrived at the mouth of the harbour. A telegram, despatched to the authorities in Rome, announcing the safe arrival of the "Division Charette" in Civita Vecchia, proved most welcome intelligence, as they had not known what to expect. A train sufficient to accommodate the force was immediately despatched from Rome to bring us in. Food and wine had been served out as soon as time allowed it to be procured.

A little after nine the train was filled, and M. de Charette, mounting the engine beside the driver, we started for the Eternal City.

The Zouave depôt, and Captain de Kermouil's company were left in Civita Vecchia, with some companies of the Cacciatori, and a small detachment of artillery. Meanwhile the train was speeding swiftly along, the banks on either side flew by, when emerging from the undulating country, the train skimmed along the water's edge—the sea running into the land at that point—and we saw close to the shore a frigate, with her broadside to the railway. There being no air to wave her flag, it was impossible to tell her nationality. Many an eye was watching the frigate, expecting to see the tongues of fire shoot out from her broadside. One breathless moment of suspense, and the speeding train was past, while a slight breath of wind disclosed the English flag to view.

The miles sped swiftly by, and but one stoppage occurred, owing to some culvert on the railway having broken down. About two miles from Rome the train stopped; we descended, and formed in our respective companies. The order to advance being given, the troop was speedily in motion, anxious to set foot once more within the walls of the Eternal City, and rejoined the comrades who awaited us. Emerging from the thick cane plantations that grew on either side of the railway, the line of march ran along the banks of the Tiber; on one side we were entirely sheltered from observation, while on the other the city gradually unfolded itself to view; dome after dome of the beautiful churches rose in the picture among the solemn monuments of antiquity. Every step and every glance brought to the heart some happy reminiscence. When within a quarter of a mile of the walls, the river side was left, and as we gained the high road, the Porta Portese appeared in view. The old and venerable gate was covered with mattresses; earthworks had also been thrown up in front of it. Nearer and nearer drew the little band, till rounding the earth-works, we entered the gate. Crowds of people came to see the march through the city. Travel-stained and dusty uniforms bore witness to the toils endured by our troop, and words of welcome exhibited the sympathy of the Romans for us. The events of those few days will not soon be forgotten by those engaged in them, each one of whom can testify to the daring and genius of our able Lieut.-Colonel, the brave De Charette, who conducted this masterly retreat with consummate skill, under no ordinary dangers and difficulties.

CHAPTER XXVIII.

EVENTS OF SEPTEMBER, 1870—DIARY OF A ZOUAVE OFFICER DURING THE SIEGE — BRAVE CONDUCT OF GENTLEMEN RETURNING TO THE CORPS, ETC.

THE letter mentioned in the last chapter but one, together with an appeal to the ex-Zouaves from another quarter, made a profound impression upon me, and other old Zouaves with whom I was in correspondence. We now felt that if ever our presence were required as defenders of the Holy Father and of the Eternal City, *now* was the time, and having been appealed to, we began to consider it a point of honour to return to the post of danger.

After two or three days' reflection, I began to make arrangements, and on Sept. 8th wrote and gave notice that I intended to give up the business I was managing, in order that I might return to the Zouaves as soon as possible. I made known my intention also to my old comrades of the corps, and three of them, R——, Raymond, and Weetman, declared their intention of accompanying me. Before, however, we had made the necessary arrangements preparatory to leaving England, came the unlooked-for intelligence of the surrender of Rome to the Italians, which took place Sept. 20th. Thus, much to our chagrin and disappointment, we were compelled to remain at home, and abandon our design of returning to the Eternal City.

Of the events which led to the surrender of Rome to the troops of the Robber King, I cannot do better than insert the following summary, kindly furnished me by two friends, who bore a very prominent share in the defence.

Sept. 10th, 1870.—Ponza di San Martino arrives in Rome

with Victor Emmanuel's letter to the Pope, and is received by the Holy Father.

13th.—At 9.30 a.m. I receive orders to assemble immediately at Trinità dei Monti; I am then ordered to Porta Pia, from which point to the river is occupied by the Zouaves.

It was on this day that the memorable combat of Sergeant Shee with a troop of Italian Lancers took place. This skirmish of the brave Sergeant and four other Zouaves against half a squadron of Lancers exhibits in bold relief the courage of these five men. Their company, the 6ième du 3, having been ordered to reconnoitre the enemy, had occupied Monte Mario at 5 a.m. The gallant Sergeant commanded the advanced guard, which took up a position about 600 yards ahead of the company. A cavalry-man was seen advancing, but was supposed to be a Pontifical Dragoon, for an orderly was expected with despatches; as he neared the post, the Zouaves perceived their mistake—he was an Italian, and behind him rode half a squadron of Lancers. On perceiving the Zouaves, they immediately deployed, and cut off the Sergeant and his four men from the rest of the guard. The first volleys fired dismounted some of the Lancers, and on their approach Sergeant Shee unhorsed and killed the sergeant of the troop. This first encounter resulted in a loss to the enemy of one killed, nine wounded, and two prisoners. The Italians now retreated over the hill near, and just as the Zouaves, congratulating themselves on their marvellous escape, were preparing to depart, they were again attacked by *ten* to *one*. The Italians demanding a surrender, the Zouaves replied that no such word was understood by them. The enemy paid dearly for every wound the Zouaves received. At length all his men being wounded and made prisoners, the Sergeant, now himself also wounded, was left alone to sustain the unequal contest, and after placing several of the enemy *hors de combat*, he fell insensible, from the effect of a fearful blow on the head, which, cutting his *kepi* in two, inflicted another severe wound. He was taken for dead, and awaking from his stupor, found himself on a cart with several dead bodies, but electrified the Italians by an enthusiastic shout of "Viva Pio Nono!" He had received nine lance and sabre wounds; at the Italian camp his wounds were dressed, and every care was taken of him, and he met there his brave men, all of them badly wounded. (He has now completely recovered, but he is justly proud of his scars, received in defence of the holiest of causes.)

14th.—Captain de Fabbri's company skirmish on Monte Mario.

15th and 16th.—Both quiet; occupied in filling sand-bags and completing the barricades outside the gate.

17th.—The Italians cross the Tiber, between the Ponte Molle and Teverone, the Swiss Carbineers retiring from the Ponte Nomentano, and the Antibes Legion from the Ponte Mammole. The enemy by this flank movement invests the city on the south side. Columns are seen advancing from the direction of Albano. We get into position two rifled 12-pounders, instead of the two field-pieces.

18th.—The anniversary of Castel Fidardo. The Italian Lancers showing in groups, the garrison of Macao send them some shots. The Bersaglieri occupy the Osteria della Barocche, 2000 metres from the Porta Pia, near the Convent of S. Agnese fuori le mura; I send a shell to dislodge them.

19th.—Captain de Couissin, of the 3 du 1 Zouaves, and Captain du Raquier, of the Swiss Carbineers, occupy the Villa Patrizi, just outside the gate (Porta Pia). Some shots are exchanged by the skirmishers, with no loss to our side, but some of the Italians are hit.

20th.—During the night batteries were placed by the enemy in the Villa Dies, about 800 yards from the Porta Salara, and also in the Villa Albani. At 5 a.m. the first shot is fired; after fifteen minutes the two half companies —of Zouaves and Swiss—retire from the Villa Patrizi, and the bombardment becomes hot. About 6, one of my two guns is dismounted, the enemy's fire takes us *en echarpe*, and we cannot command their position. I send off the *caissons* and the other gun, spiking the injured one. Lieutenant Vicomte de Montcabrier, Sub-Lieutenant Tortosa, and Sergeant-Major Capialli di Carife—two Neapolitans—distinguish themselves in this operation. The sand-bag parapet of the barricade is knocked to pieces; I close the iron grilles, and get half of the company on to the parapet to the right of the gate, that on the left being useless and unapproachable, except by a ladder. At 7 o'clock the fire becomes terrible, and as we have but our rifles to depend on, the enemy advance their cannon to 400 metres, but are obliged to fall back to 500, then to 600, and finally to 800 metres.

8 o'clock.—By this time the Police and Excise Offices on the inner side of the gate are knocked to pieces, the gate-front is injured and part of the parapet; about half-past 8, they—the enemy—place some guns on the road, and send shells through the arch of the gate, these sweep the Via di Porta Pia and the Via del Quirinale as far as Monte Cavallo. My gun, with others, is placed at the fountain of Moses, opposite the Madonna della Vittoria, to enfilade the enemy if he should assault the gate, whilst the Zouaves at the gate are to take the enemy in flank from the shrubbery. The Maresciallo and the men round the piece are knocked over, the guns are drawn down to the Quattro Fontane, where they still command the gate.

9 o'clock.—The Swiss company at my right is recalled. I refuse to quit without a positive order addressed to myself; I place my reserve under shelter of the wall and in the bushes, the other section keeps up the fire from the parapet. I send a few men to replace in part the Swiss. I have no news from the regiment, and there is a report that a breach has been made, and that the Porta del Popolo has been taken.

10 o'clock.—I received orders from General Zappi, through Colonel Jeannerot, to retire to the Piazza de' Termini, passing through Macao. I find the last gun leaving Macao under Lieut. de Falaiseau. A second line of defence is being established by the Zouaves and the Swiss ($2\frac{1}{2}$ companies of Zouaves and 3 companies of Swiss); we place bundles of straw, and the men in skirmishing order. General Zappi

now orders us to cease, as the resistance is over. We place a gun and my company at the entrance of the Macao to prevent the enemy's advance, but these are withdrawn as the Corso, Pincio, &c., are occupied.

We receive notice of the capitulation; the men are furious, and a scene ensues for more than half-an-hour, they break their rifles and fling about their cartridges.

We are sent into the cloister of Michael Angelo, at Santa Maria degli Angeli, and carry in straw, &c., in the evening we pile arms on the Piazza, where the Italians bivouac.

21st.—*Grand defilé* of the troops on the Corso; horrible orgies going on until after midnight.

From the above diary it will be seen with what bravery and fidelity the Pontifical troops fought to defend Rome, until the moment when, by orders of the Holy Father, they were commanded to lay down their arms; the obedience to this order,—*i.e.*, to surrender while they felt themselves unconquered—was the highest sacrifice Pius IX. could have demanded of his Zouaves. To fight and to shed their blood in his defence, this they willingly did, but to surrender to the wretched Italians, the instruments of sacrilege and robbery, this indeed was the greatest trial to which they could be subjected; thus, although the majority of the Pontifical troops recollected that obedience is a soldier's first duty, and acquiesced at once in the orders of the Sovereign Pontiff, yet it can occasion no great surprise, that in their fit of astonishment at the capitulation, some few should have given vent to their disappointment as related above.

On calm reflection, every one will see that the Holy Father was guided in his decision, in this affair, by the greatest prudence; for, had he not made any resistance at all to the superior forces of the Italians, they might have distorted his conduct into an approval of their iniquitous spoliation; on the other hand, had he made a prolonged resistance, in the face of the immensely superior strength of the Italian army, the ultimate result must have been the same, and his enemies would have had a pretext for accusing

17—2

him of sacrificing many valuable lives to no purpose. Thus in deciding to resist the forcible seizure of Rome, and at the same time issuing orders to General Kanzler, to capitulate should a breach in the walls be effected, we may conclude that Pius IX. chose the happy medium, and acted with the most consummate wisdom.

The following letter, which appeared in the *Evening Freeman* of September 29, 1870, contains a few additional particulars. The writer was an old Zouave, who returned to rejoin the corps at this critical juncture: he shall speak for himself :—" I arrived in Rome at midnight on the 21st, to find, alas! that I was too late to take part in its defence. I did not know till I was close to the gates, having driven from Civita Vecchia—there being no train—that the Italians were inside the walls. The siege lasted five hours. Our troops numbered 8,000, with 30 guns. The Italians, in number 65,000, with 150 pieces of siege artillery, played with fearful effect on the walls and gates, and it was only when resistance any longer was perfectly fruitless, that the Papal troops laid down their arms. Our enemies entered *by force while the capitulation was being arranged*—soldier-like conduct! They were accompanied by the *emigrati* men, who had been exiled for political offences, or, having been condemned in Rome for murder and every abominable crime, had escaped into Italy. These opened the Roman prisons, and then the work of blood commenced. No one's life is safe now. The solitary Zouaves who may be found, are butchered in the streets. I saw, yesterday morning, a poor Zouave led, all alone, down the Corso to slaughter. The gendarmes are thrown into the Tiber, and we are conquered, *par exemple!* by *soldiers*. Our townsman, Captain de la Hoyde, is the talk of everyone—his conduct, his bravery was worthy of an Irishman. He defended the Porta Pia magnificently— forty guns played on it. Of all in Rome there were two whose names will be remembered. Monsignor Stonor stood the whole time of the fight among bursting shells and balls falling as thick as hail, giving Absolution. Mrs. Stone, the personification of heroism, was *at her post*, always the spot of the greatest danger and need, tending her poor wounded.

"Our men are all prisoners. The Irish and English are to be sent to Genoa, where Monsignor Stonor is at this moment going, to have every care taken of them, and have them at once sent to England.

"I am, Sir,

"BARTHOLOMEW TEELING."

The heroism of one distinguished lady has been recorded in the commencement of this work, and corroborated by General Kanzler's report, and also by Mr. Teeling in the letter just quoted. The succeeding narrative, kindly furnished me by a friend, describes the courage under fire, and the presence of mind shown by another English lady during the siege of Rome.

"Rome, September 23rd, 1870.—I leave for Civita Vecchia to-night . . . . my heart beats fast still. I am so afraid of the mob. I was on Dr. Torriani's staff of the ambulance, the only lady. On Saturday I mounted my red cross on my arm and went to see Father Alfieri at the St. Jean de Dieu, to enroll myself for hospital work. He asked me to do ambulance work, as there were plenty of ladies for the hospital. The request took me aback, but I said yes! so he sent me to tell different people to go to certain points at the first firing of cannon. Early on Sunday I went to Holy Communion at St. Peter's, and then I called upon Ceccarelli, the head surgeon, at Santo Spirito. He sent me to the Termini to join Torriani. This pleased me, for almost all my friends were up there. I got a room in which to take shelter, and passed Sunday and Monday in running errands, invested with the red cross, which was *then* my protection, now alas! my life would not be safe if it were seen. On Monday I was at the Tre Arche when the sortie was made, which resulted in two wounded Zouaves and many wounded amongst the enemy. Just as I was getting some refreshment, a Captain of the Roman Legion ran up to me and said, 'Madame, on vous demande, il y a deux blessés.' The poor fellows were brought in, neither of them dangerously wounded.

"I said a tiny word to Our Lady that she would strengthen me for the sight of blood, and she did, for I was able then and next day to do all that was required of me.

"That day we had no more wounded, so at night I lay down without undressing, but I could not sleep, for I knew the dawn would bring sad work. At a quarter to five I heard the first boom, I arose at once, and was at the ambulance before five o'clock.

"The doctor laughed, and said I was in a hurry; no wounded could come yet. The firing was fearfully heavy—the balls coming thick over the Porta Pia. Then I heard a shout—'Signora, Signora, un ferito.' I ran across and found one poor fellow, who had been working at the fortifications -he was lying in a pool of his own blood; he was covered with blood, while his face was as pale as death; I had him removed on a cart. His wound was not mortal so far, but it was terrible to behold. Directly afterwards others were brought in. We were in the midst of the fire—cannon balls came whizzing by us, so we were obliged to pick up our basins, bandages, etc., and make for S. Maria degli Angeli. We were soon compelled to quit this also, and to remove to the Hospital of the Forçati, close by. There the wounded came in thickly, so we had no time but to do what was absolutely necessary for them, and send them to S. Spirito. At ten o'clock we heard that the Italians were in, Captain de la Hoyde having received orders to surrender.

"Then the scene was terrible. They brought the Zouaves who had been defending Porta Pia into the Piazza de' Termini. They were crying like children at having been ordered to surrender. . . . . I was then ordered to remain there for an hour, in case any more wounded came in, and then to go to Santo Spirito. Then began my real peril; I was advised to take off my red cross, and did so. I started off dusty, dirty, covered with blood, and a large bundle of bandages and lint under my arm. Not a carriage was to be seen. When I arrived at the Piazza di Spagna I saw a carriage, which I felt sure I should get, as I had often employed the driver before. The man, however, instead of allowing me to get into the carriage, cried out aloud, 'Andate in Inghilterra, amica dei Zouavi.' Then a man, dressed as a gentleman, thrust his face against mine and ordered me to cry, 'Viva Italia.' I refused, when others who were near came and spat upon me, and knocked me about. I escaped from them, and arrived safe home with my bundle. I washed, changed my dress, ventured out again, and went on foot to S. Spirito, where Dr. Torriani told me that they had more nurses than wounded, so my services were not required. He recommended me to go home—'easier said than done.' When I left the hospital I passed through side streets, as I was afraid of insults in the large thoroughfares. Passing over the iron bridge into the Via Giulia, I met a poor woman, one of my *protegées*, who, unluckily, was so pleased to see me that she drew attention to me by her demonstrations of joy. There were some two or three hundred Bersaglieri near the Carceri Nuovi. Some one told them who I was, and I was beset. They gathered round me, shouting 'Bruta Papalina, amica dei Zouavi,' again and again. Some spat upon me, others hustled me; however, they failed to make me quicken my pace. I passed through them without real injury, but in deadly terror. I arrived home in safety. The night following was one of terror; houses were pillaged, women insulted, and many outrages committed under the plea of looking for Zouaves.

"On Wednesday I went to the Piazza of St. Peter; all the Zouaves were there. It was a heartrending sight, and I stayed only long enough to do some business, and then left. The Holy Father came out to the balcony and gave his solemn Benediction, after which he raised his arms to heaven, and then buried his face in his hands. 'Viva Pio Nono, Papa e Re!' rose in shouts from his faithful soldiers. The Swiss fired a salute. Almost immediately the Zouaves were marched off, and the men are now scattered to the four winds of heaven. That same afternoon I was disturbed by a ring at the bell. I was rather suspicious, as I was well aware of the outrages which were then being committed in Rome, so I signed to my landlady to be quiet while I went to the door, peeped through the little hole, and slipped the bolt and lock, for I saw before me a villanous looking ruffian, with a long knife in his hands, which, together with his short sleeves, were covered with blood. I kept quiet, pretending that no one was there, while he continued knocking and ringing for a few minutes, which seemed to me an age; at last he went away.

"I left Rome on Saturday, the 24th of September, for Civita Vecchia, where I rendered what little services I could to the Zouave prisoners; but I was obliged to leave Civita Vecchia that same evening, having received an order from General Cerotti to do so. He also intimated to me that I was not to loiter on my way out of Italy, as I was known to be a friend to the Zouaves. ..... I am now safe out of Italy, and breathe more freely. I never thought I could have gone through so much."

In an account written for the *Freeman* by a *Chevalier* of Pius IX., the loss of the Papal troops in sustaining the attack on the Eternal City is stated to have been one hundred and fifty men and five officers killed, while the loss of the enemy is estimated to have been as high as two thousand men *hors de combat*. This correspondent confirms Mr. Teeling's statement as to the cowardly conduct of the ruffians and *canaglia*, who followed the Italian army into Rome, in attacking defenceless Zouaves in the streets. Even the Italian Bersaglieri, men pretending to the name of *soldiers*, disgraced their profession by an act of cowardly assassination, which he relates as follows:—"A young Belgian nobleman—an officer of Zouaves, who distinguished himself highly by repelling the enemy at the breach—was walking quietly along with his fellow-soldiers, after they had been taken prisoners; he still retained his sword, and this attracted the attention of some Bersaglieri, who demanded it. He laid his hand upon the hilt, and said, in a quiet but firm tone, '*Jamais!*' Immediately half-a-dozen bayonets were buried in his body, and, in order to finish their victim, one of the ruffians put his rifle to the young Zouave's head and blew his brains out!" These assassins are the men sent to Rome to represent modern *civilization*, and to accomplish *Italian unity!* Can a good cause need the aid of assassination ?

I have mentioned, in the commencement of this chapter, how my intention of returning, with several friends, to rejoin our regiment was frustrated. We have seen Mr. Teeling trying to accomplish the same object, and arriving a day after the battle. In the following " Journal of a Pontifical Zouave," published in the *Freeman*, and copied into the columns of *Catholic Opinion*, we shall observe how three brave men passed through the Italian lines, and joined their comrades inside the city during the siege of Rome :—

"It was evident Bixio meant to lose no time in his meditated attack on the Eternal City, as his troops were on the move by three o'clock on the morning of the 19th. We could hear the quick tramp of the cavalry, and the heavy rolling of the artillery on the old Roman pavement beneath us. Exciting still further the cupidity of our *vetturino* (coachman) by another payment of a hundred francs to take us, if possible, twenty miles nearer to Rome, we followed the Piedmontese, and soon overtook their rear-guard. We were obliged to give precedence to a carriage belonging to one of the army surgeons, and so had ample time to note the appearance of the Piedmontese troops, marching in single file on our right and left. No wonder the Archduke Albert should have had so little trouble in driving them before him on the day of Custozza, as it may be safely said they dare not engage any army of Europe of equal numbers for an hour with the faintest prospect of victory. The men have a careworn, prematurely aged look, and seemed utterly broken down after a short march. They are sadly wanting in stamina and *esprit de corps*. On the whole, they leave one the impression that they lack the most essential quality in the soldier's character—indomitable pluck! It is but just to add, however, that they are likely to fight most valiantly against the Pope's little army, not a tenth of their number.

Clad simply in a coarse blue coat, buckled around the waist, dirty unbleached canvas trousers, and an ill-shapen shako, their *tout ensemble* is wretched in the extreme.

"The bugles having sounded a halt, we pushed on past long trains of baggage-waggons and commissariat carts until we suddenly found ourselves again face to face with General Bixio, who seemed in no enviable mood, pacing to and fro on the roadway. He was evidently troubled lest his superior, Cadorna, who commanded 40,000 men on the side of the Porta Pia, should enter Rome first, and so rob him of his coveted laurels.

"'Why press on so eagerly with my army?' 'Our desire to be present at the operations.' '*Mais la guerre comme la guerre!* Your place on the march is at the rear, and not in the midst of my troops. You enjoy the excitement of the war?' 'Most men do, but this is not war!' '*C'est une petite affaire à présent*—to-morrow you shall see. Those pet lions, the Zouaves, know how to fight; a rising in the streets (which ought to have occurred ere this, our friends being in the city for some weeks) will place them between two fires! Their destruction is inevitable, as their presence in Rome is a menace and a danger to Italian patriots!' (The foregoing colloquy is set down to General Bixio.)

"At length Bixio allowed us to proceed as far as his advanced post, two miles distant, with a warning not to attempt to pass the lines at our peril. We were soon apprised of the limit in question by the appearance of a number of dragoons and Bersaglieri posted near a ruined osteria. The officer in command told us we should remain about the place, another way of saying we were under arrest.

"Leaving our *impedimenta* in the carriage to disarm suspicion, we expressed a wish to get a sight of Rome if possible, and climbed the height overhanging the road, the officers making no objection. Here we held council, in full view of the Piedmontese. The dragoons, with the exception of those acting as videttes, were lounging in the shade, their horses picketed close by; our *vetturino* was consoling himself with some water, the only thing to be had. Both my friends, Messrs. Tracy and Kenyon, though fully aware that the seizure of the despatches would necessarily involve their fate in mine if captured, like true Zouaves, unhesitatingly declared their readiness to accompany me at all hazards. At that moment, catching a glimpse of St. Peter's glorious dome in the distance, we could no longer brook delay, as we were only twelve miles from the Eternal City, and had given no parole to the Piedmontese.

"Turning the crest of the hill, we descended rapidly, and keeping along the valley, made a detour to avoid the road, as the dragoons cannot easily follow across country. Soon we left Bixio's army far behind us. Mile after mile we hurry on, gaining fresh impulse at every step, as we see St. Peter's, more and more clearly defined, towering in all its majesty against the sky. Not a sound disturbs the awful stillness which reigns around. It would, indeed, seem as if the world stood still before the commission of the dreadful crime on the morrow. But it is the calm which portends the storm; ere many hours elapse the cannonade will thunder far across the Campagna, and make the shepherds cower in their huts on the slopes of the hills. On and on we press, with an ardour fast becoming a fever of excitement to reach the goal of our hopes, utterly regardless of the danger of falling in with Cadorna's cavalry scouts endeavouring to cut off communication with the devoted city.

"At last we are under the fortifications! Friends recognise us from above, Mr. Edmond de la Poer, M.P., Major Lewis, and Captain Coppinger, who are on guard, rifle in hand, on the walls. We are told the Porta Angelica is not far off. Our hearts were full of gratitude for the privilege so signally accorded us of being able to join our comrades before the assault. We arrive at the gate, and show our passports to the officer on guard. We enter Rome! *Evviva il Papa Re!*

"Once inside the walls I hasten to deliver the despatches, the one to Cardinal Antonelli, at the Vatican, and the others I place in the hands of Colonel Allet, at the head-quarters of the Zouaves, on the Pincio. Our brave old commander welcomed us back to the corps with all that kindness of manner which has so endeared him to the hearts of the Zouaves. As no news had reached the city for several days, we reported the affair at Civita Vecchia, the advance of Bixio's army, and the certainty of an attack on Rome next morning. Enrolled once more in the Zouaves, and attached to the company of Captain D'Arcy, who won his spurs at Castel Fidardo, where General Lamoricière, in admiration of his heroic valour, called him *Le Brave D'Arcy*, we quickly got into uniform, and drove to the Gate of St. John Lateran. At the front everywhere we were greeted by some old comrades, but especially by my friend the Chevalier Lynch, a crusader for the third time, he having served in 1860 and 1867.

"Owing to the continuous movement of detachments during the night from post to post along the walls, fourteen miles in circuit, we were unable to join our own company until the morning.

"The attack, as we expected, commenced at five o'clock, and lasted until half-past ten. For five hours a storm of shot and shell raged against the Eternal City, girt around by a circle of fire, and assailed by 65,000 Piedmontese. Bixio thundered at the Porta San Pancrazio, while Angioletti menaced the gate of St. John Lateran, Cosnez the Porta San Lorenzo, Ferrero appeared before the Porta San Paolo, Masi threatened the Porta del Popolo, and Cadorna in person took up position before Porta Pia. Not content with attacking the defenders on the walls, the enemy in many instances threw the shells over our heads into the town, causing considerable damage at every explosion.

"Our artillery vigorously responded at all points, while each time the Piedmontese Bersaglieri—our boasted rivals—attempted to break cover and dash into the open, they were swept down by the ceaseless discharge from the Remington rifles of the Zouaves.

"By this time many beautiful villas near the walls were complete wrecks, and fires broke out in various parts of the city; yet the cannonade only grew the more fast and furious. At length Cadorna succeeded in making a breach in the wall near the Porta Pia, which was held with a desperate resistance by Captain De la Hoyde and the Zouaves under his command. At this juncture Colonel de Charette, with strong detachments, was hurrying to the breach, when a white flag was raised, and General Zappi rode up to him with peremptory orders to cease fighting and stop the rush of the Zouaves.

" To this Colonel de Charette demurred, until he was satisfied it was by the express command of the Pope."

This writer confirms the statement here brought forward by two others, that the Piedmontese seized the opportunity afforded them by the armistice to enter the city at the breach while the capitulation was being arranged.

The next two chapters—one of which relates to the events of September, 1870—have been kindly furnished by an intimate friend and comrade of mine. He took part in the late defence of Rome.

CHAPTER XXIX.

THE SIEGE FROM ANOTHER POINT OF VIEW—FAREWELL OF THE ZOUAVES TO THE HOLY FATHER—THEIR RETURN HOME—ITALIAN SOLDIERS AT GENOA.

ON Monday, September 10th, 1870, many rumours were rife in Rome of menacing dangers, of the advent of Garibaldi, and, still worse, of the invasion of the then still remaining dominions of the Pope by the armies of Victor Emanuel. The events which were rapidly succeeding each other in France gave much appearance of truth to the latter report, which was confirmed by the coming to Rome of the Envoy of the Robber King, who had this same day asked the consent of the Holy Father to the entry of the Italian troops into the city, on the absurd pretext of maintaining order, which had never been disturbed.

Yet with all these tales of ill omen circulating through the city, and fresh from his interview with the messenger of the Italian Bandit, Pius the Ninth never for a moment hesitated about fulfilling his intention of blessing the waters of the Aqua Pia, the large fountain of which was this day to play for the first time in front of the railway station. Along with a Zouave friend I walked up to the large square before the railway station, and got there just as His Holiness drove up. He was received by the assembled crowd, composed entirely of Romans, with the greatest enthusiasm; but one fact struck us much,—the entire absence of military (save those on duty), who were wont usually to come in crowds to spectacles of this kind. But their absence only proved how real was the love of the Romans for their Pontiff-king. General Kanzler, commander-in-chief, and a few other officers were in immediate attendance on the Pope, and after these and a few of the Roman nobility and dignitaries, and officials of the Waterworks had, after the blessing of the water, paid their homage to the Holy Father, the latter returned amid loud cheering to the Vatican.

As we were leisurely returning towards the centre of the town, we saw no soldiers in the streets, and so we at once went to our quarters to discover the cause of this unusual fact. There we found nearly all the men under arms, while some had already been sent to the walls and gates to aid in putting them in a state of defence. A telegram had just been received from a frontier town, saying that the Italian troops, in spite of all law, without a single reason or just pretext, had already dared to begin their sacrilegious march against the Eternal City.

Next day every military preparation possible was complete. The troops were all at their allotted posts; artillery bristled at the gates and along the old and almost useless walls; the ambulances were prepared, while from all the many hospitals of Rome floated the black flag, denoting to the enemy the places where the sick were.

My company and four other companies of Zouaves, some of the French Antibes Legion, a battery of artillery, a squadron of dragoons, and some foot and horse gendarmes, were posted in the Piazza Colonna, as also many ambulance waggons, bearing the cross of the Geneva Convention. Our duty was to maintain order in the centre of the town, and to act as a reserve to the troops at the walls. The former duty was light, thanks to the good sense of the Romans, who, although many agents of the secret societies were urging them to revolt, remained perfectly quiet, and many even gallantly enrolled themselves in the Urban Guard, whose members any soldier would be proud to own as comrades in arms. They, like ourselves, debarred from fighting the enemy, nobly exerted themselves in the dull but important duty of patrolling the city, thus grandly showing themselves to be at once brave soldiers, true citizens, and loyal subjects.

We slept on straw under the colonnades of the Piazza, where we were kept till Monday, the 19th. Owing to the residence of the Commandant de Place and of the Director of Police being near it, this Piazza was a point of great interest and excitement during this time, aides-de-camp and orderlies arriving each instant with information of the enemy's movements and doings, who, it seemed to us, were a long time in commencing the attack. But here it was as always, "conscience making cowards" of them, and they were striving hard, by many wily schemes and offers, to obtain a peaceful entrance. In vain. Their messengers were foiled in all their attempts to gain this, and on Monday we heard the first cannon fired at 5 a.m., in the direction of the Pincio.

About ten o'clock we received orders to proceed to the Lateran Gate, in front of which the enemy was erecting batteries. From there a lieutenant with twenty men, myself among the number, were sent to the convent at Santa Croce, where, along with some gendarmes and squadriglieri, we were posted along the old wall near there. A fire of musketry was kept up along parts of the walls between our men and some Italians who were prowling around, examining the weak points of the walls. A few cannon shot were fired, and a successful one was aimed from a nine pounder near where we were. A house outside the walls had been occupied by about two hundred Bersaglieri, and it was deemed necessary to dislodge them therefrom, as it commanded an extensive view of the walls and of the position of the troops stationed near the three-arched gate of the railway. Accordingly this cannon, loaded with grape, was discharged at this house; a yell arose from within it, the walls were riddled with shot, and a moment after not a man of the enemy was visible within the house.

Some Italian line soldiers from a vineyard near the walls exchanged a few shots with some of our little detachment, but our men dislodged them without loss to ourselves. An artilleryman serving the cannon mentioned above had a bullet pass through his forage cap without doing him any injury.

A skirmish took place near us, at the Porta Maggiore, in which a few of our Zouaves were wounded. At night all was quiet, save an occasional rifle shot fired by some of the advanced posts.

It fell to my duty to visit our sentinels posted along the walls, and as I walked along them I could see the enemy's camp fires burning for miles, I may say, around, and I could distinctly hear bugle calls.

As I was speaking to one of the sentries, some kind individual from without, attracted by the light of a torch which we had with us, sent a bullet whistling over us, to remind us of our rash exposure of ourselves.

At midnight, the Squadriglieri having relieved us, we retired to rest on some straw strewn along the large corridors of the Convent of Santa Croce. But as "weariness can snore upon the flint," so I enjoyed a sound sleep, from which I was awaked about 5 a.m. by a horrid whizzing noise, which in some dreamy, hazy way, I fancied was an express train rushing past the spot where we lay. But a fellow Zouave soon ended my delusion by shaking me, while he exclaimed, "Still asleep, come, the bombardment has begun." And so indeed it had.

The roar of the cannon was now incessant, and looking towards the interior of the city, we saw many little white puffs of smoke and jets of flame shoot up, denoting where a shell had fallen. On going up on the walls, I could perceive two batteries, one near the Cemetery of St. Lorenzo, and one in front of the Lateran Gate.

The former was pounding away with great skill and energy, and with considerable effect at the weak Railway Gate, while the second, with less true aim, was striving to destroy the Lateran Gate. We could see the shells bounding along the Lateran road, and an osteria or inn outside the Gate was soon destroyed, but as yet the Gate itself was unharmed, and two of our guns placed near it were doing considerable damage to the enemy, and a thick black smoke was seen to rise from a farm-house near their battery, set on fire by our shells, which was said to be occupied by some of the Italian Staff. Although the enemy's fire was well-directed on the whole, many of their shells fell wide of or beyond their mark, as, for instance, several shells from the St. Lorenzo battery fell within a short distance of us, in the garden where we were posted, and two burst on the roof of Santa Croce, doing no material harm beyond sending a few tiles flying over our heads, and enveloping us in a cloud of dust.

As far as I could judge, many shells, supposed to be directed against the Lateran Gate, were purposely aimed with a high elevation, in order to fall, as they did, into the centre of the city, among the non-combatants, there to produce a moral Bismarkian effect.

The firing all round the city was kept up with great energy on both sides till near ten o'clock, when along the walls the bugle-call *Cessez le feu* sounded, and to our grief we beheld the white flag flying from different parts of the walls. But we could not realize that the struggle was over; some more sanguine ones even imagined that the enemy, tired of fighting, wished again to parley with us. But all our hopes either of fighting on, or of having brought the enemy to such terms, were ended by the coming of our lieutenant, who told us that orders had been given to agree on terms of capitulation, and soon after we beheld the flag of Italy, still bearing on it the cross of Savoy, as if in mockery of the king who had sold his birthright, planted in front of the now burning Lateran Gate.

It is not my purpose here to discuss our chances of ultimate success against a well-equipped army, which, on the testimony of an Italian officer, consisted of more than 50,000 men, we being only about 12,000 men of all arms. Suffice it to say that the Holy Father could not have exacted a more trying sacrifice from his soldiers, than by thus requiring of them the yielding up of their arms almost without a struggle.

Here let me record an example of that contempt which throughout the whole of their unjust proceedings, the Italian authorities showed for the usages of civilized warfare.

It has always been held dishonourable, while a flag of truce is flying, and terms of surrender are being discussed, to advance to the attack of a city, yet this the Italians did, for we, who were stationed, as I before said, near the church of Santa Croce, saw a train, bearing two Italian flags, come up almost to the ruined gate of the Railway, filled with troops, evidently with the view of assaulting the same gate should terms not be agreed on, while we could distinctly see also numbers of troops massing on the roads leading in the direction of the same gate. Is such a movement of troops under such circumstances, and for such a purpose, lawful, and in accordance with the customs of war?

About two o'clock in the afternoon orders came for us to retire from our positions to the Piazza of St. Peter's, where we found the majority of our little army gathered together. On our way thither, we passed through large crowds of anxious-faced Romans, but all, without exception, were well-conducted and respectful in their demeanour towards us.

We passed the night in the Piazza of St. Peter's, its paving stones for a bed, and our knapsacks for pillows. All Rome, except the Leonine city and the Castle of St. Angelo, was occupied by the Italians. When morning came our officers informed us of the terms of the capitulation, and conveyed to us the thanks of the Holy Father for our services, and the praise of our general for our conduct during the time we had been under his command. Our pay was given us, up even to this day.

Some English Zouaves and myself then went to a café to obtain a little refreshment, which we much needed. While there our brave Lieutenant-Colonel de Charette entered, and we asked him to do us, some of his English Zouaves, the honour of taking something with us. Having been served, he told us he had always been well pleased with his brave English Zouaves, and with tears in his eyes, he added:—"Three times have I fought in the cause of the Pope, the first time at Castelfidardo and Ancona, where I was made prisoner; the second time I fought victoriously at Mentana, and now, the third time, his Holiness wills us to throw down our arms;" but brightening up, he continued, "*Mes enfants*, may we again meet for the same cause, under happier circumstances, but while my sword is no longer required here, I go to use it against my country's enemies." So saying, he shook each of us by the hand and left us. Before the siege began, he distinguished himself by the skill and daring with which he made a forced march from Viterbo to Rome, getting there without any loss, in spite of the Italian General Bixio's endeavours with a superior force to intercept him.

About mid-day the bugles called us to arms for the last time. The troops were all drawn in the large square of St. Peter's, preparing to march out, when at a window of the Vatican, to our great joy and consolation, we beheld our beloved Holy Father. At the same instant, our noble Colonel Allet, thirty-five years a soldier of the Pope, drawing his sword, cried in a loud voice, "*Mes enfants! Vive Pie Neuf!* There arose from the whole army such a shout as perhaps has never, nor ever will again be heard. It came from the hearts of all who were there. At that moment, all our different nationalities, all our different feelings, all we had endured, even the great sacrifice we were making in thus laying down our arms at the Pope's command without a fight, all for the moment were forgotten at the sight of his venerable person. Our only desire was to strive with our tongues to express to him our love towards him, and our devotion to his cause. Long the cheering continued, the bands playing "*Viva Pio Nono!*" Then a moment we were silent as we presented arms and knelt to receive his blessing. Ere we stood up again, he was gone, seen alas! by many of us, for the last time. Never shall I forget this parting scene, and I would it had continued longer, for such a "parting is such sweet sorrow."

Silently and with heads bowed down, and heavy hearts, we quitted the city we had fondly hoped to hold against all enemies, leaving him whom we loved a prisoner of the basest and most treacherous of foes. As we defiled among the troops awaiting on the Piazza their turns to leave, I noticed many young men, manly young fellows, weeping like children, and many an old veteran, bearing on his breast the medals for the African, Crimean, Italian or Danish and Austrian campaigns, furtively wiping away the tear that stole unbidden down his bronzed and weather-beaten face.

We left Rome by the Porta Angelica, marching round the back of the Vatican to the Gate of St. Pancras. And here let me thank for her kind prayer some, to me unknown, English lady, who, standing near the Porta Cavallegieri as we passed it, exclaimed in heartfelt accents "Poor fellows! May heaven preserve them!" · At St. Pancras Gate we found the Italian troops of different arms drawn up along the road, their Generals on horseback near the gate, along with our three Generals on foot. We marched past with fixed bayonets, our bugles sounding, our officers saluting our own Generals as we passed them, the Italian troops presenting arms, and their bands playing while we defiled past them. I heard not a single insulting or rude remark from any of the Italian soldiers, but on the contrary an Italian captain exclaimed as we passed, "What fine young men!" and many seemed surprised at our discipline and military bearing, the poor fellows having been taught to believe that Papal Zouave was another term for an assassin. We threw down our arms in a large field near the Pamphili Gardens, and then set out on our march to Ponte Galera, a railway station eight miles off. We had our knapsacks, great coats, and other private property we had about us, left us, and we were allowed to march without any regard to rank or order, along the road. The heat being very severe, the little and partial rest that we had lately had, an insufficiency of food, and the cheerless position of prisoners of war, rendered this march, though short, still very trying. At Ponte Galera, being arranged by regiments, we awaited the arrival of trains to convey us to Civita Vecchia. At length our turn came to start, just as it became dark. We were crammed into railway carriages, fourteen men or more into one compartment, but in spite of want of space, I had a most refreshing sleep on the way. On waking I found we had got to our journey's end, where, till near eleven p.m., we were kept waiting in the station, while the different nationalities composing our regiment were separated and marched off to different quarters. While here we suffered much from thirst and cold, for September nights in Italy are often damp and chilly, and we were thirsty from our hot dusty march, and from the closeness of the railway cars into which we were packed. Thanks to a Dutch fellow Zouave, I was enabled partially to quench my thirst with a few drops of lemonade he had, by some means or other, obtained from the *buffet* of the station. But many were bitterly complaining of thirst, and the Italian authorities did not deem it necessary for us even to see a drop of water till next day. At length we English, along with some of the Dutch and Swiss Zouaves, were marched off to the Bagni, or convict establishment outside the town, where we lodged in the large rooms used by the convicts for sleeping in. But of the latter there were none, and on asking an Italian soldier where they were, he answered, "Freed and gone to Rome." Such were the men who had come to regenerate and liberate the City of the Popes from their tyranny, and to restore order therein! And, be it clearly understood, these men were no political prisoners, but men convicted of forgeries, murders, and such like crimes.

Till next day we were shut in, 250 men in one room, sleeping on straw strewn on the stone floor, but it was not till mid-day that we each received a small loaf, a couple of ounces of cheese, and a thimbleful of rum. Till then we were kept without food, though a few among us, through the kindness of the soldiers, not of the authorities, were enabled to buy from them a few grapes and apples, some bread and wine. Almost all the private soldiers of the Italian army, as far as it lay in their power, treated us with the greatest good feeling and kindness. Not so those in power. Water was not supplied to us until after the cheese and bread had been served out, and then in such a small quantity that some did not get any. At five in the evening we were allowed out for half an hour into a small yard to breathe a little fresh air. While here a few of our officers were allowed to come and see us.

At about eight in the evening we were marched down to the port, where we were embarked on board barges, into which we were so closely packed that their gunwales were almost flush with the water.

In these noyade-like boats we were taken off to the screw steamer, Liguria, which sailed for Genoa at 10 p.m. Although a small vessel, 750 men were stowed away in her. The hold was filled, the cabins crowded, and locomotion on deck was simply impossible, owing to the numbers of men lying there; even the sailors had the greatest difficulty in doing their work. I thought myself lucky in getting a place to lie down on, on the quarter-deck, thus avoiding the intolerable closeness down between decks. I fancy few slavers were ever more heavily freighted with human beings than this good ship. Providentially we had fine weather, and a calm sea. During the time we were on board we were given only two meals of maccaroni soup with a little meat in it, with a small allowance of wine each. It was served out in large tins, each containing portions for twenty men, and the confusion and trouble to get even this was immense, owing to the overcrowded state of the vessel, and as for getting to the water-butts to get a drink, it was first, a matter of skill to steer thither without treading some one to death, and then a fight to keep your turn for drinking when you got there. All that night in the cold, and all next day in the heat of a broiling sun we lay cooped up, some below, some on deck lying close one to another, like fish packed in wooden boxes for the London market. At dusk we entered the port of Genoa, and a barge having been brought alongside of us, those below rushed on deck thinking we were about to land, but it being too late for landing, the barge sheered off, and we were doomed to pass another night on board, our discomfort being increased by those who had come up on deck remaining there, and we slept so crowded together, that where I was, we were sleeping, or rather longing to sleep, one on the top of another. I never had, and hope never to pass again such a night, for when the morning came, I scarce knew if I had a bone left unbroken in my body, and the cold and damp mist of the harbour had quite benumbed us. At daybreak we landed, and each of us having been given an eating tin, a spoon, and a small blanket, we were formed by fours and marched through Genoa about four miles uphill, and inland to a Fort Montirati. While passing through the outskirts of Genoa, we were kindly allowed by the officer in charge of us, to enter some of the shops and buy wine and bread and such-like things. The people of this part of Genoa were most kind, in some cases even refusing payment for what we took. I drank in one shop some country wine, for which the goodman of the shop refused my money, saying, "his wine was for the Pope!" And many more instances could I tell, of how these poor people strove to show their love for Pio Nono, by kindness to his captive soldiers. On our way through the town we were greatly pleased to see again our energetic and indefatigable chaplain, Monsignor Stonor, and to speak to his useful assistant Mr. T——, who told us how the former had followed us from Rome to Civita Vecchia, and on here, and he promised that our return to old England would be speedy.

As usual we slept on straw, at the fort, having made ourselves some soup from meat and rice, and bread supplied us by the Italian authorities. Early next morning, Sunday, before daybreak, all the English were assembled together and marched back to Genoa, to the large barracks of St. Benigno, near the port. While we passed through the town we were much stared at, but though many people were about in the streets, we received no insults, more than from one man, who asked "Where we had left the Pope?" In many places about the town large placards were posted up with " Viva Roma, the capital of Italy," printed in large letters on them.

In these barracks we were quartered till the 1st of October, sleeping as usual on straw, but being allowed to go where we liked in the barracks, receiving the same food as the Italians, as also the same daily pay, and being allowed free use of two really excellent cantines. Our Chaplain was untiring in his efforts in supplying us with all necessaries, such as clothes, boots, and such-like things, while at the same time he had chartered a large screw steamer to convey us home.

The poor Italian soldiers envied us our lot. Most of them were married men, called out in consequence of late events, and they almost all declared, that had they been sent against Rome they would not have fired a shot. They are badly fed; a mess of maccaroni or vegetables in the morning, a small piece of meat and some soup with maccaroni in the evening, a loaf of bread every other day, and an occasional small quantity of wine, or coffee, make up their bill of fare.

Their pay is five centimes a day. On Sundays they are purposely kept working till late in the day to prevent their going to church, no military Mass ever being said for them. To be known as a religious man is a bar to all promotion, and thus most of their officers are men without any religion, and whose conversation is too disgusting for a gentleman, let alone a Christian, to take part in. But this order of things has only been in force since the usurpations of Victor Emmanuel commenced, and thus some of the officers who had entered the army before them are of a much better kind. The poor privates were mostly good men, forced into the life by the odious conscription. They did all that lay in their power to make us comfortable, offering to mend our clothes and shoes for us, and even to share their beds with us. At night it was our custom to recite aloud in English our prayers together. The first night we noticed one Italian soldier quietly enter our room, and kneel in an out-of-the-way corner, next night there were several, and each successive night more. Poor fellows, they could not pray in their barrack-rooms, and came thus amongst us, although they understood not our language, to unite with us in doing, what to them was, I may say, an impossible and forbidden thing. What a shame to call a kingdom Catholic, whose soldiers are not allowed to practise even this much religion! In fact, our stay had quite made us brothers to these Italian soldiers.

The 1st of October we embarked on board the *India* for Liverpool, after a sorrowful parting with the good-hearted Italian soldiers, among whom our coming had entirely dispelled the notions so earnestly inculcated by the Italian government and the *Times*, that all Papal Zouaves were bloodthirsty brigands and ferocious mercenaries.

CHAPTER XXX.

VISITORS TO ROME—A SAD INCIDENT—ORGANIZATION AND DISCIPLINE.

From Christmas till the end of the Carnival, and again during Eastertide, Rome is inundated with floods of visitors. All nations are represented, but the most numerous are the Americans and English, who come in such numbers that one is almost inclined to believe that the possession of the Eternal City has passed into the hands of the Anglo-Saxon race.

I think we should not be very well pleased if our members of parliament were not better representatives of their constituencies than some of our English travellers are of the British nation. Many, nay the majority of our travelling compatriots, are an honour to the nation to which they belong, and are the cause of Englishmen being loved and respected among many foreigners. But alas, there is a minority, and not I fear a very small one, who bring their fellow-countrymen into contempt and even hatred. The short transit across the 'narrow seas,' besides deranging the inner man, seems also to turn their heads.

From quiet, order-loving, respectable citizens, they, on landing at Ostend or Calais, become insolent, unmannerly, gaping rovers. Every Frenchman to them is a poor, half-starved wretch, to be treated more like a dog than a Christian. Every shopkeeper, or hotel-waiter is to understand at once their loud-roared incomprehensible jargon, under pain of entering Dante's Inferno. Churches were built for them to walk about in with creaking boots, and in family parties of ten or twelve, or as places where they may rest and regale themselves on ham-sandwiches and sherry, as I myself have seen done in Rome. But the list of their vulgarities might be prolonged *ad infinitum.* Happily they who act thus are comparatively few, but yet enough in number to make Englishmen disliked abroad.

Many too, of our compatriots have queer habits and do eccentric things. An Englishman's "tub" is a foreigner's wonder, although some of our French friends, in their imitation of our customs, have also adopted it. In Rome, in consequence of the reckless way a Briton too often exposes himself to the dangers of the climate, there is a saying, "That none but Englishmen and mad dogs walk in the sun." The former also do not pay sufficient attention to acquiring, before they leave home, even a knowledge of the rudiments of the language and outline of the manners of the people among whom they are about to go. I remember one evening walking near the church of the Gesù, being accosted by one, who, although trying to disguise it, was evidently a minister of the Church by law established in England. "Zouave," said he, in unmistakably Anglo-French, "*quelle est la chemin pour le Corso?*" At once guessing his nationality, I answered, "Oh, the way to the Corso, is that it?" I hope I did the man no permanent harm, but for a moment he was struck dumb and breathless. Could it be, an Englishman in the livery of a Papal hireling? Oh no! "You are an Irishman, doubtless?" he said, slightly recovering from his first shock. "No," I answered, "every inch an Englishman." But the good man seemed to doubt my word, and after thanking me for showing him his way, left me with a most bewildered and puzzled expression of countenance.

Some of our High Church friends abroad join as if they were Catholics in all the devotions and practices of the Holy Roman Church, but some of the Low Church party go to an opposite extreme, to show their dislike to us. A friend of mine, being in the Sistine Chapel, when the Pope was carrying in procession the Blessed Sacrament, happened to be behind an Englishman of the bigoted type, who, when all were kneeling refused to do likewise. Whereon my friend behind him gently pulled the tailcoat of him, who, amid the bending crowd, remained erect. Of course, my friend did not expect him to kneel to the Sacred Host, but only wished him to pay that homage, which all men of all creeds could without scruple, pay to the Pope as King. Our stubborn countryman, feeling the pressure exerted on his garments, turned round to my friend, and in a solemn and severe way, remarked, "Render to Cæsar the things that are Cæsar's." "Just so, it is all I desire," replied my friend, delighted at his opponent's apt quotation.

Oftentimes those who have little acquaintance with the language, are placed in awkward positions. We all know the tale of the Englishman, who leaving a ball, having been courteously helped by a foreign gentleman to put on his coat, handed him a franc, which being indignantly refused, thought "garsoon" wanted more, and tendered him a larger sum. A friend told me that one bright moonlight night, being desirous of visiting the Colosseum, and not having the proper pass for entering, asked the sergeant of Zouaves on guard to allow him in, which he did, and after seeing the ruins, on going away, my friend offered the Sergeant a small gratuity. To the confusion of my friend, the Sergeant, drawing himself up proudly, said:—"*Monsieur, je vous remercie, mais je suis sergent aux Zouaves Pontificaux.*" My friend erred through ignorance, and often afterwards laughed over the adventure with a member of one of the noblest French families, the Zouave sergeant of my tale.

A few weeks before the seizure of Rome by the Italians, a sad event occurred, of which the blame, if blame there was, many journals wished to throw on the Zouaves. I was walking past the church of St. Andrea della Valle with another English Zouave corporal, when a Dragoon officer came riding along the street, and told us in a hurried way, to hasten to the Campo dei Fiori, as firing and a disturbance of some kind was going on there. On coming there, we saw some one firing from an upper window of the Dutch

Zouaves' Club, which stands at one end of the Piazza. On our way here we passed two poor men wounded in the legs, being helped along by some Zouaves. At first we thought an *emeute* had broken out. The shops in the neighbourhood were closed, and the square of the Campo dei Fiori was deserted, and shots were being fired from different quarters up at the before-mentioned window. Running up to the gateway of the Dutch Club, and getting under it, to shelter ourselves from the bullets that were rapidly being shot from the window above us, we learnt that the cause of all the disturbance was a poor maniac. In a short time the adjutant of the Third Battalion, M. de Pavi, came up with a small force of armed Zouaves, and mounting the stairs, broke open the door, and disabled with a revolver-shot the madman who was preparing to fire at him. The maniac was a Dutchman who had come from Holland to join the Zouaves, but, on account of his evident insaneness, he was rejected by our Doctors, and subsequently having evinced dangerous symptoms, was removed to the Lunatic Asylum of Santo Spirito Hospital. After having been kept here sometime, he was, by order of the authorities of the asylum, liberated. Being a Dutchman, he was permitted by those in charge of the Dutch Club, to frequent it during the time while he was awaiting his return home, and it was during this time that he found his way into a room where some rifles of the employés of the club were kept, and providing himself with two weapons and eighty rounds of ammunition, he placed himself in a room alone, locked the door, and opened fire on all passers by, thus wounding two men and a woman and child, and a Zouave, the latter dangerously. A Zouave corporal, Brandler by name, of my company, had his trousers pierced by a bullet close to his knee, which made a black graze along his drawers without actually wounding him. The whole blame of the affair rests with the authorities of the Lunatic Asylum, one of whom, was, I believe, dismissed on account of this affair.

The lunatic did not, at any time, belong to the corps of Zouaves, and he fired indiscriminately on civilian and

Zouaves alike. But notwithstanding this, as the affair had taken place at one of the Zouave clubs, a handsome collection was made of 1500 francs, to aid those civilians who had suffered by this lamentable occurrence.

It may be interesting here to give a brief outline of the composition, organization, promotion and discipline of the corps. On New Year's day, 1870, the Papal Zouaves formed a regiment of four battalions, of six companies each, and of a Depôt Battalion of four companies, together with a company called *La compagnie hors range*, composed of officers' servants, of the tailors, shoemakers, and armourers, and of the bandsmen and *Sapeurs* of the regiment.

The numerical strength of the different companies varied much, and as new recruits arrived, and old soldiers left, the same company would vary much in its strength at different periods. About one hundred men was the supposed complement of men to each company, but often it was but sixty or even less, while occasionally the numbers increased immensely. At the time of the taking of Rome by Victor Emmanuel's troops, the 5th company, 3rd battalion, numbered nearly 150 men.- I should, therefore, think, about the beginning of 1870, the corps numbered about 3500 men in all. Of these the most numerous were the Dutch, then the French, and after these the Belgians, Canadians, English and Irish, Swiss, Germans, and Italians. Spain, Portugal, and many other nations sent their representatives, including three or four blacks, and one Chinese.

As all the orders and words of command were in French, the majority of the officers were French.

The supreme command of the regiment was vested in the Colonel, M. Allet, a native of Switzerland. Next to him was M. de Charette, the Lieutenant-Colonel.

Each battalion was under the command of a Commandant, and each had a Captain-Adjutant-Major, nearly corresponding to the Adjutant in the English army, and an Adjutant corresponding to an English Sergeant-Major, and who, like the latter, carrying a sword, and wearing a uniform very like an officer's, yet only ranked as a *sous-officier*, or non-commissioned officer.

Each company had three officers, a Captain, a Lieutenant, and a sub-Lieutenant. Under these were the Sergeant-Major, the Sergeant-Fourrier, an assistant to the Sergeant-Major, four common Sergeants, and one Sergeant *du Tir*, to look after the rifles and ammunition of the company. Also, there were eight full Corporals, and a certain number of "*fonctionnaires*" or lance-Corporals. One Corporal, or *fonctionnaire*, was always named "*caporal d'ordinaire*," and his duty was to superintend the buying of meat, &c., and the cooking of the food for each company.

The men of the band were under the immediate supervision of a *Chef de Musique*, with the rank of Lieutenant, and a *sous-Chef de Musique*, along with a Sergeant-Major, Sergeants, and Corporals of the band.

The payment of the soldiers was managed thus.—*Le Capitaine Tresorier*, a Captain especially appointed for the purpose, aided by his staff of clerks, composed of a sub-Lieutenant, two Sergeants, four Corporals, and some privates, received the money from the Intendant of the Division. This, every five days, was given out to each Sergeant-Major, who in turn divided it among the Corporals of his company, who in their turn paid it to the men of their squads.

The ordinary pay of the private soldier was three sous per diem, which, by good and steady conduct could be increased to six sous per diem, and be further increased by promotion.

Discipline was of course carried out by the officers, sergeants, and corporals; the right of inflicting punishments being invested in each proportionately to rank. Thus, a Corporal could inflict a punishment of two days in the *salle de police*, or four days' confinement to barracks, while the Colonel could award fifteen days' imprisonment or the same number of days in the *salle de police*. Trivial offences and breaches of discipline were punished by *corvées*, *i.e.*, fatigue duties, or by punishment drill. Greater offences, such as coming late to the *appel* or roll-call at night were punishable by confinement in the *salle de police*. The difference between *salle de police* and prison has been explained in Chapter V.

But in cases of great and serious crimes, the accused was brought before either a Council of War, or a Council of Discipline, both corresponding to our Courts-Martial. The first-named was presided over by a *Chef de Bataillon*, or Commandant, and was composed of a Captain, a Lieutenant, and a sub-Lieutenant, and if the prisoner was a private, or of other grade, by one other member, his equal in grade. The case was got up and stated by the *Capitaine Auditeur*, an officer who had especially studied the law, and who acted as a kind of prosecutor, assisted by a *Sergent-Auditeur*. The prisoner could choose his own defender, either a civil lawyer or often a clever comrade, to make out his defence. This Council could inflict the highest penalties, such as death or dismissal, or life imprisonment. It sent its finding for approval to the Minister-at-Arms, along with any remark the Regimental Colonel might see fit to make. The Council of Discipline was formed much in the same way, but could only award short terms of military imprisonment, or not more than six months' service in the *Compagnie de Discipline*, (including men of bad conduct, who were sent there to be reformed), and were kept under control by the severest discipline, each breach of which rendered the offender liable to another month's service in the company.

Perhaps one of the most sad and solemn sights I witnessed during my Zouave life, was the carrying out of the sentence of a *Conseil de Guerre*. I have often seen them carried out in the barrack square on more ordinary offenders, but on this occasion which I am about to describe, the *execution militaire*, as it is termed, was more than usually impressive. The prisoner was a young man, descended from a good old Legitimist French family, and had served some time in the Papal Zouaves, and had risen to the rank of Sergeant-Major. But, unfortunately, before he had long occupied this somewhat responsible position, he became acquainted with some young men of fast and expensive habits, and unable to do all they did with the little money he had of his own, he had borrowed some more from the public money that passed through his hands, intending to pay it back as soon as his own money should come to him from France. But he failed in doing so; the money he had taken had to be accounted for, and nothing but disgrace and punishment was left him to look to. So he deserted, but was arrested near the frontier by some Gendarmes, one of whom he severely injured in endeavouring to escape from them. Brought back to Rome, a *conseil de guerre* found him guilty, and sentenced him to death!

An early summer's sun was gilding with its morning rays the many domes of the Eternal City, and its brilliant light had awakened nature from her sleep, the hum of men setting about their daily toil is heard in the city, and the voices of the feathered songsters singing their morning prayer to their Creator make the gardens of the city thrill with their merry notes. But in the courtyard of the Castle of St. Angelo, under the dark shadow cast by Hadrian's tomb, and amid the damp mists from the river, which the sun's rays are not as yet strong enough to dispel, there resounds the tramp of armed men and the clashing of arms. The words of command are given in a quick, audible, yet low tone of voice, and the gathering soldiers quickly array themselves around the courtyard in a hollow square. Detachments of all the regiments of the Papal army are there. Dragoons with their long sabres and short carbines, and burnished helmets, o'ertopped with horsehair, form one side of the square, along with some Gendarmes with cocked hats and white crossbelts, all dismounted. Red-trousered men of the line, dapper little Chasseurs, broad-shouldered Swiss Carbineers, and grey-clad white-gaitered Zouaves compose the other three sides.

A small part of one side of the square falls back, and leaves an opening as the bugles commanding attention break the death-like silence that reigns. The officers stand out in front of the men, who face inwards, the Colonel and some superior officers stand together at one end of the inside of the square, the buglers of the assembled troops facing them at the other end. Then through the opening, escorted by a half-dozen Zouaves with fixed bayonets, the condemned man is led in, looking pale and abashed, dressed in a black suit of civilian clothing, with his military cap and great coat over them. Then, standing between his guards, facing the Colonel, with uncovered head he listens to the reading of the sentence, which the Captain *Auditeur* reads aloud. Stating his crimes—and after saying that the Council of War finding them proven, condemns him to the last penalty of the law, death—the sentence goes on to say:—" Whereas, the Court, taking into consideration extenuating circumstances, recommends the prisoner to mercy, wherefore the Minister at Arms annuls the first sentence, and condemns the prisoner to degradation of rank, expulsion from the Corps of Zouaves, and awards him five years of hard labour in the galleys." The whole is signed and approved of by the Minister at Arms, the Colonel, and members of the Court. An Adjutant then walks up to the prisoner, pulls off the regimental buttons of his great coat, strips him of it, and gives him a gentle blow with the butt of his gun, to denote his expulsion from the Corps. The prisoner is then marched past the assembled troops, while the buglers march behind him playing a quick march; having made the circuit of the square, he is then handed over to the civil authorities. The prisoner, a tall handsome youth, seemed to feel his situation deeply while the sentence was being read, but while being marched past his comrades was in a kind of stupor, walking along mechanically, but when this was over, and the Gendarmes came to take him in charge, as one of them took his hands and adjusted the handcuffs to his wrists, at the touch of the iron he started, blushed deeply, and wept bitterly. The dread reality of his position was now fully realized.

Promotion in the corps was by selection, and all were obliged to enter as privates. From private to Corporal and then to the rank of Sergeant and Sergeant-major, candidates were chosen by the Captain, their names sent in, along with their qualifications, to the Colonel, who took the names of those he thought most capable, and gave them the coveted grade. For promotion to the rank of sub-Lieutenant and higher, the names were sent in by the Colonel to the Minister-at-Arms, who presented those names he selected to the approval of His Holiness, who signed their commissions.

Of course slight favouritism occurred occasionally, but as a general rule, the promotions were most fair. A capable, intelligent, and well-conducted soldier was sure of promotion up to the rank of Sergeant-major quick enough, but, on account of the few vacancies, promotion to the rank of officer was slow.

CHAPTER XXXI.

THE USURPATION — THE POPE A PRISONER — FRANCE — LIBERTY, EQUALITY, FRATERNITY — CONSOLATION — HEROISM—CONCLUSION.

> Eternal Rome! thou city of the great,
>   Æterna Urbs! I raise my soul to thee!
> Thy silent voice and high historic fate
>   Have charm'd my mind as sweetest melody.
>
> Blest home, and centre of the Christian fold,
>   Thy highest destiny hath won my heart:
> What grief now fills my soul as I behold
>   Injustice reign, thy glory all depart!
>
> But this shall never last; as one who runs
>   May read, in lessons oft repeated, past;
> St. Peter's bark a mightier storm outliv'd,
>   And outlives still, though troubles thicken fast:
> Great Pius will the bark in safety guide,
> And conq'ring all, to port will swiftly ride.

THE events related in connection with the Zouaves, in the last chapter but one, referred to their return to their respective homes, in consequence of the surrender of the garrison of Rome to the superior force of Victor Emmanuel.

This forcible usurpation of the remaining States of the Church was the commencement of another series of robberies and sacrileges which the Catholic Church and the Supreme Pontiff have had to experience at the hands of that misguided and unhappy monarch. As a consequence of that act of spoliation the Holy Father is virtually a subject and prisoner in his palace, the Religious Orders are being deprived of their monasteries and convents, the city of Rome has been filled with escaped convicts and assassins, so as to make it unsafe at times to walk through its streets; and lastly Victor Emmanuel has not improved the condition of Italy by his yielding to the *party of action*, or rather in anticipating that party in their designs on the Eternal City. In fact, since the occupation Rome has occasioned the greatest trouble to the Italian Government. Witness the stormy debates in the Italian Chamber on the "Transfer of the Capital," and the stupid imposture of the "Guarantees." The revolutionary party is not satisfied; the secret societies have not yet attained their ends, *i.e.*, the overthrow of the kingdom of Italy, and the establishment of that *universal republic* whose delights and blessings the *reds* and *Communists* of Paris have lately exhibited to the world; and while the bankrupt kingdom seems likely to come to an untimely end, in the mean time the Romans behold the prospect of vastly increased taxation, the detested conscription, and the probability of a decreased trade consequent on the absence of the usual number of visitors from all parts of the world.

As regards the statement of the Pope being virtually a prisoner, the following extracts from the *Unità Cattolica* may be cited in proof of it :—

"Vincent Gioberti called Pio Nono a prisoner when he was at Gaeta, the guest of the King of Naples, who treated him with all the affection of a most devoted son. Here are the words of Gioberti, 'The Neapolitan sojourn was "a fatal slavery."' Now if the Pope were declared a prisoner because he was a guest of the King of Naples, and the 'Septembrists' themselves, such as Lanza, Mamiani, &c., said then that he was 'under the pressure' of the Bourbon, who can imagine for a moment that he enjoys liberty to-day or independence of any sort under the command of Bixio and Cadorna? . . . . . . We know too well how all the conquests of the Italian States commenced with the imprisonment of bishops. In Tuscany they imprisoned Cardinal Corsi, Archbishop of

Pisa; in Bologna, Monsignor Canzi; in Imola, Cardinal Baluffi; .... at Milan, Monsignor Caccia; at Piacenza, Monsignor Ranza; at Benevento they maltreated Cardinal Riario Sforza, &c., &c. ...... Who can blame us, then for being in the greatest anxiety about our Holy Father, Pius the Ninth?

"'Dogs,' say we to the ministers of Italy, 'what have you done with your Father and ours?'"

Another reason why the Pope is not perfectly free, is that in his communications with the Catholic Episcopate of the world he is subject to the control of the Italian authorities of the Roman post, and his letters and documents are liable to be intercepted at any moment.

Many persons visiting the Holy Father, or known for their fidelity to him, have been, since the occupation, subjected to insult, interruption, and annoyance in their passage through the streets of Rome.

But the most conclusive proof of the fetters imposed upon him was furnished in the seizure by the Italian government of every Italian journal which published the Encyclical Letter of the Holy Father on the usurpation of Rome, dated November 1st, 1870, for while these very papers cited the fact of their publishing this document of the Pope as a proof that all his acts were free, the ground was immediately cut from under their feet, and the fallacy of their argument displayed by the confiscation of every one of the journals which had dared to print it.

Thus is brought home to us the fact that, although as yet the personal liberty of the Pope has not been actually interfered with, yet he does not enjoy that entire freedom of word, and act, and communication which belonged to him as a Sovereign, and which is requisite to his dignity and authority as Supreme Head of the Catholic Church, comprising two hundred millions of Christians.

Some of the greatest Protestant statesmen of the age, and particularly M. Thiers and M. Guizot, have strongly advocated the proposition *that the Sovereign Pontiff must always be perfectly free and independent of every other authority.*

If the present sad state of Rome and Italy is such as to cause the gravest apprehensions in the mind of every well-wisher to the cause of religion and good government, that of Paris has lately presented a sadder aspect still. Here we behold the horrors and crimes of the Reign of Terror repeated,—generals and peaceful citizens murdered in cold blood, and shot down by armed mobs,—the archbishop and his priests imprisoned and assassinated,—the ministers of religion denied access to the unhappy prisoners,—churches closèd by order of the "Commune,"—the name of God ignored and denied.

Here we see the *red republican* doctrines of *liberty, equality,* and *fraternity* interpreted by its professors, the Socialists, Communists, and *Franc-maçons*, and other secret societies, who have inaugurated the late terrible civil war.

Amidst so much that we see to cause us the saddest reflections, we may still glean some elements of consolation in the great movement of sympathy with the wrongs of our Holy Father the Pope, which has set in amongst the Catholics all over the world, and which has been expressed in mass meetings in America, in Ireland, in England, in Belgium, and in Germany, as well as in the numerous addresses laid at the foot of the Pope from the inhabitants of so many countries, including even the small island of Malta. Another element of consolation comes to us from the courage and patriotism which have been so signally displayed by the French Pontifical Zouaves during the late unfortunate French war, and which proves that bravery and love of country still animate one part at least of the army of that *fair France* now so much prostrated. The recital of the heroic deeds of General de Charette and his brave followers will, I think, form an appropriate conclusion to this work—already perhaps too long. Mr. George Goldie writes as follows to the *Tablet* of December 24th.—"Whatever may be the sympathies of your readers . . . . they will not refuse their generous admiration for the Christian chivalry of the Pontifical Zouaves. The incidents I have endeavoured to string together below are all derived from authentic sources.

"On reaching France after the capitulation of Rome, the ex-Pontifical Zouaves first assembled at Tarascon, and from thence were ordered to Le Mans to complete their military organization under their Colonel, M. de Charette.

"Nearly all the officers and *sous-officiers* were there assembled, and numerous volunteers of the most Catholic and noble families, side by side with the humble but devoted peasantry of Brittany, Anjou, &c., flocked beneath the banner of this Christian legion. . . . But meanwhile the older soldiers were sent forward to the seat of war, and as early as the 11th or 12th of October, those companies were already engaged in active operations, and it was, thanks mainly to this handful of men, who for seven hours held the Prussians in check at the entrance to Orleans, that General de la Motterouge was enabled to withdraw the main body of his army. The most exaggerated accounts of the losses of the ex-Pontifical Zouaves were circulated both by the French and English journals; happily, however, only fifteen were killed and wounded . . . . Every time they have since appeared in the field, has only confirmed and increased their renown and glory." The writer then relates several other details, and describes the heroic devotion of the Zouaves at Patay near Orleans—a former battle-field, the scene of one of the victories of Jeanne d'Arc—where they threw themselves between their retreating countrymen and the advancing Prussians, leaving the field strewn with their glorious slain. "The affair took place on Friday, the 2nd of December—I quote from the letter of one of the Zouaves to his father, dated the 6th of December:—'I promised you some details of the sad but glorious day of Friday; sad, because it witnessed some of the purest blood of France poured out; glorious, because it proved to our country that there are yet amongst her children those who are ready to sacrifice themselves to save her honour. General de Sonis had assumed the command of the 17th *corps d'armée*, of which we formed a portion. An intimate friend of our Colonel, M. de Charette—whose bravery, piety, and true nobility of sentiment he shares—it was under his command that we attacked Brou, which was first entered by my battalion led by Charette. On reaching the village the General and Colonel threw themselves into each other's arms in the presence of their men. But the affection and esteem of General de Sonis for our corps did not stop there. He reserved to us the honour to serve as an example to all the army, to offer to France and the enemy the spectacle of devotion to our cause, and that bravery through which God has so often given success to our arms.' It was under a white banner, bearing on one side the Sacred Heart with the legend, *Sacré Cœur de Jesus, sauvez la France,* and, on the reverse, *Saint Martin, patron de la France, priez pour nous!* that the Zouaves marched to battle. ' On Friday, we reached the little village of Patay at an early hour, where we expected to pass the day. The cannon growled at a distance of three or four leagues, but, as we formed the reserve of the *corps d'armée* which was engaged, we had little idea that the hour of sacrifice was at hand for us. The General and the Colonel had both approached Holy Communion in the morning. About mid-day we received orders to be in readiness. It was rumoured that De Sonis wished to make a *reconnaissance* in the direction of the battle that was going on, but so little did we expect to be engaged, that those who were fatigued by the constant marches of the previous days, remained in camp, and were not ordered to raise the tents. Our second battalion followed us at a considerable interval, and was thus prevented from sharing in the action. The cannonade appeared to be drawing near us, and the General, believing that our presence might prove opportune, led us towards the left flank of the troops already in action. Ranged in line, we were exposed to the fire of several batteries—the object of which appeared to be to turn our flank —without our being able to use our weapons. The shells falling in our ranks killed and wounded about a dozen of our men. Suddenly, Colonel de Sonis galloped along our line, and pulling up beside our Colonel, cried out to us, *Mes amis, je compte sur vous!* Our only response was a simultaneous shout of *Vive le Général*, repeated again and again; joy shone in every eye, and the presence of danger made way to the keen desire to prove ourselves worthy of the noble task confided to us. In an instant we were ready, and with fixed bayonets we advanced at the double towards a little plantation which crowned a height, and was occupied by 1500 Bavarians; 350 Zouaves advanced, the General with his staff leading, with De Charette at his side, and behind them the Baron de Troussures at the head of his battalion.'

"It was a splendid sight to see these young men advancing as if on parade, ranged in a line with their flag, without deigning to answer by a shot the murderous fire of the enemy. There first fell Lieutenant de Boischevalier, Major de Bourget, and Sergeants de Villemarais and de Vougué. The advanced line was so shattered that it was in vain the ranks were closed up, the fallen could not be replaced! The Bavarians seemed at this moment to be seized with amazement, possibly by a sentiment of admiration, they remained stupefied by such audacity, and fired at random or ceased firing altogether. Just as the Zouaves entered the wood, Colonel de Charette fell, his horse being shot, but quick as lightning he disengaged himself, and ran as fast as he could to General de Sonis, who still charged at our head, and disappeared in the smoke. As soon as the enemy felt the points of the bayonets, they fled in utter confusion. Carried on by their ardour, the Zouaves passed through the wood in pursuit; unhappily they were alone, their leaders had fallen, and there was no one to check the pursuit when the end and object of the combat had been gained. On the opposite side of the hill, the wooded crest of which was now occupied by the victorious Zouaves, extended another wood, beyond a plain, and beyond that a fortified and loopholed village, occupied by the enemy in force. It was in following the fugitive Germans across this plain, that the mere handful of Zouaves were exposed to a terrible reprisal, for sixty out of the

350 alone regained their camp! But the retreat was worthy of the attack. Slowly—with a *sang-froid* worthy of the veteran troops, under a hail of bullets, shells and shot, disputing every inch of ground till they reached the cover of the wood they should never have left, the Zouaves withdrew, and thence in good order, and together, the glorious fragment reached their camp.

"Alas! the glory of the fight had been dearly bought. M. de Vertanon had left his rifle to carry the flag; he fell dead at the verge of the little wood. M. de Traversay, sergeant-major, was on his left, and M. Jacques de Bouillé at his right. A ball struck down M. de Traversay as he was about to catch up and bear forward the fallen flag. M. Jacques de Bouillé seized the glorious emblem, which served as a target to the enemy, and waving it over his head, he rushed with a loud hurrah into the wood, which was swept by the Zouaves. Beyond the wood this young and generous volunteer—who had left his young wife, his two children, and his life of ease and luxury, to take his place as a simple soldier amongst the Zouaves, was shot dead, and a young Zouave, whose name has unfortunately not been recorded, had the honour of bearing back the flag of the battalion intact to the camp. M. le Marquis de Bouillé (father of the young man named above, and who, at an age when men may fairly rest, had brought his fifty-five years to serve as a volunteer, giving up a life of splendid ease and ample wealth for his country's cause,) was also wounded, and a late report states he is since dead. His son-in-law, M. de Casenove, had his wrist broken. M. Ferdinand de Charette, brother of the Colonel, was shot in the arm. M. Hervé de Kersabiec was taken prisoner. MM. de la Brosse, de Bois-chevalier, de Maquillé, de Sièvre, de la Touche, and many others, equally distinguished by birth and gallantry, were grievously wounded.

"The General de Sonis was captured by the Prussians, lying helpless from his wound, beside his dead charger. It has been said that, touched by his chivalric bearing and Christian fortitude, the Prussian officer in command gave him his liberty, and restored him to his wife and family of nine children. Of M. de Charette, the most painfully contradictory rumours are afloat. He was wounded in the thigh, and with a devotion worthy of his character, he forbade his soldiers to expose themselves by carrying him off the field. Since, it has been stated that he was a prisoner, but there seems good reason to hope he has escaped from the hands of the Prussians, and is at Poitiers." (The event proved that the brave Zouave Colonel did escape from the Prussians; he recovered quickly from his wound. His services to his country were subsequently recognized by the Government of the day, and he was raised to the rank of General.)

The recital of these acts of self-sacrifice and heroism afford some ground for consolation in the present critical position of France, and of the Holy See; for certainly we may entertain some hope that the country which produces men so truly devoted and heroic, contains in itself the germs of a new and vigorous life, which, now that the fruits of infidelity and atheism have exhibited their innate decay and corruption, will shoot forth and become once more the legitimate pride of France, whose King may yet make reparation for the crimes of the Secret Sects against God, the Blessed Sacrament, and our Blessed Lady, by showing himself to be, as of old, the Eldest Son of the Church.

THE END.

www.ingramcontent.com/pod-product-compliance
Lightning Source LLC
Chambersburg PA
CBHW030013240426
43672CB00007B/935